Fiction by American Women: Recent Views

Edited, with an Introduction by
WINIFRED FARRANT BEVILACQUA

National University Publications
ASSOCIATED FACULTY PRESS
Port Washington, New York // 1983

Manufactured in the United States of America

Published by
Associated Faculty Press, Inc.
Port Washington, N.Y.

Library of Congress Cataloging in Publication Data
Main entry under title:

Fiction by American women.

(National university publications)
Contents: Introduction / Winifred Farrant Bevilacqua —The sentimentalists / Mary Kelley—Thanatos and Eros: Kate Chopin's The awakening / Cynthia Griffin Wolff— [etc.]
1. American fiction—Women authors—History and criticism—Addresses, essays, lectures.
2. Feminism and literature—Addresses, essays, lectures. I. Bevilacqua, Winifred Farrant, 1947-
PS151.F54   1983   813'.009'9287   83-2816
ISBN 0-8046-9315-3

Cover design for

Fiction by American Women:
Recent Views

The illustration is a handmade quilt.
The pattern is called Roman Stripes.
Quilting has long been one endeavor in which women
could express themselves creatively. It has been
and continues to be an important American art.

This contemporary rendering of a traditional pattern
in sophisticated color combinations gives the
quilt a mix of traditional with contemporary.
This echoes the range of American fiction
written about in this book. The fine interweaving
of pattern and needlework are not unlike that
of written creative work.

Cover designed by
Ron McClellen

The quilt by
Ginny McDowell McClellen

Cover photo by
Michael McClellen

To Nicola and Pat

CONTENTS

PREFACE

In recent years, a growing number of literary scholars have made a conscious and continuing effort to study the relationship between literature and female reality and to deepen our knowledge of the aims and achievements of women writers. The essays in this book provide a sampling of one part of this scholarship, criticism that considers and evaluates fiction by American women. The nature of past critical commentary on female authors and the directions and main concerns of contemporary research are discussed in the introductory chapter. Of the ten essays which follow, one is a general study presenting a fresh interpretation of popular literature by women in the last century; the other nine are in-depth explorations of works by outstanding individual authors from the nineteenth and twentieth centuries: Kat Chopin, Edith Wharton, Willa Cather, Gertrude Stein, Katherine Anne Porter, Flannery O'Connor, Sylvia Plath, Toni Morrison, and Erica Jong. Written by expert teachers and critics, these essays investigate with care issues of central importance in understanding the writers and works they treat. Since some reflect the newer feminist perspectives while others take more traditional approaches to the literature they examine, they also demonstrate diverse ways in which women's fiction can be profitably explored. They have been selected both to indicate the seriousness and sensitivity with which critics are currently studying women's writings and to provide a solid foundation for an intelligent appreciation of the authors discussed. I also hope that this book will help stimulate in the college student engaged in formal study of American literature and women writers, and in the informed general reader pursuing an interest in female American authors, a greater awareness of the range, intensity, and richness of women's literary accomplishments in the United States.

Winifred Farrant Bevilacqua
Arona, Italy
April 1983

ACKNOWLEDGEMENTS

Barbara Harrell Carson, "Winning: Katherine Anne Porter's Women," from *The Authority of Experience: Essays in Feminist Criticism* (Amherst: University of Massachusetts Press, 1977), pp. 239-256. Copyright © 1977 by University of Massachusetts Press. Reprinted by permission of University of Massachusetts Press.

Judith Fetterley, " 'The Temptation to Be a Beautiful Object': Double Standard and Double Bind in *The House of Mirth*," *Studies in American Fiction*, Volume 5, no. 2 (Autumn 1977), pp. 199-211. Copyright © 1977 by Northeastern University. Reprinted by permission of *Studies in American Fiction*.

Blanche H. Gelfant, "The Forgotten Reaping-Hook: Sex in *My Antonia*," *American Literature*, Volume 43, no. 1 (March 1971), pp. 60-82. Copyright © 1971 by Duke University Press. Reprinted by permission of Duke University Press.

Mary Kelley, "The Sentimentalists: Promise and Betrayal in the Home," *Signs: Journal of Women in Culture and Society*, Volume 4, no. 3 (Spring 1979), pp. 434-446. Copyright © 1979 by The University of Chicago Press. Reprinted by permission of The University of Chicago Press.

Joyce Carol Oates, "The Visionary Art of Flannery O'Connor," *Southern Humanities Review*, Volume 7, no. 3 (Summer 1973), pp. 235-246. Copyright © 1974 by Joyce Carol Oates. Reprinted by permission of Joyce Carol Oates.

Marjorie G. Perloff, " 'A Ritual for Being Born Twice': Sylvia Plath's *The Bell Jar*," *Contemporary Literature*, Volume 13, no. 4 (Autumn 1972), pp. 507-522. Copyright © 1972 by the Board of Regents of the University of Wisconsin System. Reprinted by permission of the University of Wisconsin Press.

Joan Reardon, "*Fear of Flying*: Developing the Feminist Novel," *International Journal of Women's Studies*, Volume 1, no. 3 (May-June 1978), pp. 306-320. Copyright © 1978 by Eden Press Women's Publications. Reprinted by permission of Eden Press Women's Publications.

CHAPTER 1

Introduction

Winifred Farrant Bevilacqua

For centuries literature has been an art form to which women have contributed brilliantly. Yet literary critics have not always dealt fairly and sensitively with women writers, because of cultural and personal conditioning and prejudices which have made it difficult for them to appreciate and to assess the value of women's writings. Women writers themselves have always been aware that, simply because of their gender as authors, their work might be misunderstood, belittled, or even derided. In a few lines from her "Prologue," Anne Bradstreet, America's first poet of consequence, summed up some of the most frequent complaints against female artists:

> I am obnoxious to each carping tongue,
> Who says, my hand a needle better fits,
> A poet's pen all scorn I should thus wrong;
> For such despite they cast on female wits:
> If what I do prove well, it won't advance.
> They'll say it's stolen, or else, was by chance.

Similarly, in the late seventeenth century, the British poet Anne Finch expressed in her "Introduction" her certainty that whatever faults critics would find with her poetry would in the end be attributed to their having been "by a Woman Writt," for

> Alas! a woman that attempts the pen,
> Such an intruder upon the rights of men,
> Such a presumptuous creature is esteem'd
> The fault can by no vertue be redeem'd.

In the nineteenth century, women writers were so often assessed in terms of usually negative group stereotypes and viewed as women first and as artists second that many of them sought refuge in a male pseudonym or otherwise denied their female identity. Mary Ann Evans chose to publish *Adam Bede,* her first novel, under the name George Eliot so the book could be judged on its own merits and not as the work of a Lady Novelist. Charlotte, Emily and Anne Brontë selected the sexually neutral pseudonyms of Currer, Ellis, and Acton Bell because, as Charlotte commented in her 1850 introduction to *Wuthering Heights,* "we had a vague impression that authoresses are liable to be looked upon with prejudice; we noticed how critics sometimes use for their chastisement the weapon of personality and for their reward a flattery which is not true praise." These authors' attempts to make it possible for their works to be evaluated impartially, however, did not succeed. Their books were dissected by gender conscious critics who, certain of the innate qualities of male and female literary talent, were determined to discover the sex of the creator.

Earlier in this century, Virginia Woolf reported that when she began to do research for her essay "Women and Fiction" she was shocked to find that most existing studies on the topic had been written by "angry" men. Speculating on the effects of their hostile and narrow attitudes on women writers, she recounted the fate of a hypothetical "wonderfully gifted" sister of Shakespeare who, after having learned that being a poet and playwright was unthinkable for a woman of her time, killed herself one winter's night. Woolf believed that even those gifted women of the past who survived disillusionment and persevered in their careers must have had their contributions to literature shaped, and in some cases probably crippled, by the persistent stereotypes and preconceptions about the nature of female literary talent with which they had to contend.

In the United States, not all literary critics have displayed overt prejudices about female authors, and some women's writings have been given a place of honor within the literary canon. But an unwillingness to grant women writers full equality with males has long been implicitly transmitted in the choice of texts that college students of both sexes have been assigned to read in literature courses. Most of these texts provide a predominantly male point of view on such general issues as growing up, seeking an identity, interpersonal relationships, male and female sexuality, the struggle to be an artist, the tensions between individual aspirations and external reality, and learning to deal with social and political problems. Women writers have been accorded relatively brief coverage in the standard literary histories, and in many of the influential critical studies designed to explore the essential spirit and style of a particular literary period or of the national literature as a whole, they have received much less emphasis than males or have been ignored.

When American women writers have been discussed, they have often been forced into limiting categories. Sometimes, only parts of their total work or selected aspects of their central concerns have been considered. Sarah Orne Jewett and Kate Chopin were for many years described primarily as skillful practitioners of "local color" fiction, an interesting but secondary tributary of the American literary mainstream; Edith Wharton was almost always viewed as a lesser Henry James, not as a serious artist working in her own way with her own subject matter; few studies of Katherine Anne Porter stressed her interest in portraying women or her critiques of the roles offered them in Southern society. Black women writers and artists from other minority groups were rarely studied at all. Biases and oversights such as these have finally begun to disappear in recent years, as the American literary tradition has become subject to a revision aimed at including female perspectives, and as many scholars, dissatisfied with conventional responses, have started to subject women writers to a rigorous reexamination, attempting significant confrontations with well-known authors and returning with reawakened attention to their less famous counterparts.

This renewed attentiveness to women writers can in part be attributed to the resurgence of feminism in America and to the resulting interest in all aspects of women's experiences which it has fostered. Generated by the enormous changes in women's lives since World War II, the contemporary women's movement in the United States finds some of its ideological roots in Simone de Beauvoir's *Le Deuxieme Sexe,* published in France in 1949, and in America, as *The Second Sex,* in 1953. In this seminal study of woman and her historical and contemporary situation in Western culture, de Beauvoir, a wide-ranging thinker with strong existentialist and feminist leanings, examines her subject matter from social, historical, biological, psychological, mythological, and literary standpoints. Her thesis is that women's development as free and independent beings and their achievements in many of the endeavors they have undertaken have been hindered by the fact that they have generally been forced to occupy a secondary place in the world in relation to men, not out of any biologically imposed necessity but because of elaborate educational traditions, cultural patterns, and social structures firmly under the control of men.

At the start of the 1960s, concepts similar to those advanced by de Beauvoir began to gain currency in the United States. In 1961, a presidential commission appointed by John Kennedy began investigating and documenting social and economic discrimination against American women; its preliminary report, *American Women,* was completed in 1963. In that same year, Betty Friedan's *The Feminine Mystique,* a study of the causes and effects of the discontents of middle-class American women, which presents in a somewhat less problematic way ideas like those in *Le Deuxieme Sexe,* heralded the rebirth of the women's movement, a movement that had been more or less moribund in this country since the post-suffrage era.

In the years that have followed, scholars from various fields—sociologists, anthropologists, historians, psychologists, theologians, and philosophers—have continued to demonstrate the vitality and originality of the feminist-influenced perspective in opening up fresh areas of investigation and in leading to stimulating interpretations of familiar or hitherto overlooked material. Drawing on each other's research and on the diverse bodies of thought that have come to compose the interdisciplinary field of women's studies, and guided by advances in theory within their own disciplines, such scholars have reassessed social and cultural traditions, reevaluated and challenged received ideas about women, searched out and studied buried records of women's lives, and gathered information necessary to formulate alternative hypotheses about women and about human nature. A few of the excellent studies which have been produced are

The Woman in American History (1971) by Gerda Lerner, *Man's World, Woman's Place* (1972) by Elizabeth Janeway, *Beyond God the Father* (1973) by Mary Daly, and *The Mermaid and the Minotaur: Sexual Arrangements and Human Malaise* (1976) by Dorothy Dinnerstein.

A body of critical studies on the relationship of women and literature has also begun to accumulate. It focuses on goals similar to those of the scholars working in other fields, namely, to rescue women's literary past from misconception and neglect, to argue for the excellence of women's works, and to revise some of the basic concepts of the discipline of literary criticism so that it may encompass female experience and female creativity with greater clarity and precision than before. This criticism, much of which has been influenced by feminist viewpoints and feminist thinking, has in its relatively short history, developed and followed several related lines of inquiry, including systematic reexamination of the biases in past critical commentary on female authors, recovery of lost works by women writers, investigations of the role that gender plays in creativity, and exploration of aspects of women's literary history.

A variety of scholars, chief among them Mary Ellmann in *Thinking About Women* (1968), have demonstrated that in the past literature by women was often misread and misunderstood because certain presuppositions about female talent were so pervasive that they came to be considered accurate descriptions of women's writings. Some of the recurring stereotypes they have identified are that women typically exhibit excessive reliance on autobiography, have the habit of focusing on trivial subject matter, and operate from intuitive rather than analytic sensibility. Such scholars have in fact argued that the characteristic reluctance of so many earlier critics to speak of women writers without reference to their sex is to be attributed not to the perception that women might create a separate, different, and equally significant literature, but rather to the conviction that their writings are inherently less important than men's. They have likewise demonstrated how the early critics' failure to disengage the prevalent concept of woman from her work often led them to substitute a discussion of the writer's personal life for a thoughtful analysis of her fiction or poetry. When they did praise her literary production as containing brilliant insights, they often denied it credibility as a consciously created art by saying that the author, as a woman, could not have been fully aware of the implications of her observations, be they about the situation of women, society at large, or the human condition.

The growing awareness of the stereotypes and mistaken emphases in earlier commentary on women writers has impelled modern critics to seek out those books by women which have been neglected or otherwise ignored by traditional scholarship, to reevaluate them and to document the circumstances which led to their being forgotten or deliberately buried, and sometimes to help restore them to circulation in reprintings generally accompanied by meticulous and insightful commentary placing them in their literary, cultural, and social contexts. In this way, certain original and complex works such as Rebecca Harding Davis' *Life in the Iron Mills* and Charlotte Perkins Gilman's *The Yellow Wallpaper,* to name two exciting rediscoveries in America that have been reissued by The Feminist Press, have once again been made known and easily available to the general public and to literary critics.

Another primary task of contemporary scholars has been to provide better conceptual frameworks for the study of women writers. This undertaking has inevitably involved them in the longstanding and as yet unresolved debate about whether and to what extent the consciousness of being a woman affects the workings of the literary imagination. Some critics assert that the whole question of sex should be considered irrelevant in literary studies because the marks of a true writer, which it is the function of the critic to illuminate, are originality of style and uniqueness of vision. Others, sensing a distinctively female voice and vision in literature by women, have instead maintained that fictional language, structure, and content are at least in part determined by the sex of the creator. Although avoiding sweeping generalizations about the nature of the female mind, these latter scholars have continued to search for evidence of a demonstrable relationship between creativity and gender. They, of course, do not attempt to encompass in their theories all writings by women, a body of literature so vast and varied as to escape any final definition, but focus on those texts in the making of which gender, along with all the other factors on which artists draw, seems to have played a significant role. Among the vexing questions which they have tried to answer in their rigorous reexaminations of groups of women writers have been whether these writers have been possessed of a strong awareness of themselves as women, whether they have developed a literary tradition different from men's, and whether their works invariably, albeit sometimes covertly, contain discourses about the situation of women in their contemporary worlds.

A few of the critics who in different though complementary ways have followed this course of investigation are Patricia Meyer Spacks, the late Ellen Moers, and Sandra Gilbert and Susan Gubar. Their books, all based on an impressive range of scholarship and offering often very original interpretations of both highly esteemed and less well-known authors, have in very little time brought the study of women's literature to a remarkable level of sophistication. Through their delineation of certain issues crucial to a more precise understanding of women's literary achievements, they have opened new prospects and set high standards for future research.

In *The Female Imagination* (1975), Spacks surveys prose fiction and auto-biography by women in the Anglo-American tradition over the last three centuries; she individuates a number of frequently recurring themes and issues, among them the conflict between passivity and moral growth, the problems of altruism and of taking care of other people, the psychological effects of social conditioning on female adolescents, and the complex motives that underlie the woman's choice of the artist's role. The lingering presence of these concerns and the similarities in the ways in which they are presented, she believes, support the idea that "a special female self awareness" emerges in women's literature in every period.

Moers' *Literary Women* (1976) examines such topics and themes as work, money, sexuality, social justice, and private fears and rebellions in literature by major French, English, and American women writers from the mid-eighteenth century to the present day. In each case, she traces the influences these writers had on one another, both in terms of the confidence which they derived from knowing that other women had managed to write and of the inspiration which they received from reading each other's work.

Interested in highlighting the interrelations and tensions between literature by women and literature by men, Gilbert and Gubar, in *The Madwoman in the Attic: The Woman Writer and the Nineteenth Century Literary Imagination* (1979), explore how British and American women writers in the last century responded to the male literary tradition and to its images of women. Building on Harold Bloom's theory of the "anxiety of influence," which posits that truly creative artists are inevitably at odds with their literary predecessors, they maintain that before female writers in the Victorian Age could assert themselves as artists, they had to confront the two "paradigmatic polarities"—angel or monster—in terms of which earlier writers had depicted women. The authors conclude that many female writers resolved this problem by revising or inverting these very images, transforming the monsters into madwomen who lashed out at patriarchal institutions, and the angels into heroines afflicted with limiting psychological problems. These writers, they further suggest, used their angels and madwomen, along with a host of other strategies and literary devices, to express their own subversive desire to challenge social and literary conventions.

Whatever their approach, all of these critics' investigations of the difficulties faced by women writers from the eighteenth century onwards as they struggled for self-definition and self-expression in a literary culture not always sympathetic toward them have invited the reader to look at the phenomenon of female creativity from a new perspective. They have generated the kind of fresh social insight that also makes their work a contribution to the growing awareness of women's unique history. Moreover, their examinations of women's literature in relation to itself and to aspects of the larger tradition have shown that it is possible to view some women's writing both as an imaginative continuum repeating certain patterns, themes, and issues, and also as a dynamic body of literature that develops and changes.

A history of American women writers, presenting the type of richly detailed overview offered by Elaine Showalter in *A Literature of Their Own: British Women Novelists from Brontë to Lessing* (1977), has yet to be written. Such a history would examine these writers' changing conditions of authorship, the extent of their participation in or alienation from the dominant literary movements and trends of their times, and their responses to literature by American men; it would also attempt to determine the common characteristics of their works and whether they share a literary heritage separable from the national tradition. Stimulating studies of chapters in this literary history have, however, been provided by such critics of American women writers as Ann Douglas, Nina Baym, and Barbara Christian.

Douglas in *The Feminization of American Culture* (1977) and Baym in *Woman's Fiction: A Guide to Novels by and about Women in America, 1820-1870* (1978) reconsider from quite different points of view that vast body of best-selling fiction by nineteenth-century women writers. Douglas, concerned with delineating the complicated relationship between historical reality and the literature which both reflects and creates it, studies the lives of representative middle-class women writers and liberal Protestant clergymen, and analyzes their fiction, poetry, sermons, consolation books, and magazine pieces of every kind. She argues that these women and clergymen produced this literature in an attempt to overcome their marginal social status by achieving influence over the mass audience. In so doing, she maintains, they debased the culture by sentimentalizing it and helped create the "passive consumerism and anti-intellectualism which characterize modern mass culture."

Baym instead offers a mainly literary analysis of popular fiction by women. She first identifies and explicates the "single tale" which this fiction tells over and over, the story of the trials and hardships which lead a young heroine to achieve a personal identity and to learn to balance the demands of the self with the needs of others, and then discusses the evolution of this tale in books by Catharine Sedgwick, Susan Warner, E.D.E.N. Southworth, Augusta Jane Evans, and a host of other writers. Unlike Douglas, she holds that this literature represents "a protest against long-entrenched trivializing and contemptuous views of women" and is therefore less sentimental and conservative than is usually believed.

Barbara Christian is one of the critics who in the past few years have made an effort to break the silence surrounding black women writers and who have begun to argue that because of the cultural and social experiences these writers have been obliged to share, they constitute an identifiable literary tradition. Her *Black Women Novelists: The Development of a Tradition, 1892-1976* (1980) is the first full-length study to trace the stages of this tradition. After following the development from colonial times to the 1960s of such stereotypical images of the black woman as the Mammy, the tragic Mulatta, and the Conjure Woman, and discussing their impact on the work of black female artists from Frances Harper to Gwendolyn Brooks, she provides detailed analyses of fiction by three contemporary authors: Paule Marshall, Toni Morrison, and Alice Walker. She focuses on each writer's particular vision of the black community and on her distinctive artistry, and considers the ways her books reflect and attempt to overcome the legacies of racism and sexism.

In addition to books like these, there has been a growing body of criticism devoted to deepening our appreciation of the aims and methods of individual female writers in the United States. Although by no means unified in their methodological commitment or choice of topic, the authors of these studies have all contributed in some degree to what can be seen as a collective effort to provide the bases for thinking about the national experience and identity, and the human condition, in a way that includes women. And they have all tried to reinterpret the literary past along the lines suggested by Adrienne Rich, that is, through "re-vision—the act of looking back, of seeing with fresh eyes, of entering an old text from a new critical direction."

Attesting to the vitality and authority of much of this scholarship are the well-focused essays in this volume, which show critics responding in new ways to fiction by some of America's finest female authors. These critics manifest a willingness and ability to approach fiction by women with an open mind, a belief that revealing answers can be found when new questions are asked, and a commitment to providing insights that are fresh, accurate, and compelling. The topics they consider range from examination of the ways women writers present and evaluate the larger society and general human problems to elucidation of their views on the roles women play and on the female search for selfhood, and from studies of their characteristic styles and fictional strategies to attempts to discern whether it is possible to speak of a feminine aesthetic.

The essays by Judith Fetterley and Barbara Harrell Carson scrutinize the situation of women in society as revealed in the fiction of Edith Wharton and Katherine Anne Porter. Wharton's Lily Bart, the central character of *The House of Mirth,* has most often been viewed as a symbol of the waste of an individual's resources in a particular social and historical milieu. To demonstrate that Lily's tragedy is instead closely related to her being a member of a sexual class, Fetterley highlights the many ways in which Lily is victimized by her patriarchal society, especially by its cult of the woman as a beautiful object, its double standard of social behavior, and, its conception of marriage as an economic transaction. Carson's essay focuses on Porter's sensitive and complex handling of women's social roles and psychological problems in the "Miranda stories," nine pieces about the Rhea family. According to Carson, the tracing of young Miranda's gradual liberation from inherited modes of behavior and thought is meant to indicate the painful route women must follow if they are to achieve independent and honest lives, while the eventual failures of the elder women in the Rhea family to express an authentic selfhood show the tragic consequences of emotional bondage to familial, social, and cultural norms.

Female perspectives on women's roles in society and in the home are similarly discussed by Mary Kelley in her survey of popular literature by a dozen nineteenth century writers. Kelley attempts a mediation between the divergent interpretations of this literature offered by such critics as Ann Douglas and Nina Baym—the view that it thoroughly supports the status quo and the one which finds it implicitly subversive. Detecting both satisfaction and discontent in the novels, short stories, and essays she studies, Kelley explores the secular and religious ideals and the social and cultural realities which gave rise to these contradictory feelings, and comments perceptively on the tensions they created in the plots, characterizations, and messages of women's writings.

In studying Gertrude Stein and Erica Jong, writers intensely aware of their identities both as women and as artists, Cynthia Secor and Joan Reardon try to determine to what extent their concepts of womanhood influenced the evolution of their craft. In an analysis of *Ida, A Novel,* Secor asserts that Stein's lesbian perspective enabled her to write in a unique way about such matters as the struggle for selfhood and interpersonal relationships. She also suggests that Stein's efforts to develop a mode of narration devoid of references to myth, ritual, and other cultural artifacts may have been undertaken in response to having been born a female artist in a predominantly patriarchal tradition. In her discussion of *Fear of Flying,* Reardon illustrates how Jong first presents her heroine's journey to maturity through traditional images and formal structures but then rejects these conventions in favor of experimentation with a distinctively female idiom and the development of a time sequence in the plot that parallels the heroine's menstrual cycle. She interprets these changes as a conscious attempt by Jong to put into practice her conviction that women writers need to come to terms with their own bodies if they are to speak in their own voices.

To clarify the personal dramas of characters in works by Kate Chopin and Sylvia Plath, Cynthia Griffin Wolff and Marjorie G. Perloff use insights from modern psychology. R.D. Laing's description of the schizoid personality and its typical patterns of behavior furnishes Wolff with a vantage point from which to analyze passages in Chopin's *The Awakening* that reveal the splits and stresses within the heroine's character and to examine in some detail her relationships with other people. Her analysis supports her contention that this heroine, rather than being the victim of repressive external forces, is destroyed by her own psychological fragility. In the opening section of her study of Plath's *The Bell Jar*, Perloff also draws on Laing's research to explain the existential dilemma of Esther Greenwood, the novel's narrator and central character. She then shows how Plath links Esther's private psychosis to her larger social situation, pointing out her skill in using Esther to reveal the state of female consciousness in the 1950s and in making even her most intimate experiences emphasize the ills of American society in that decade.

The other essays in this collection, by Blanche H. Gelfant, Joyce Carol Oates, and Susan Willis, illuminate the particular craft and vision of the authors they treat. Writing about Willa Cather's *My Antonia,* Gelfant overturns some common critical assumptions about this novel and brings to light its hidden complexities. She discards Jim Burden as a reliable narrator, because in recounting the past he suppresses its disquieting and threatening aspects. She also notes in the book a consistent linking of love and death and argues that this theme is as central to the story as is its celebration of the American frontier. Moreover, by showing how a number of the episodes usually considered extraneous fit into the overall pattern of the narrative, she refutes the idea that the novel is marred by the presence of some poorly integrated material.

Joyce Carol Oates provides insight into Flannery O'Connor's literary imagination through a study of the often violent and physically brutal revelations into the realm of the spiritual experienced by her characters in the stories in *Everything That Rises Must Converge.* She argues that O'Connor's revelations are illustrative of a view of the relationship between the secular and the sacred which resembles in part ideas expressed by the Christian philosopher Tielhard de Chardin and which links her to other visionary artists like Dostoyevsky, Kafka, and D.H. Lawrence. She also discusses how readers who do not share O'Connor's austere world view can nonetheless appreciate and interpret her work.

Susan Willis describes the problem at the center of Toni Morrison's writing as being how to maintain an Afro-American heritage once black social and cultural forms undergo the disruptions and transformations which inevitably accompany social, economic, and historic change. She shows that in her four novels, *The Bluest Eye, Sula, Song of Solomon,* and *Tar Baby,* Morrison analyzes the particular kinds of alienation and repression which derive from the black community's changing relationship to the ideology and lifestyle of the bourgeois class in strategic moments in modern black history in the United States. Her discussion of this author's literary techniques focuses on the ways in which her images, metaphors, and sensual descriptions allow her readers to understand the psychological and social effects of change on her characters and to perceive these characters' relationship to their black heritage and to the society as a whole.

CHAPTER 2

The Sentimentalists:
Promise and Betrayal In The Home

Mary Kelley

The sentimentalists, especially those who focused upon woman and her role in the family and society, have long been objects of neglect, dismissal, and scorn. Hawthorne's oft-repeated outburst that "America is now wholly given over to a d----d mob of scribbling women" was echoed a century later by Leslie Fiedler's ridicule of "the purely commercial purveyors of domestic sentiments."[1] Adopting a more fruitful perspective, other critics have chosen instead to concentrate upon the social and cultural values articulated by this popular and highly influential group of nineteenth-century writers of fiction. Generally the assessments have been strikingly dissimilar, even contradictory, as the interpretations of Alexander Cowie and Helen Waite Papashvily illustrate. Cowie painted the sentimentalists as ultraconservative, claiming that their fiction "functioned as a sort of benign moral police, whose regulations were principally comprised under the heads of religion and morality."[2] He contended that the image of woman in the fiction was that of a complacent, contented, protected lady; that the writers were undeviating in their banal support of the status quo: "Keen feminist arguments are met by the stock replies that women have intuition but not reason, that they may lose feminine graces in the pursuit of rights, and that men will deteriorate too if the need for chivalry is removed."[3] In direct contrast, Papashvily argued that the fiction betrayed an insidious distaste for the status quo and its male custodians, and that it "encouraged a pattern of feminine behavior so quietly ruthless, so subtly vicious that by comparison the ladies at Seneca appear angels of innocence."[4] In Papashvily's view, these writers believed that "female superiority had to be established and maintained";[5] their fiction, she insisted, constituted a virtual act of insurrection.

Such divergent perspectives as Cowie's and Papashvily's presented distorted assessments by defining the entire body of the literature in terms of certain specific aspects which they treated in isolation. By drawing upon nearly 200 volumes of novels, short stories, and essays written by the twelve women who were the major producers of this prose, as well as upon their personal papers

11

which comprise several thousand letters, journals, and diaries, it is possible to offer an interpretation that not only encompasses the perspectives of Cowie, Papashvily, and others, but even goes beyond them.[6]

Moralists *non pareil,* the sentimentalists have been regarded as the foremost proponents of the nineteenth century's cult of domesticity. It is true that they subscribed to the traditional separation of spheres. As directed by God and in the interests of familial and societal order and stability, the wife was to defer to her husband as head of household.[7] The husband was responsible for conducting the affairs of society and for providing material support for the family. The wife's appointed function was to be the architect of the home—christened Eden. But to perceive the sentimentalists as simply sweet singers of domestic blissfulness, as songsters of the lives of idle, submissive, ornamental middle-class housewives is to ignore the strains in their fiction. In their effort to entertain, instruct, and share grievances with an audience that numbered in the hundreds of thousands, they imparted a contradictory message. They wrote of their domestic dream and revealed a deep discontent. In a hopeful vision of womanly glory, they promoted as a female archetype a strong, commanding, central figure in the home; a supportive and guiding redeemer for her husband; and model and teacher of rectitude for children; and a reformer of and servant to an American society judged to be in dire need of regeneration. The emphasis always was on woman's selflessness and her service to the needs of others.

But the positive, forceful message rode and was partly generated by an undercurrent of dissatisfaction and despair. The determination to enhance woman's image and role represented a simultaneous attempt to protest the status of their female contemporaries and the moral condition of their country in the nineteenth century. Despite their assent and belief in woman's posture as one of deference to a male head-of-household, the glorification of woman as superior being was tantamount to a protest that she had to defer to an erring, inferior husband; the promotion of woman as strong and independent underlined her predicament as a dependent forced to rely upon an unreliable male; and the wonderment at woman's work implied a rejection of the characterization of woman's status as inferior. And in spite of their belief in the domestic as woman's properly restricted sphere, they were apprehensive that woman's position was dependent upon the stability of the family and fearful that, because of the burden of household duties and the demands of serving the needs of others, woman's autonomy was diminished and her individuality denied. Melodramatic and simplistic though the plots may be, wooden and stereotyped though the characters may appear, the protest in the novels and stories frequently preempted the prescription. In the prescription and the protest lay the promise and the betrayal of the nineteenth-century woman.

The sentimentalists did not write in a vacuum. Premature death and debilitating illness, financial fluctuations and domestic instability touched their own lives as children and as mature women. In a century of upheaval, movement, and turmoil, status was uncertain and social stability tenuous. America was economically and geographically expanding and changing and the agrarian and rural landscape was becoming industrial and urban. A nation dedicated to material progress invited the pursuit of the dollar, wild speculation, and rampant opportunism. The response of these writers was to express a nostalgia for an imagined past and a demand that society return to supposedly traditional, more communally oriented values. Their familial experience revealed to them the reality of the mutual dependence of human beings and they insisted that an increasingly pervasive individualism yield to an older ethic that gave precedence to the community—to the needs and desires of others. They deplored society's materialism and called for reimmersion in the spiritual. These goals, they believed, could only be achieved by women whom they promoted as superior, selfless, strong beings, and whom they heralded as society's moral guardians, reformers, and judges. The family, glorified as a source of virtue and as a sacred refuge from an increasingly competitive, fragmented, and transitory society, was regarded as the arena in which woman would fulfill her exemplary, anointed role.

The sentimentalists perceived a moral vacuum in a country that lacked a central authoritative force, and moved to fill it by dispensing prescription disguised as fantasy. As the daughters and wives of clergymen, legislators, journalists, educators, merchants, and jurists they came from families that provided a leading, prominent, active citizenry, accustomed to the tradition of overseeing its society's values and its nation's direction. As women they were restricted to the private domestic sphere, but as writers they in effect sought to comment upon and influence the very public life in which they had no part. They exercised the role without the title. In their unceasing efforts to proselytize their readers, they transformed the fiction into didactic essays, speaking directly to their readers in prefaces or intruding in the pages of their melodramas as author or omniscient narrator. Some even added footnotes. Uncertain of themselves as artists, they harbored no doubts that their art should have a moral purpose. All would have agreed with the view expressed by Augusta Evans Wilson in a letter to a friend: "Should not excelsior be the Watchword and motto of the true artist? Is not an artist a great reformer whose instructions are pictorial? Art should elevate, should refine, should sanctify the heart."[8] Echoing Wilson's credo, Mary J. Holmes wrote: "I mean always to write a good, pure, natural story, such as mothers are willing their daughters should read, and such as will do good instead of harm."[9] A model for society, Augusta Evans Wilson's heroine, Edna Earl, stood as the fictional counterpart of the sentimentalist writer: "The fondest hope of Edna's heart was to be useful in 'her day and generation'— to be an instrument of some good to her race...."[10] As a writer, herself, she did not desire popularity "as an end, but as a means to an end—usefulness to my fellow creatures."[11]

Self-appointed critics of their society, the sentimentalists did not, however, stand alone in their demand that Americans adopt alternative values. Their attitudes were the secular equivalent to the righteous, reformist ethos of Protestantism. Their views reflected the convictions espoused by the Protestant ministry in various denominations. All twelve of the writers were committed Protestants. Most maintained close ties with ministers; three married members of the clergy. As writers, they regarded themselves as preachers of the fictional page. Catharine Maria Sedgwick, for example, earnestly professed to the clergyman William Ellery Channing that "neither pride nor humility should withhold us from the work to which we are clearly 'sent,' "[12] Mary Virginia Terhune's heroine, Phemie Hart, perceives her purpose as a writer to parallel that of the minister: "If God had given me strength, it seemed to me that I should help the weak, if courage, I ought to cheer the desponding. If knowledge were mine, it should be shared with those who were ignorant."[13] Mirroring their clerical counterparts, the sentimentalists expressed the belief that their labors were totally dependent upon, and directed by, God's beneficence. In reply to Dorothea Dix's praise of *The Wide, Wide World,* Susan Warner rejected any credit for herself: "I do not deserve your commendations,—not in anywise. You say 'God bless me' for what I have done,—nay but I say 'Thank him for it,' and I wash my hands of all desert in the matter."[14] Maria Cummins ascribed all of her efforts to heaven; "If I have ever done anything worth doing, it has been through the motives and spirit" of God.[15] Harriet Beecher Stowe went so far as to exclaim that God, himself, had penned *Uncle Tom's Cabin.*

For the sentimentalists, piety involved more than an inner conviction. Love of God was expressed by love of others. To submit to the will of God did not imply passivity. Selflessness did not mean simple self-denial. One served God by actively serving others. Heroines and readers alike are told to obey God's command and defer their own needs and interests to those of others. Maria McIntosh's Augusta Moray is predictably admonished by an equally predictable figure, her minister, to "Get away from yourself—let your sympathies and work be no longer for yourself. . .but for the needy and sorrowing wherever you find them; and let your trust, your reliance be not on yourself, not on any human arm, but on God."[16] "Learn above all things," the headmistress of a female academy says sternly to Maria Cummins's Mabel Vaughan, "to beware of self-love, and cultivate to the utmost a universal charity."[17] The heroines prove able students. E.D.E.N. Southworth's Catherine Kavanaugh "lived only for the good of others," having "grown to believe that there was no individual happiness for herself except in the service of others."[18] While the first, primary duty was to serve family, frequently anyone in need, or in need of reformation, became "family." The "ideal woman"—strong, active, and independent—is to serve family and community. The "fashionable woman" is a prominent object of derision and shame in the fiction not only because she symbolized the corrupting materialism of the age but because she lent credence to the notion that the middle-class woman was idle, narcissistic, and unproductive. The writers were adamant in their insistence that theirs was not a leisured class; theirs was not a philosophy of leisure.

Although the sentimentalists espoused the ministers' view that both man and woman were prone to the sin of selfishness, they chose to focus upon man's, and not woman's, transgressions. Man demonstrated his lack of piety by disregarding the needs of others. Novel after novel, story after story, repeated the melodramatic tale of man's obsessive quest for wealth and social position. They agreed, too, that human beings must strive for regeneration, but they stressed man's need of woman's aid to reform. Writing to her brother, Henry Ward Beecher, Harriet Beecher Stowe repeated the claim and the complaint that "it is the women who hold the faith in the world. The mothers and wives who suffer and must suffer to the end of time to bear the sins of the beloved in their own bodies."[19] These writers saw themselves as their brother's keeper, a term which was paradoxically more fitting for them than the clergy. Whereas ministers perceived themselves as responsible for the reformation of all human beings, regardless of sex, the sentimentalists called upon women to reform men whose sins most directly threatened the family.

Throughout the incredible events in the fiction, the bizarre and complicated plots, the heroine's superior character is apparent and her dominating presence felt. The pious, deferential chaste wife, while she could not be openly proclaimed the authoritative figure in the home, is directed to guide and influence her husband and becomes absolutely vital to his moral well-being. Harry Henderson in Harriet Beecher Stowe's *My Wife and I* describes his mother's power over his father as the "spiritual and invisible" power of the "soul over the body," a "subtle and vital power which constantly gains control and holds every inch that it gains." However manipulative it may seem, the influence of Henderson's mother upon his father is, according to Stowe, stabilizing and uplifting. Gradually, and surely, she becomes his "leader and guide," and he in turn begins to exhibit "new and finer traits of tenderness and spirituality [that pervade] his character and his teachings." The father, himself, admits that his wife "made me by her influence."[20]

Given the superiority of the female, it was logical for her to claim sole right to care for her children. Parton's "A Mother's Soliloquy" delineates the complete moral and physical dependence of the child upon the mother: "I am the centre [of the child's] little world; its very life depends upon my faithful care." The language is saccharine, the tone maudlin, but the point is clear: "It is my sweet duty to deck those dimpled limbs—to poise that tiny, trembling foot. Yet Stay,—my duty ends not here! A soul looks forth from those blue eyes—an undying spirit, that shall plume its wing for ceaseless flight guided by my erring hand."[21] The sentimentalists insisted that woman alone must train her children in virtue: "It is *her* hand which God appointed to trace the first character on man's unwritten mind," wrote Caroline Lee Hentz.[22] And Mary Virginia Terhune hoped her female readers could recognize the "grandeur of the work assigned to them." In fact, the writers claimed, as Terhune put it, that women were "the architects of the nation's fortunes, the sculptors, whose fair or foul handiwork is to outlast their age, to outlive Time, to remain through all Eternity."[23] Glorifying womanhood, the writers sought to impress on their female readers a domestic brand of noblesse oblige.

The wife and mother was appointed the architect of a home that was to embody perfection. "Home was her true sphere," wrote Caroline Howard Gilman, "there everything was managed with promptitude and decision."[24] While the supposedly responsible, reliable husband and father absented himself from the family on a daily basis in order to provide for its support and meet his obligations to the community, the wife and mother, as the family's vital, living center was so essential to the functioning of the home that its very existence could not be imagined without her. Likening the home to the church, Harriet Beecher Stowe stated that it was the "appointed sphere for woman, more holy than cloister, more saintly and pure than church and altar. . . . Priestess, wife, and mother, there she ministers daily in holy works of household peace."[25] The home was the only realm in which woman was supposed to reign. Anointed the moral guardian for all society, she was called upon to transform its values, and yet she was to achieve that goal within the confines of the home. As Catharine Maria Sedgwick suggested: "By an unobtrusive and unseen process, are the characters of men formed, at home, by the mother, the first teacher. There the moral nature is fixed." "I cannot believe that it was ever intended," Sedgwick stated categorically, "that women should lead armies, harangue in the halls of legislation, bustle up to ballot-boxes, or sit on judicial tribunals."[26] The boundaries of woman's realm could not be enlarged or her role extended, warned Augusta Evans Wilson, "without rendering the throne unsteady, and subverting God's law of order. Woman reigned by divine right only at home."[27] Glorified as a divinely appointed station for woman, as a haven for man, and as a moral setting for the rearing of children, "home" was an Eden. Maria McIntosh dubbed it "the nursery of pure and high thoughts."[28] The source of virtue, the home was ipso facto the source of happiness. Mary Virginia Terhune rejoiced: "Home! wife! peace! Sweet synonyms that sum up the rapturous emotions of many a satisfied heart."[29]

The shining image that the sentimentalists sought to promote, however, is eclipsed by the graven image they actually projected. The domestic dream proffered, it vanishes in due course. Prescription runs aground in the protest of the fiction. Of course, it was not the conscious intention of the sentimentalists to transmit to their readers a predominantly negative image of woman's role in the family and society. But their fiction is an apt illustration of D.H. Lawrence's remark on American literature in general: "Never trust the artist. Trust the tale."[30] As "artists" they intended to impress on their readers the example of superior heroines serving family and nation. They tried to project the Edenic image, the perfect home for their readers' worship and emulation. Nevertheless, the "tales" subverted their intentions. The novels and short stories coalesce into one long melodrama of heroines trying valiantly to meet the challenges of woman's role with partial success and little satisfaction. The glorified, heroic role envisioned for the wife is frequently seen as confining and stultifying. Social and economic disaster, sickness and death plague the performance of her roles. The achievement of Eden frequently eludes them and the ameliorative impact of their superior self-sacrificing nature is continually undermined by the impurity of those around them.

Although the writers did not hesitate to damn fashionable women obsessed with self-gratification who abandoned hearth and home as the focus of existence, most often, the villain was man. Impious, abusive of his privileged position as head of household, a trifler and despoiler of woman's sexual virtue, man was the threat to the domestic dream. At times, he is indifferent to the family's welfare, forgets or refuses to be a provider, neglects his children, and fails to abide by his wife's moral example. At other times, he is well-meaning but weak and irresponsible, incapable of performing his assigned role. That all men in the fiction are not evil incarnate tells us that the writers were not motivated by a vengeful hatred of men. The "ideal man" does make his infrequent appearance and his portrait amounts to a study in the feminization of the male. This male hero seeks above all to serve the needs of others, particularly of women. Nor did the sentimentalists think that every erring man was hopeless. In the most optimistic of instances, the morally flawed male is ultimately receptive to woman's moral direction. Led by the angels of mercy, man's self-concern gives way to concern for others, the harm done to others is rectified, the moral lesson imparted, and the novel or story concludes with the overwhelmed male bathing his mate in bathetic praise, and the woman, deluged in tears, consenting to continue as his mentor.

But man is not always redeemed in the fiction and there are not always happy endings. From the thicket of plots and subplots emerges the reprobate who is unresponsive to woman's ministrations, the unregenerated male whose corrupt values and destructive acts have a lasting impact. To such a man, money and social position are far more important than his intimates. Caroline Lee Hentz's *Rena: or, the Snowbird* accents man's quest for wealth and social position at all costs, including the seduction and betrayal of women, and the total neglect of familial obligations. Herbert Lindsay's finale is to commit suicide, but not before becoming Hentz's spokesman, in a lament that underlines the grievances women hold against men. "I have chilled her by coldness, bruised her by harshness—yet she loves me still. Oh! woman, woman! great and marvelous is thy love! Ill-requited, wronged and suffering woman! surely there must be a heaven for thee if not for transgressing man!"[31] Herbert strikes the mournful note that reverberates through the sentimentalists' fiction.

By dwelling upon the immoral, at times, depraved, tyrannical male and his pillage of woman and the family, the sentimentalists revealed their dismal and dire prognosis of nineteenth-century society. The self-concerned, aggressive male in their fiction symbolizes the rampant, destructive individualism which they were convinced was preempting a higher commitment to community. Repudiating the prevalent notion that goods stood for greatness, the writers disdained materialism as the damnable worship of the golden calf. Not only did man's mania for money cloud his judgment, it corrupted his virtue. Materialistic, individualistic, immoral man appears again and again in their pages as the bellwether, the diseased product of a society obsessed with the money that bought privilege and power.

Man proves to be the leading villain in a play that was supposed to be an idyll of the home. Just as the chief beneficiaries of woman's reformation are man and the family, so the primary victims of man's immoral behavior are woman and the family. Instead of reformer, woman ends up the victim. The divinely ordained symbol of the home, on the one hand, woman also appears as thwarted, dissatisfied, and dejected, as physically and emotionally overburdened. In *Recollections of a Housekeeper,* Caroline Howard Gilman speaks of the "cares [that] eat away at her heart." Demands made upon her are unceasing as each "day presses on her with new toils, the night comes, and they are unfulfilled; she lies down in weariness, and rises with uncertainty." Gilman bemoans the fact that "many a woman breaks and sinks beneath the wear and tear of the frame and the affections."[32] Maria McIntosh added her own note of distress for woman's plight: "Work—work—work, till heart and hand fail, till the cloud gather on her once sunny brow, and her cheeks grow pale, and friendly consumption come to give her rest from her labors in the grave, or the throbbing brain and over-anxious heart overpower the reason, and a lunatic asylum receive one more miserable inmate."[33] Citing an officer's report for the Retreat of the Insane in Hartford, Connecticut, McIntosh emphasized its claim that many young women sought refuge in "lunatic" hospitals, unable or unwilling to do battle any longer with their domestic circumstances. The primary architect of a home that was to embody peace, order, and perfection, woman was demoralized in her restricted sphere, denied the benefits of emotional and intellectual stimulation. In *Husbands and Homes,* Mary Virginia Terhune angrily charged that confinement and isolation "have racked and strained muscle and nerve, turned our daily bread into ashes, blunted our perceptions to all that was once beautiful to the sight, pleasant to the ear, stimulative to the intellect."[34]

The defects of man and the burdens of domesticity made it difficult if not impossible to create the idealized home and family. The sentimentalists had hoped to advance the nuclear family as the critical institution for the maintenance and reform of the social fabric, but as protestors they disclosed imperfections in its structure that precluded an adequate performance of its function. Death was its own final drama of the unrealized familial Eden. If the mother died, the husband might continue to provide material sustenance but was unsuited to discharge the responsibilities of his wife. His inadequate care promised wayward sons and daughters. Caroline Lee Hentz's Bryant Clinton is denied the "gentle, yet restraining influence which woman in her purity and excellence, ever asserts. . . ."[35] Encouraged to gamble by his father, Bryant goes into debt, robs a helpless widow, and is finally imprisoned. Because Augusta Temple's father instills the belief that physical appearance is more important than her conduct, he renders her "vain from adulation, and selfish from indulgence."[36]

When the father died, on the other hand, the mother was not prepared or encouraged to earn a livelihood for herself and her children. The widow and her children, isolated from both relatives and society, were left stranded in the home without adequate means of support. But it was the fate that awaited children when both parents died that signaled the final destruction of the nuclear family. No figure is either treated with greater emotion or sentimentality, or endures greater hardship and privation than the orphan who appears in the work of every writer. Maria Cummins's Gertrude Flint is the archetypal orphan. Cared for by a cruel old woman, Gertrude is totally neglected—"scantily clad, in garments of the poorest description. . .her complexion was sallow, and her whole appearance unhealthy." She is also denied affection: "No one loved her. . . . No one treated her kindly; no one tried to make her happy, or cared whether she were so."[37] Many, like Gertrude, are condemned to orphan asylums. In *Rose Clark,* Sara Parton describes the suffering resignation of orphans with their closely shaven heads, "lackluster eyes, stooping forms and pale faces. . .the hopeless, weary look on those subdued faces."[38]

The shift from prescription to protest and beyond in the fiction of the sentimentalists is accompanied by a critical and sometimes bitter disillusionment. This shift in tone symbolized a fall from innocence. In the interests of prescription and entertainment, the sentimentalists began with a blueprint of what family life in nineteenth-century America should be only to end by issuing what was a report on the condition of family life in nineteenth-century America. In the words of Mary Virginia Terhune, the writers became involved in "writing hard things and heavy to be borne by the young with whom hope is reality, and thoughts of love dearer than promise of life, wealth, and honor; but he who sketches from nature must, perforce, oftentimes fulfill the thankless task of iconoclast."[39] The writers attempted to project an ideal image of the home, the family, marriage, and domesticity, but the contrast between intention and realization is evident throughout. The fiction of the sentimentalists is, finally, expressive of a dark vision of nineteenth-century America, and not, as they wished, of the redemptive, idyllic, holy land.

CHAPTER 3

Thanatos and Eros: Kate Chopin's *The Awakening*

Cynthia Griffin Wolff

After its initially dramatic reception, *The Awakening* slipped into an unde-served state of neglect; now, partly as a result of the new feminist criticism, the pendulum has swung in quite the other direction, and Chopin has been hailed as an early advocate of women's rights. Edmund Wilson sees *The Awakening* as an anticipation of D.H. Lawrence in its treatment of infidelity.[1] Kenneth Eble maintains that "the novel is an American *Madame Bovary,* though such a desig-nation is not precisely accurate. Its central character is similar: the married woman who seeks love outside a stuffy, middle-class marriage."[2] Jules Cha-metzky is even more explicit: "What does surprise one is the modernity. . .of Mrs. Chopin's insights into 'the woman question.' It is not so much that she advocates woman's libidinal freedom or celebrates the force of the body's prerogatives. . . .What Kate Chopin shows so beautifully are the pressures work-ing against woman's true awakening to her condition, and what that condition is."[3]

There are differences, of course, among these evaluations, but the underlying similarity is unmistakable: all see the power of the novel as growing out of an existential confrontation between the heroine and some external, repressive force. Thus, one might say that it is the woman against stifling sexual standards or that it is the woman against the tedium of a provincial marriage. Chametzky offers, perhaps, the most detailed explanation: "The struggle is for the woman to free herself from being an object or possession defined in her functions, or owned, by others."[4] Certainly elements of the novel serve to confirm these interpretations, especially if one takes seriously some of the accusations leveled by the heroine in moments of anger or distress. Edna is disillusioned by marriage; to her "a wedding is one of the most lamentable spectacles on earth" (p. 172).[5] Even so, the contemporary readings of the novel which stress Edna's position as a victim of society's standards do not capture its power; for although it is not a great novel—perhaps it is even a greatly flawed novel because of the elusiveness of its focus—reading it can be a devastating and unforgettable experience. And such an experience can simply not grow out of a work whose importance lies in the fact that it anticipates Lawrence or that it is a sort of American *Madame Bovary*. Such evaluations are diminishing. The importance of Chopin's work does not lie in its anticipation of "the woman question" or of any other question; it derives from its ruthless fidelity to the disintegration of Edna's character. Edna, in turn, interests us not because she is "a woman," the implication being that her experience is principally important because it might stand for that of any other woman. Quite the contrary; she interests us because she is human—because she fails in ways which beckon seductively to all of us. Conrad might say that, woman *or* man, she is "one of us."

It is difficult to define Edna's character as it might have existed before we meet her in the novel, for even at its opening such stability as she may have had has already been disrupted. We do learn something of her background. She is the middle child of an ambiguously religious family. "She comes of sound old Presbyterian Kentucky stock. The old gentleman, her father, I have heard, used to atone for his week-day sins with his Sunday devotions. I know for a fact, that his race horses literally ran away with the prettiest bit of Kentucky farming land I ever laid eyes upon" (pp. 171-172). The family has two faces, then: it "sins" (during the week) with its racing and land-grabbing; and it "atones" (on Sundays) with pious condemnations. The character of each of the daughters reflects this contradiction. So Margaret, the oldest "has all the Presbyterian undiluted" (p. 172); she is "matronly and dignified, probably from having assumed matronly and house-wifely responsibilities too early in life, their mother having died when they were quite young. Margaret was not effusive; she was practical" (pp. 43-44). She was also, quite possibly, in her remote and disapproving way, the principal mother-figure for Edna. Janet, on the other hand, "the youngest is something of a vixen" (p. 172). Edna, caught between the two extremes, can live comfortably with neither portion of the family's double standard; instead she tries to evolve a habit or manner which will accommodate both.

The attempt to internalize this contradiction combines with other of Edna's psychic needs to produce an "identity" which is predicated on the conscious process of concealment. In some sense there are two Ednas: "At a very early period she had apprehended instinctively the dual life—that outward existence which conforms, the inward life which questions" (p. 35). Therefore she is very little open to sustained emotional relationships because those elements of character which she might want to call her "real" self must remain hidden, revealed only to herself. "Edna had had an occasional girl friend, but whether accidentally or not, they seemed to have been all of one type—the self-contained. She never realized that the reserve of her own character had much, perhaps everything, to do with this" (p. 44). Not that Edna *wants* to be so entirely alone. On the contrary, the cool distancing tone of her "visible" character conceals an ardent yearning for intensity, for passion. So Edna provides the passion she needs in the only manner which seems safely available to her— through daydreaming.

Edna often wondered at one propensity which sometimes had inwardly disturbed her without causing any outward show or manifestation on her part. At a very early age—perhaps it was when she traversed the ocean of waving grass—she remembered that she had been passionately enamored of a dignified and sad-eyed cavalry officer who visited her father in Kentucky. She could not leave his presence when he was there, nor remove her eyes from his face, which was something like Napoleon's, with a lock of black hair falling across the forehead. But the cavalry officer melted imperceptibly out of her existence.

At another time her affections were deeply engaged by a young gentleman who visited a lady on a neighborhood plantation. It was after they went to Mississippi to live. The young man was engaged to be married to the young lady, and they sometimes called upon Margaret, driving over of afternoons in a buggy. Edna was a little miss, just merging into her teens; and the realization that she herself was nothing, nothing, nothing to the engaged young man was a bitter affliction to her. But he too, went the way of dreams.

She was a grown young woman when she was overtaken by what she supposed to be the climax of her fate. It was when the fact and figure of a great tragedian began to haunt her imagination and stir her senses. *The persistence of the infatuation lent it an aspect of genuineness. The hopelessness of it colored it with the lofty tones of a great passion.*

The picture of the tragedian stood enframed upon her desk. Any one may possess the portrait of a tragedian without exciting suspicion or comment. (pp. 45-46, italics added)

The emotional change here must be described as the development of an increasingly resistant barrier between the "real" external world and that world which was most authentic in Edna's experience—the inner world of her fantasies. Thus her libidinal energies are focused first on a real man who is in some ways genuinely available to her; he is apparently unmarried, unattached and a frequent visitor to the family home. Still, he is a good deal older than she, and his chief attraction seems to be his resemblance to Napoleon (and perhaps the romantic aura attached to his having been a cavalry officer—one calls to mind the clanging spurs which echo in Edna's memory as she is drowning). The next object of Edna's affections is manifestly unavailable since he is engaged to her sister's friend, and although the realization that she was "nothing, nothing, nothing to the engaged man" may have made Edna consciously miserable, there is a form of safety, too, in nothingness. The passion is never expressed, always controlled, with only the substantial threat of "dreams" which melt away. Characteristically, she reserves her greatest passion for a figure of pure fantasy, the tragedian whose picture one can possess "without exciting suspicion or comment."

Given the apparent terror which genuine emotional involvement inspires in Edna, her marriage to a man like Léonce Pontellier is no accident. No one would call him remarkable; most readers might think him dull, insensitive, unperceptive, even callous. Certainly he is an essentially prosaic man. If one assumed that marriage was to be an intimate affair of deep understanding, all of these qualities would condemn Léonce. Yet for Edna they are the very qualities which recommend him. "The acme of bliss, which would have been marriage with the tragedian, was not for her in this world" (p. 47); such bliss, indeed, is not for anyone *in this world*. It is a romantic illusion, a dream—defined by its very inability to be consummated. What is more, the intensity of dreams such as these may have become disturbing to Edna. So she chooses to marry Léonce; after all "as the devoted wife of a man who worshiped her, she felt she would take her place with a certain dignity in the world of reality, closing the portals forever behind her upon the realm of romance and dreams" (p. 47). The marriage to such a man as Léonce was, then, a defensive maneuver designed to maintain the integrity of the two "selves" that formed her character and to reinforce the distance between them. Her outer self was confirmed by the entirely conventional marriage while her inner self was safe—known only to Edna. An intuitive man, a sensitive husband, might threaten it; a husband who evoked passion from her might lure the hidden self into the open, tempting Edna to attach her emotions to flesh and blood rather than phantoms. Léonce is neither, and their union ensures the secret safety of Edna's "real" self. "It was not long before the tragedian had gone to join the cavalry officer and the engaged young man and a few others; and Edna found herself face to face with the realities. She grew fond of her husband, realizing with some unaccountable satisfaction that no trace of passion or excessive and fictitious warmth colored her affection, *thereby threatening its dissolution*" (p. 47, italics added).

If we try to assess the configuration of Edna's personality when she comes to Grand Isle at the novel's beginning, we might best do so by using R.D. Laing's description of the "schizoid" personality. As Laing would describe it, the schizoid personality consists of a set of defenses which have been established as an attempt to preserve some semblance of coherent identity. "The self, in order to develop and sustain its identity and autonomy, and in order to be safe from the persistent threat and danger from the world, has cut itself off from direct relatedness with others, and has endeavoured to become its own object; to become, in fact, related directly only to itself. Its cardinal functions become phantasy and observation. Now, in so far as this is successful, one necessary consequence is that the self has difficulty sustaining any *sentiment du réel* for the very reason that it is not 'in touch' with reality, it never actually 'meets' reality."[6]

Laing's insights provide at least a partial explanation for elements of the novel which might otherwise be unclear. For example, Edna's fragility or susceptibility to the atmosphere at Grand Isle (as compared, for example, with her robust friend Madame Ratignolle, or the grand aloofness of Madame Reisz) can be traced to the circular ineffectiveness of the schizoid mechanism for maintaining identity. To be specific, such a person must be simultaneously alert to and protected from any invitation to interact with the real world since all genuine interactions leave the hidden "real" self exposed to potential danger. Vigilance begets threat which in turn precipitates withdrawal and renewed vigilance.[7]

More important, interpersonal relationships can be conceived of only in cataclysmic terms; "there is a constant dread and resentment at being turned into someone else's thing, of being penetrated by him, and a sense of being in someone else's power and control. Freedom then consists in being inaccessible."[8] Such habits of mind comport with Edna's outbursts concerning her own relationships.

Certainly her rather dull husband seems not to notice her except as a part of the general inventory of his worldly goods: thus early in the novel he is described as "looking at his wife as one looks at a valuable piece of personal property which has suffered some damage" (p. 4). Yet his attentions, such as they are, are rather more indicative of indifference than otherwise. Indeed, at every point within the narrative when he might, were he so inclined, assert his "rights," he declines to do so. After the evening swimming party, for example, when he clearly desires sexual intercourse and his wife does not wish to comply, he utters but a few sharp words and then, surprising for a man so supposedly interested in the proprietary relationship, slips on a robe and comes out to keep her company during her fitful vigil (see pp. 78-81). After their return to New Orleans, he reacts to Edna's disruption of her "wifely functions" with but momentary impatience; he does not attempt coercion, and he goes to the lengths of consulting a physician out of concern for her well-being. Even when Edna has taken up residence in her diminutive "pigeon house" Léonce decides to leave her to her own ways. His only concern—a small-minded one, to be sure—is to save appearances.

It is hard to cast such an ultimately insignificant man in the role of villain—compared with a man like Soames Forsyte or with some of the more brutal husbands in Chopin's short stories. Léonce is a slender vehicle to carry the weight of society's repression of women. Yet Edna sees herself as his possession, even as she sees herself the prisoner of her children's demands. Her dying thoughts confirm this fixation: "She thought of Léonce and the children. They were a part of her life. But they need not have thought that they could possess her, body and soul" (p. 302). Now if Léonce is not able to rise to the occasion of possessing her body and soul, the children as they are portrayed in the novel, seem to exercise even less continuous claim upon her. They are always accompanied by a nurse whose presence frees Edna to pursue whatever interests she can sustain; what is more, they spend much of their time with their paternal grandmother, who seems to welcome them whenever Edna wishes to send them. Her emotional relationship with them is tenuous at best, certainly not demanding and by no stretch of the imagination stifling. "She was fond of her children in an uneven, impulsive way. She would sometimes gather them passionately to her heart; she would sometimes forget them" (p. 47). Given the extraordinary latitude that Edna did in fact have, we might better interpret her feelings of imprisonment as projections of her own attitudes and fears. The end of the novel offers an ironic affirmation of such a view, for when she returns home from Madame Ratignolle's accouchement, even her apparently positive expectations with regard to Robert follow the same familiar definition: "She could picture at that moment no greater bliss on earth than possession of the beloved one" (p. 291). The wording is somewhat ambiguous—she might possess him, he might possess her, the "possession" might be understood as a synonym for sexual union—still the key word here is *possession*, and it is Edna's word.

Possession, as descriptive of any intense emotional involvement, is both tempting and terrifying. To yield to possession is to become engulfed, to be nothing. The antiphonal emblematic figures that appear like phantoms while Edna is staying at Grand Isle reflect the dilemma. On the one hand there are the lovers, intimate, always together, seemingly happy, a beckoning vision of replenishment which carries always with it the fear of annihilation. And then there is the woman in black, the emblem of the self-destroyed in a bizarre act of self-preservation, withdrawn from all personal interaction—"safe" and "free."

One solution for the problem Edna faces would be to formulate a way to have her relationship with Robert without ever *really* having it. Temporarily she does effect such a solution, and she does so in two ways. First, while she is at Grand Isle, she systematically denies the possibility of an adult relationship with him; this denial takes the form of her engulfing him ("possessing" him, perhaps) by a kind of incorporation of his personality into her own. She accepts his attentions, his services, his affection; and in so far as these are important to her, she comes to regard them as extensions of her own will or desire. Robert is not conceived of as a separate, individuated being, and thus she repeatedly is surprised and dismayed when his actions unaccountably (to her) deviate from her wishes. We can see this aspect of their relationship very early in a trivial incident when Robert leaves her one evening and fails to return. "She wondered why Robert had gone away and left her. It did not occur to her to think he might have grown tired of being with her the livelong day. She was not tired, and she felt that he was not. She regretted that he had gone. It was so much more natural to have him stay, when he was not absolutely required to leave her" (p. 103). This scene and Edna's reaction is a foreshadowing of the much more distressing separation when Robert leaves for Mexico. "But can't you understand? I've grown used to seeing you, to having you with me all the time, and your action seems unfriendly, even unkind. You don't even offer an excuse for it. Why, I was planning to be together, thinking of how pleasant it would be to see you in the city next winter" (p. 114). She finds it difficult, if not impossible, to separate his will or his wishes from her own, to acknowledge his existence independent of hers. Only after he has left can she safely *feel* the intensity of passion that later comes to be associated with him; and she can do so because once physically absent, he can be made magically present as a phantom, an object of her own imagination, a figure which is now truly a part of herself. She has reawakened the cavalry officer, the young engaged, the tragedian; "for the first time she recognized anew the symptoms of infatuation which she had felt incipiently as a child, as a girl in her earliest teens, and later as a young woman" (p. 116). As a woman, however, Edna wants more.

Thus she evolves a second solution by which she can have a relationship with Robert without being forced to fuse the outer and the inner "selves" that comprise her identity. This stratagem is the affair with Arobin. She can respond sensually to the kiss which initiated their relationship precisely because she has no feeling for him. Her feelings are fixed safely on the *image* of Robert; "there was Robert's reproach making itself felt by a quicker, fiercer, more overpowering love, which had awakened within her toward him" (p. 219). And this arrangement frees her from anxiety, leaving only a "dull pang of regret."[9] When Robert does, in fact, return, the problem of fusing the outer world with the "real" world within returns with him; and, as before, the fantasy is easier to deal with. "A hundred times Edna has pictured Robert's return, and imagined their first meeting. It was usually at her home, whither he had sought her out at once.

She always fancied him expressing or betraying in some way his love for her. And here, the reality was that they sat ten feet apart, she at the window, crushing geranium leaves in her hand and smelling them, he twirling around on the piano stool" (pp. 256-57).

Robert's return and his sensuous awakening to her kiss (pp. 282-84) precipitates the final crisis from which she must flee. She cannot, in the end, yield her "self" to the insistence of his passionate plea to stay; and his own subsequent flight destroys the fantasy lover as well. Both of Edna's selves are truly betrayed and barren, and she retrenches in the only manner familiar to her, that of a final and ultimate withdrawal. As Laing says: "If the whole of the individual's being cannot be defended, the individual retracts his lines of defence until he withdraws within a central citadel. He is prepared to write off everything he is, except his 'self'. But the tragic paradox is that the more the self is defended in this way, the more it is destroyed. The apparent eventual destruction and dissolution of those in schizophrenic conditions is accomplished not by external attacks from the enemy (actual or supposed), from without, but by the devastation caused by the inner defensive manoeuvres themselves."[10]

This description of Edna's defensive patterns is an invaluable aid in understanding the novel; however, taken alone it does not lead to a complete explanation. We can understand, perhaps, why Edna's act of self-destruction seems the logical culmination of other apparently nondestructive behavior, but we cannot yet comprehend the manner of her dissolution, nor the significance to Edna (which must have been central) of Madame Ratignolle's accouchement or of Edna's own children, who seem to haunt her even though their *physical* presence scarcely enters the novel. More important, the tone of the novel—perhaps its most artistically compelling element—cannot yet be described or explained in any but the most general terms as a reflection of Edna's schizoid affinity for fantasy. Even the title of the work, *The Awakening,* suggests a positive quality with which Edna's systematic annihilation of self (albeit from the most "self-preserving" motives) seems oddly at variance. Thus though we might accept the psychic anatomy defined by Laing as schizoid, we must go beyond simple categorizing to understand the novel as a whole.

We might begin with the title itself. Surely one unavoidable meaning of the title has to do with Edna's secret "real" self. She had married a Creole and yet she "was not thoroughly at home in the society of Creoles. . . .A characteristic which distinguished them and which impressed Mrs. Pontellier most forcibly was their entire absence of prudery. Their freedom of expression was at first incomprehensible to her, though she had no difficulty in reconciling it with a lofty chastity which in the Creole woman seems to be inborn and unmistakable" (pp. 22-23). The unfamiliar mode of conduct which seems most puzzling to Edna is the ability to have affect—to show feeling, even passion—without going beyond certain socially approved limits; that is, it is not just the "freedom" of the Creole society but the coupling of that freedom with a confident sense of decorum, "lofty chastity," which confounds her. "A book had gone the rounds of the *pension.* When it came her turn to read it, she did so with profound astonishment. She felt moved to read the book in secret and solitude, though none of the others had done so—to hide it from view at the sound of approaching footsteps. It was openly criticized and freely discussed at table. Mrs. Pontellier gave over being astonished, and concluded that wonders would never cease" (pp. 23-24). As we have seen, "freedom" for Edna has always meant isolation and concealment, an increasingly sterile and barren existence; now suddenly she finds herself among people who have a different kind of freedom, the freedom to express feelings openly and without fear. What a temptation to that insistent inner being whose authenticity Edna so feverishly guards from attack! For this is a self which is starving—and Grand Isle offers nourishment in bounteous abundance.

However, danger lies in the possibility that this hidden self will emerge as voracious, omnivorous and insatiable. Such a fear is probably always present in the schizoid personality; for these defense mechanisms "can be understood as an attempt to preserve a being that is precariously structured. . . .The initial structuralization of being into its basic elements occurs in early infancy. In normal circumstances, this occurs in such a way as to be so conclusively stable in its basic elements (for instance, the continuity of time, the distinction between the self and not-self, phantasy and reality), that it can henceforth be taken for granted: on this stable base, a considerable amount of plasticity can exist in what we call a person's 'character'."[11] (It is precisely this plasticity which Edna observes among the Creoles and which she finds not shocking but deeply puzzling because it is absent in her own personality.) It is at this most elementary level that Edna's hidden self subsists. "The orientation of the schizoid personality is a primitive oral one, concerned with the dilemma of sustaining its aliveness, while being terrified to 'take in' anything. It becomes parched with thirst, and desolate."[12] And out of this desolation Edna's "self" ventures forward to seek resuscitation and confirmation.

The awakening is a sensuous one. It is important, however, not to accept this term as an exclusively or even primarily sexual one. To be sure, Edna's awakening involves a liaison with Arobin, and the novel leaves little doubt that this attachment includes sexual activity. Yet it would be naive and limiting to suppose that Edna's principal complaint ought to be described in terms of sexual repression (though she might find it reassuring to do so). Gratifying sexual experience cannot be isolated from sensuous experience in general, and entering into a sexual relationship is an act which necessarily "awakens" memories—echoes, if you will—of earlier sensuous needs and experiences. As Freud has observed, the mind is unique in its development, for "only in the mind is such a preservation of all the earlier stages alongside of the final form possible."[13] Now a reader of Chopin's novel might find herself more absorbed by the apparently genital aspects of Edna's sensuous life, the love affair with Robert and the attachment to Arobin; after all, this is in some sense the "appropriate" level for the expression of passion in an adult woman. The narrator, however, directs our attention in a different direction. "That summer at Grand Isle she began to loosen a little the mantle of reserve that had always enveloped her. There may have been—there must have been—influences, both subtle and apparent, working in their several ways to induce her to do this; but the most obvious was the influence of Adèle Ratignolle. The excessive physical charm of the Creole had first attracted her, for Edna had a sensuous susceptibility to beauty" (p. 35).

Why is Adèle and not Robert singled out as the primary force that rouses Edna from her slumber? Our introduction to Adèle gives some hints. "There are no words to describe her save the old ones that have served so often to picture the by-gone heroine of romance and the fair lady of our dreams" (p. 19). If some portion of Edna's self has been arrested in dreams, perhaps Adèle is the embodiment of those dreams. And yet, despite the "spun-gold hair" and blue eyes, she is scarcely a conventional heroine. Her beauty derives its power from a sense of fullness, ripeness and abundance. Her very essence might be described as a kind of plump succulence, and the narrator reverts to terms of nourishment as the only appropriate means of rendering her nature. She had "two lips that pouted, that were so red one could only think of cherries or some other delicious crimson fruit in looking at them. She was growing a little stout, but it did not seem to detract an iota from the grace of every step, pose, gesture" (p. 20). Her hours are spent delightfully (to her) in mending and sorting children's clothes, and she is pregnant—a fact which pleases her and becomes her principal topic of conversation—when Edna meets her. She might have been painted by Renoir. She is, in Edna's terms, the quintessential "mother-woman."

Though Edna's own instincts for mothering are fitful, she is clearly attracted to the bounty of Adèle's nature, allowing herself to slip into caressing intimacy like a grateful child. "Madame Ratignolle laid her hand over that of Mrs. Pontellier, which was near her. Seeing that the hand was not withdrawn, she clasped it firmly and warmly. She even stroked it a little, fondly, with the other hand, murmuring in an undertone, 'Pauvre cherie.' The action was at first a little confusing to Edna, but she soon lent herself readily to the Creole's gentle caress" (p. 43). So far as one can tell, this is the first sensuous contact that Edna has had with anyone—perhaps in her conscious memory, certainly since adolescence. "During one period of my life," she confides to Adèle, "religion took a firm hold upon me; after I was twelve and until—until—why, I suppose until now, though I never thought much about it—just driven along by habit" (pp. 42-43). This sensuous awakening loosens Edna's memory, and her mind drifts back through childhood, recalling the enveloping sea of grass, the succession of phantom lovers. "Edna did not reveal so much as all this to Madame Ratignolle that summer day when they sat with faces turned to the sea. But a good part of it escaped her. She had put her head down on Madame Ratignolle's shoulder. She was flushed and felt intoxicated with the sound of her own voice and the unaccustomed taste of candor. It muddled her like wine, or like a first breath of freedom" (p. 48).

The almost blinding intensity of this episode between Edna and Adèle contrasts vividly with the emotional paleness of Edna's real-world interaction with Robert (which must not be confused with her fantasies about him, especially after he leaves, nor with her increasingly narcissistic appreciation of her own body). Thus Edna's coming to rest upon Adèle's shoulder with trusting openness is preceded by an episode between Edna and Robert which is similar in action and yet altogether different in tone. "During his oblivious attention he once quietly rested his head against Mrs. Pontellier's arm. As gently she repulsed him. Once again he repeated the offense. She could not but believe it to be thoughtlessness on his part; yet that was no reason she should submit to it. She did not remonstrate, except again to repulse him quietly but firmly" (p. 29). Several things must be noted here: Edna views Robert's action not as sensuously stimulating but as an imposition, even an affront; her resistance betrays no conflict (that is, the narrator does not suggest that she was tempted by the possible sexual content of his gesture or that she felt threatened or guilty), quite the contrary; her attitude is cooly distant. But then Robert is a man whose quasi-sexual flirtations are not to be taken seriously.

In many ways his patterns of behavior are similar to Edna's, and to some extent, this similarity makes him non-threatening. He does not seek genuine emotional or sexual involvements, preferring to attach his affections to those women who are "safely" unattainable. "Since the age of fifteen, which was eleven years before, Robert each summer at Grand Isle had constituted himself the devoted attendant of some fair dame or damsel. Sometimes it was a young girl, again a widow: but as often as not it was some interesting married woman" (p. 25). His psychic life is more firmly rooted in the world than Edna's; he does not pursue figures of pure fantasy. Still, his propensity for playing the role of hopeless, love-sick youth is so well known as to be able to be anticipated by those who know him. Thus "many had predicted that Robert would devote himself to Mrs. Pontellier when he arrived" (p. 25). His attentions, gratefully received by a number of the ladies, more often than not take the form of ministering to their creature comforts; he fetches bouillon for Adèle, blankets and shawls for Edna.

Indeed, an astonishing proportion of that part of the novel which deals with Edna's sojourn at Grand Isle is paced by the rhythm of her basic needs, especially the most primitive ones of eating and sleeping. If one were to plot the course of Edna's life during this period, the most reliable indices to the passage of time would be her meals and her periods of sleep. The importance of these in Edna's more general "awakening" can be suggested if we examine the day-long boat trip which she makes with Robert.

There is an almost fairy-tale quality to the whole experience; the rules of time seem suspended, and the mélange of brilliant sensory experiences—the sun, the water, the soft breeze, the old church with its lizards and whispered tales of pirate gold—melts into a dreamlike pattern. It is almost as if Edna's fantasy world had come into being. Indeed, there is even some suggestion that after the event, she incorporates the memory of it into her fantasy world in such a way that the reality and the illusion do, in fact, become confused. Later on in the novel when Edna is invited to tell a true anecdote at a dinner party, she speaks "of a woman who paddled away with her lover one night in a pirogue and never came back. They were lost amid the Baratarian Islands, and no one ever heard of them or found trace of them from that day to this. It was pure invention. She said that Madame Antoine had related it to her. That, also, was an invention. Perhaps it was a dream she had had. But every glowing word seemed real to those who listened" (pp. 182-83).

Yet even this jewel-like adventure with Robert is dominated by the insistence of the infantile life-pattern—sleep and eat, sleep and eat. Edna's rest had been feverish the night prior to the expedition; "She slept but a few hours" (p. 82), and their expedition begins with a hurried breakfast (p. 84). Her taste for sight-seeing, even her willingness to remain with Robert, is so overwhelmed by her lassitude that she must find a place to rest and to be alone. Strikingly, however, once she is by herself, left to seek restful sleep, Edna seems somewhat to revive, and the tone shifts from one of exhaustion to one of sensuous, leisurely enjoyment of her own body. "Left alone in the little side room, [she] loosened her clothes, removing the greater part of them. . . .How luxurious it felt to rest thus in a strange, quaint bed, with its sweet country odor of laurel lingering about the sheets and mattress! She stretched her strong limbs that ached a little. She ran her fingers through her loosened hair for a while. She looked at her round arms as she held them straight up and rubbed them one after the other, observing closely, as if it were something she saw for the first time, the fine, firm quality and texture of her flesh" (p. 93). Powerfully sensuous as this scene is, we would be hard put to find genital significance here. Reduced to its simplest form, the description is of a being discovering the limits and qualities of its own body—discovering, and taking joy in the process of discovery. And having engaged in this exploratory "play" for a while, Edna falls asleep.

The manner of her waking makes explicit references to the myth of the sleeping beauty. " 'How many years have I slept?' she inquired. 'The whole island seems changed. A new race of beings must have sprung up, leaving only you and me as past relics' " (p. 96). Robert jokingly falls in with the fantasy: "You have slept precisely one hundred years. I was left here to guard your slumbers; and for one hundred years I have been out under the shed reading a book" (p. 96). In the fairy tale, of course, the princess awakens with a kiss, conscious of love; but Edna's libidinal energies have been arrested at a pre-genital level—so she awakens "very hungry" (p. 96)—and her lover prepares her a meal! "He was childishly gratified to discover her appetite, and to see the relish with which she ate the food which he had procured for her" (p. 97). Indeed, though the title of the novel suggests a re-enactment of the traditional romantic myth, it never does offer a complete representation of it. The next invocation is Arobin's kiss, "the first kiss of her life to which her nature had really responded" (p. 218); but as we have seen earlier, this response is facilitated, perhaps even made possible, by the fact that her emotional attachment is not to Arobin but to the Robert of her fantasy world. The final allusion to an awakening kiss is Edna's rousing of Robert (p. 280); and yet this is a potentially genital awakening from which both flee.

Edna's central problem, once the hidden "self" begins to exert its inexorable power, is that her libidinal appetite has been fixated at the oral level. Edna herself has an insistent preoccupation with nourishment; on the simplest level, she is concerned with food. Her favorite adjective is "delicious": she sees many mother-women as "delicious" in their role (p. 19); she carries echoes of her children's voices "like the memory of a delicious song" (p. 248); when she imagines Robert she thinks "how delicious it would be to have him there with her" (p. 270). And the notion of something's being good because it might be good to "eat" (or internalize in some way) is echoed in all of her relationships with other people. Those who care about her typically feed her; and the sleep-and-eat pattern which is most strikingly established at the beginning of the novel continues even to the very end. Not surprisingly, in the "grown-up world" she is a poor housekeeper, and though Léonce's responses are clearly petty and self-centered, Edna's behavior does betray incompetence, especially when we compare it (as the novel so often invites us to) with the nurturing capacities of Adèle. It is not surprising that the most dramatic gesture toward freedom that Edna makes is to move out of her husband's house; yet even this gesture toward "independence" can be comprehended as part of an equally powerful wish to regress. It is, after all, a "tiny house" that she moves to; she calls it her "pigeon house," and if she were still a little girl, we might call it a playhouse.

The decision to move from Léonce's house is virtually coincidental with the beginning of her affair with Arobin; yet even the initial stages of that affair are described in oral terms—Edna feels regret because "it was not love which had held this cup of life to her lips" (p. 219). And though the relationship develops as she makes preparations for the move, it absorbs astonishingly little of Edna's libido. She is deliberately distant, treating Arobin with "affected carelessness" (p. 221). As the narrator observes, "If he had expected to find her languishing, reproachful, or indulging in sentimental tears, he must have been greatly surprised" (p. 221). She is "true" to the fantasy image of Robert. And in the real world her emotional energy has been committed in another direction. She is busy with elaborate plans—for a dinner party! And it is on this extravagant sumptuous oral repast that she lavishes her time and care (see pp. 225-37). Here Edna as purveyor of food becomes not primarily a nourisher (as Adèle is) but a sensualist in the only terms that she can truly comprehend. One might argue that in this elaborate feast Edna's sensuous self comes closest to some form of expression which might be compatible with the real world. The dinner party itself is one of the longest sustained episodes in the novel; we are told in loving detail about the appearance of the table, the commodious chairs, the flowers, the candles, the food and wines, Edna's attire—no sensory pleasure is left unattended. Yet even this indulgence fails to satisfy. "As she sat there amid her guests, she felt the old ennui overtaking her; the hopelessness which so often assailed her, which came upon her like an obsession, like something extraneous, independent of volition. It was something which announced itself; a chill breath that seemed to issue from some vast cavern wherein discords wailed" (p. 232). Edna, perhaps, connects this despair to the absence of Robert. "There came over her the acute longing which always summoned into her spiritual vision the presence of the beloved one, overpowering her at once with a sense of the unattainable" (p. 232). However, the narrator's language here is interestingly ambiguous. It is not specifically *Robert* that Edna longs for; it is "the presence of the beloved one"—an indefinite perpetual image, existing "always" in "her spiritual vision." The longing, so described, is an immortal one and, as she acknowledges, "unattainable"; the vision might be of Robert, but it might equally be of the cavalry officer, the engaged young man, the tragedian—even of Adèle, whose mothering attentions first elicited a sensuous response from Edna and whose own imminent motherhood has kept her from the grand party. The indefinite quality of Edna's longing thus described has an ominous tone, a tone made even more ominous by the rising specter of those "vast caverns" waiting vainly to be filled.

Perhaps Edna's preoccupation with the incorporation of food is but one aspect of a more general concern with incorporating that which is external to her. Freud's hypotheses about the persistence in some people of essentially oral concerns makes Edna's particular problem even clearer.

> Originally the ego includes everything, later it separates off an external world from itself. Our present ego-feeling is, therefore, only a shrunken residue of a much more inclusive—indeed, an all-embracing—feeling which corresponded to a more intimate bond between the ego and the world about it. If we may assume that there are many people in whose mental life this primary ego-feeling has persisted to a greater or less degree, it would exist in them side by side with the narrower and more sharply demarcated ego-feeling of maturity, like a kind of counterpart to it. In that case, the ideational contents appropriate to it would be precisely those of limitlessness and of a bond with the universe. . .the 'oceanic' feeling.[14]

A psychologically mature individual has to some extent satisfied these oral desires for limitless fusion with the external world; presumably his sense of oneness with a nurturing figure has given him sustenance sufficient to move onward to more complex satisfactions. Yet growth inevitably involves some loss. "The feeling of happiness derived from the satisfaction of a wild instinctual impulse untamed by the ego is incomparably more intense than that derived from sating an instinct that has been tamed."[15] To some extent all of us share Edna's fantasy of complete fulfillment through a bond with the infinite; that is what gives the novel its power. However for those few people in whom this primary ego-feeling has persisted with uncompromising force the temptation to seek total fulfillment may be both irresistible and annihilating.

Everywhere and always in the novel, Edna's fundamental longing is postulated in precisely these terms. And strangely enough, the narrator seems intuitively to understand the connection between this longing for suffusion, fulfillment, incorporation, and the very earliest attempts to define identity.

> But the beginning of things, of a world especially, is necessarily vague, tangled, chaotic, and exceedingly disturbing. How few of us ever emerge from such a beginning! How many souls perish in its tumult!
>
> The voice of the sea is seductive; never ceasing, whispering, clamoring, murmuring, inviting the soul to wander for a spell in abysses of solitude; to lose itself in mazes of inward contemplation. The voice of the sea speaks to the soul. The touch of the sea is sensuous, enfolding the body in its soft, close embrace. (p. 34)

Ultimately, the problem facing Edna has a nightmarish circularity. She has achieved some measure of personal identity only by hiding her "true self" within—repressing all desire for instinctual gratification. Yet she can see others in her environment—the Creoles generally and Adèle in particular—who seem comfortably able to indulge their various sensory appetites and to do so with easy moderation. Edna's hidden self longs for resuscitation and nourishment; and in the supportive presence of Grand Isle Edna begins to acknowledge and express the needs of that "self."

Yet once released, the inner being cannot be satisfied. It is an orally destructive self, a limitless void whose needs can be filled, finally, only by total fusion with the outside world, a totality of sensuous enfolding. And this totality means annihilation of the ego.

Thus all aspects of Edna's relationship with the outside world are unevenly defined. She is remarkably vulnerable to feelings of being invaded and overwhelmed; we have already seen that she views emotional intimacy as potentially shattering. She is equally unable to handle the phenomenal world with any degree of consistency or efficiency. She is very much at the mercy of her environment: the atmosphere of Mademoiselle Reisz' room is said to "invade" her with repose (p. 252); Mademoiselle Reisz' music has the consistent effect of penetrating Edna's outer self and playing upon the responsive chords of her inner yearning; even her way of looking at objects in the world about her becomes an act of incorporation; "she had a way of turning [her eyes] swiftly upon an object and holding them there as if lost in some inward maze of contemplation or thought" (p. 7). Once she has given up the pattern of repression that served to control dangerous impulses, she becomes engaged in trying to maintain a precarious balance in each of her relationships. On the one hand she must resist invasion, for with invasion comes possession and total destruction. On the other hand she must resist the equally powerful impulse to destroy whatever separates her from the external world so that she can seek union, fusion and (so her fantasies suggest) ecstatic fulfillment.

In seeking to deal with this apparently hopeless problem, Edna encounters several people whose behavior might serve as a pattern for her. Mademoiselle Reisz is one. Mademoiselle Reisz is an artist, and as such she has created that direct avenue between inner and outer worlds which Edna seeks in her own life. Surely Edna's own attempts at artistic enterprise grow out of her more general desire for sustained ecstasy. "While Edna worked she sometimes sang low the little air, 'Ah, si tu savais!' " (p. 149). Her work is insensibly linked with her memories of Robert, and these in turn melt into more generalized memories and desires. The little song she is humming "moved her with recollections. She could hear again the ripple of the water, the flapping sail. She could see the glint of the moon upon the bay, and could feel the soft, gusty beating of the hot south wind. A subtle current of desire passed through her body, weakening her hold upon the brushes and making her eyes burn" (p. 149). In some ways, Edna's painting might offer her an excellent and viable mode for coming to terms with the insistent demands of cosmic yearning. For one thing, it utilizes in an effective way her habit of transforming the act of observing the external world into an act of artistic creation. Thus the period during which Edna is experimenting with her art offers her some of the most satisfying experiences she is capable of having. "There were days when she was very happy without knowing why. She was happy to be alive and breathing when her whole being seemed to be one with the sunlight, the color, the odors, the luxuriant warmth of some perfect

Southern day....And she found it good to dream and to be alone and unmolested" (p. 149).

Yet when Edna tells Mademoiselle Reisz about her efforts, she is greeted with skepticism: "You have pretensions," Mademoiselle Reisz responds. "To be an artist includes much; one must possess many gifts—absolute gifts—which have not been acquired by one's own effort. And moreover, to succeed, the artist must possess the courageous soul....The brave soul. The soul that dares and defies" (p. 165). One implication of Mademoiselle Reisz' half-contemptuous comment may well be the traditional view that the artist must dare to be unconventional; and it is this interpretation which Edna reports later to Arobin, saying as she does, however, "I only half comprehend her" (p. 217). The part of Mademoiselle Reisz' injunction that eludes Edna's understanding concerns the sense of purposiveness which is implied by the image of a courageous soul. Mademoiselle Reisz has her art, but she has sacrificed for it—perhaps too much. In any case, however, she has acknowledged limitations, accepted some and grappled with others; she is an active agent who has defined her relationship to the world. Edna, by contrast, is passive.

The words which recur most frequently to describe her are words like melting, drifting, misty, dreaming, shadowy. She is not willing (perhaps not able) to define her position in the world because to do so would involve relinquishing the dream of total fulfillment. Thus while Mademoiselle Reisz can control and create, Edna is most comfortable as the receptive vessel—both for Mademoiselle Reisz' music and for the sense impressions which form the basis of her own artistic endeavor. Mademoiselle Reisz commands her work; Edna is at the mercy of hers. Thus just as there are moments of exhilaration, so "there were days when she was unhappy, she did not know why,—when it did not seem worth while to be glad or sorry, to be alive or dead; when life appeared to her like a grotesque pandemonium and humanity like worms struggling blindly toward inevitable annihilation. She could not work on such a day, nor weave fantasies to stir her pulses and warm her blood" (pp. 149-50). Art, for Edna, ultimately becomes not a defense against inner turmoil, merely a reflection of it.

Another possible defense for Edna might be the establishment and sustaining of a genuine genital relationship. Her adolescent fantasies, her mechanical marriage, her liaison with Arobin and her passionate attachment to the fantasy image of Robert all suggest imperfect efforts to do just that. A genital relationship, like all ego-relationships, necessarily involves limitation; to put the matter in Edna's terms, a significant attachment with a real man would involve relinquishing the fantasy of total fulfillment with some fantasy lover. In turn, it would offer genuine emotional nourishment—though perhaps never enough to satisfy the voracious clamoring of Edna's hidden self.

Ironically, Adèle, who seems such a fount of sustenance, gives indications of having some of the same oral needs that Edna does. Like Edna she is preoccupied with eating, she pays extravagant care to the arrangement of her own physical comforts, and she uses her pregnancy as an excuse to demand a kind of mothering attention for herself. The difference between Edna and Adèle is that Adèle can deal with her nurturing needs by displacing them onto her children and becoming a "mother-woman." Having thus segregated and limited these desires, Adèle can find diverse ways of satisfying them; and having satisfied her own infantile oral needs, she can go on to have a rewarding adult relationship with her husband. Between Adèle and M. Ratignolle there is mutual joining together: "The Ratignolles understood each other perfectly. If ever the fusion of two human beings into one has been accomplished on this sphere it was surely in their union" (p. 144). The clearest outward sign of this happy union is that the Ratignolles converse eagerly and clearly with each other. M. Ratignolle reports his experiences and thoughts to his wife, and she in turn "was keenly interested in everything he said, laying down her fork the better to listen, chiming in, taking the words out of his mouth" (p. 145). Yet this picture of social and domestic accord is indescribably dismaying to Edna. She "felt depressed rather than soothed after leaving them. The little glimpse of domestic harmony which had been offered her, gave her no regret, no longing" (p. 145).

Again, what has capitulated is the fantasy of complete and total suffusion; the Ratignolles have only a union which is as perfect as one can expect "*on this sphere*" (italics added). Yet the acme of bliss which Edna has always sought "was not for her in this world" (p. 47). Edna wishes a kind of pre-verbal union, an understanding which consistently surpasses words. Léonce is scarcely a sensitive man (that is, as we have seen, why she chose to marry him). Yet Edna never exerts herself to even such efforts at communication with him as might encourage a supportive emotional response. She responds to his unperceptive clumsiness by turning inwards, falling into silence. Over and over again their disagreements follow the pattern of a misunderstanding which Edna refuses to clarify. At the very beginning of the novel when Léonce selfishly strolls off for an evening of gambling, Edna's rage and sense of loneliness are resolutely hidden, even when he seeks to discover the cause of her unhappiness. "She said nothing, and refused to answer her husband when he questioned her" (p. 13). Perhaps Léonce could not have understood the needs which Edna feels so achingly unfulfilled. And he is very clumsy. But he does make attempts at communication while she does not, and his interview with the family doctor (pp. 168-74) shows greater concern about Edna's problems than she manages to feel for his.

The attachment to Robert, which takes on significance only after he has left Grand Isle, monopolizes Edna's emotions because it does temporarily offer an illusion of fusion, of complete union. However, this love affair, such as it is, is a genuinely narcissistic one; the sense of fusion exists because Edna's lover is really a part of herself—a figment of her imagination, an image of Robert which she has incorporated into her consciousness. Not only is her meeting with Robert after his return a disappointment (as we have seen earlier); it moves the static, imaginary "love affair" into a new and crucial stage; it tests, once and for all, Edna's capacity to transform her world of dreams into viable reality. Not surprisingly, "some way he had seemed nearer to her off there in Mexico" (p. 268).

Still she does try. She awakens him with a kiss even as Arobin had awakened her. Robert, too, is resistant to genuine involvement, and his initial reaction is to speak of the hopelessness of their relationship. Edna, however, is insistent (despite the interruption telling her of Adèle's accouchement). "We shall be everything to each other. Nothing else in the world is of any consequence. I must go to my friend; but you will wait for me? No matter how late; you will wait for me, Robert?" (p. 283). And at this point, Edna seems finally to have won her victory. " 'Don't go; don't go! Oh! Edna, stay with me,' he pleaded. . . Her seductive voice, together with his great love for her, had enthralled his senses, had deprived him of every impulse but the longing to hold her and keep her" (p. 284). And at this moment, so long and eagerly anticipated, Edna leaves Robert!

Robert's own resolve weakens during the interval, and it would be all too easy to blame Edna's failure on him. Certainly he is implicated. Yet his act does not explain *Edna's* behavior. "Nothing else in the world is of any consequence," she has said. If that is so, why then does she leave? No real duty calls her. Her presence at Adèle's delivery is of virtually no help. The doctor, sorry for the pain that the scene has caused Edna, even remonstrates mildly with her for having come. "You shouldn't have been there, Mrs. Pontellier. . . .There were a dozen women she might have had with her, unimpressionable women" (pp. 290-91). To have stayed with Robert would have meant consummation, finally, the joining of her dream-like passion to a flesh and blood lover; to leave was to risk losing that opportunity. Edna must realize the terms of this dilemma, and still she chooses to leave. We can only conclude that she is unconsciously ambivalent about achieving the goal which has sustained her fantasies for so long. The flesh and blood Robert may prove an imperfect, unsatisfactory substitute for the "beloved" of her dreams; what is more, a relationship with the real Robert would necessarily disenfranchise the more desirable phantom lover, whose presence is linked with her more general yearning for suffusion and indefinable ecstasy.

The totality of loss which follows Edna's decision forces a grim recognition upon her, the recognition that all her lovers have really been of but fleeting significance. "To-day it is Arobin; to-morrow it will be some one else. . . .It makes no difference to me. . . .There was no one thing in the world that she desired. There was no human being whom she wanted near her except Robert; and she even realized that the day would come when he, too, and the thought of him would melt out of her existence, leaving her alone" (pp. 299-300). Her devastation, thus described, is removed from the realm of romantic disappointment; and we must see Edna's final suicide as originating in a sense of inner emptiness, not in some finite failure of love. Her decision to go to Adèle is in part a reflection of Edna's unwillingness to compromise her dream of Robert (and in this sense it might be interpreted as a flight from reality). On the other hand, it might also be seen as a last desperate attempt to come to terms with the anguish created by her unfulfilled "Oceanic" longing. And for this last effort she must turn to Adèle, the human who first caused her to loosen the bonds of repression.

The pre-eminence of Adèle over Robert in Edna's emotional life, affirmed by Edna's crucial choice, is undeniably linked to her image as a nurturing figure and, especially here, as a mother-to-be. In this capacity she is also linked to Edna's own children—insistent specters in Edna's consciousness; and this link is made explicit by Adèle's repetition of the cryptic injunction to "think of the children" (p. 289).

Now in every human's life there is a period of rhapsodic union or fusion with another, and this is the period of early infancy, before the time when a baby begins to differentiate himself from his mother. It is the haunting memory of this evanescent state which Freud defines as "Oceanic feeling," the longing to recapture that sense of oneness and suffused sensuous pleasure—even, perhaps, the desire to be reincorporated into the safety of pre-existence. Men can never recreate this state of total union. Adult women can—when they are pregnant. Most pregnant women identify intensely with their unborn children, and through that identification in some measure re-experience a state of complete and harmonious union. "The biologic process has created a unity of mother and child, in which the bodily substance of one flows into the other, and thus one larger unit is formed out of two units. The same thing takes place on the psychic level. By tender identification, by perceiving the fruit of her body as part of herself, the pregnant woman is able to transform the 'parasite' into a beloved being. Thus, mankind's eternal yearning for identity between the ego and the nonego, that deeply buried original desire to reachieve the condition once experienced, to repeat the human dream that was once realized in the mother's womb, is fulfilled."[16] Adèle is a dear friend, yes; she is a nurturing figure. But above all, she is the living embodiment of that state which Edna's deepest being longs to recapture. Trapped in the conflict between her desire for "freedom," as seen in her compulsive need to protect her precarious sense of self, and her equally insistent yearning for complete fulfillment through total suffusion, Edna is intensely involved with Adèle's pregnancy.

Edna's compulsion to be with Adèle at the moment of delivery is, in the sense which would have most significance for her, a need to view individuation at its origin. For if pregnancy offers a state of total union, then birth is the initial separation: for the child it is the archetypal separation trauma; for the mother, too, it is a significant psychic trauma. It is the ritual reenactment of her own birth and a brutal reawakening to the world of isolated ego. "To make it the being that is outside her, the pregnant mother must deliver the child from the depths of herself. . . .She loses not only it, but herself with it. This, I think, is at the bottom of that fear and foreboding of death that every pregnant woman has, and this turns the giving of life into the losing of life."[17] Edna cannot refuse to partake of this ceremony, for here, if anywhere, she will find the solution to her problem.

Yet the experience is horrendous; it gives no comfort, no reassuring answer to Edna's predicament. It offers only stark, uncompromising truth. Adèle's ordeal reminds Edna of her own accouchements. "Edna began to feel uneasy. She was seized with a vague dread. Her own like experiences seemed far away, unreal, and only half remembered. She recalled faintly an ecstasy of pain, the heavy odor of chloroform, a stupor which had deadened sensation, and an awakening to find a little new life to which she had given being" (p. 288). This is Nature's cruel message. The fundamental significance to Edna of an awakening is an awakening to separation, to individual existence, to the hopelessness of ever satisfying the dream of total fusion. The rousing of her sensuous being had led Edna on a quest for ecstasy; but the ecstasy which beckoned has become in the end merely an "ecstasy of pain," first in her protracted struggle to retain identity and finally here in that relentless recognition of inevitable separation which has been affirmed in the delivery, "an awakening to find a new little life." Edna is urged to leave, but she refuses. "With an inward agony, with a flaming, out-spoken revolt against the ways of Nature, she witnessed the scene torture" (p. 288).

In this world, in life, there can be no perfect union, and the children whom Adèle urges Edna to remember stand as living proof of the inevitability of separation. Edna's longing can never be satisfied. This is her final discovery, the inescapable disillusionment; and the narrator calls it to our attention again, lest its signficance escape us. "The years that are gone seem like dreams," Edna muses, "if one might go on sleeping and dreaming—but to wake up and find—" (p. 292). Here she pauses, but the reader can complete her thought—"a new little life." "Oh! well! perhaps it is better to wake up after all, even to suffer rather than to remain a dupe to illusions all one's life" (p. 292).

One wonders to what extent Edna's fate might have been different if Robert had remained. Momentarily, at least, he might have roused her from her despondency by offering not ecstasy but at least partial satisfaction. The fundamental problem would have remained, however. Life offers only partial pleasures, and individuated experience.

Thus Edna's final act of destruction has a quality of uncompromising sensuous fulfillment as well. It is her answer to the inadequacies of life, a literal denial and reversal of the birth trauma she has just witnessed, a stripping away of adulthood, of limitation, of consciousness itself. If life cannot offer fulfillment of her dream of fusion, then the ecstasy of death is preferable to the relinquishing of that dream. So Edna goes to the sea "and for the first time in her life she stood naked in the open air, at the mercy of the sun, the breeze that beat upon her, and the waves that invited her" (p. 301). She is a child, an infant again. "How strange and awful it seemed to stand naked under the sky! how delicious! She felt like some new-born creature, opening its eyes in a familiar world that it had never known" (p. 301). And with her final act Edna completes the regression, back beyond childhood, back into time eternal. "The touch of the sea is sensuous, enfolding the body in its soft, close embrace" (p. 301).

"The Temptation to be A Beautiful Object": Double Standard and Double Bind in *The House of Mirth*

Judith Fetterley

"I don't underrate the decorative side of life. It seems to me the sense of splendor has justified itself by what it has produced. The worst of it is that so much human nature is used up in the process. If we're all the raw stuff of the cosmic effects, one would rather be the fire that tempers a sword than the fish that dyes a purple cloak. And a society like ours wastes such good material in producing its little patch of purple! Look at a boy like Ned Silverton—he's really too good to be used to refurbish anybody's social shabbiness. There's a lad just setting out to discover the universe. Isn't it a pity he should end by finding it in Mrs. Fisher's drawing-room?"[1]

Lawrence Selden's impassioned expostulation to Lily Bart in the opening movement of Edith Wharton's great novel *The House of Mirth* clearly echoes the central concern of his creator. As Wharton saw it, her problem in writing *The House of Mirth* was how to extract from her subject, fashionable New York, "the typical human significance which is the story-teller's reason for telling one story rather than another."[2] "In what aspect," she asked, "could a society of irresponsible pleasure-seekers be said to have, on the 'old woe of the world,' any deeper bearing than the people composing such a society could guess? The answer was that a frivolous society can acquire dramatic significance only through what its frivolity destroys. Its tragic implication lies in its power of debasing people and ideals. The answer, in short, was my heroine, Lily Bart."[3]

Critical commentary on *The House of Mirth* has also explored the dramatic significance of the destruction attendant upon frivolity and has often presented that significance in terms of the sense of waste conveyed by Selden's outburst. Blake Nevius writes, "Edith Wharton was one of the first American novelists to develop the possibilities of a theme which since the turn of the century has permeated our fiction: the waste of human and spiritual resources which in America went hand in hand with the exploitation of the land and forests. . ."[4] Marilyn Lyde summarizes her argument for viewing *The House of Mirth* as a tragedy by stating that the novel is tragic "in the universality of its conflict—a struggle, basically, between the world and the spirit; in the honesty of its approach to life; and in the intensity of its sense of loss."[5] James W. Tuttleton finds "the meaning of Mrs. Wharton's chronicle of the very rich" to lie "in the ruin of exquisite creatures like Lily Bart by a society which has failed to provide her, thanks to the surrender of its traditions, with that supporting 'web of custom, manners, culture' human nature elaborately spins about itself in traditional societies."[6] And Irving Howe concludes his essay as follows: "When one reads and submits to the urgencies of a novel like *The House of Mirth*, the effect is that of being held in a steady, inexorable enclosure. Mrs. Wharton's sense of the inescapability of waste—the waste of spirit, the waste of energy, the waste of beauty—comes to seem a root condition of human life."[7]

What neither character, nor critic, nor author recognizes, however, is the precise nature of who and what is being wasted. The critical discussion is carried on in terms of the "universal" and the "human"; and while the focus of Wharton's sense of waste is clearly not Selden's, her appraisal of Ned Silverton being that he is not valuable enough to be wasted and her sympathies being firmly located in the image of the suffering his frivolity exacts from the women who support him in it, nevertheless, she nowhere consciously addresses the implications of the fact that her symbol of social waste is specifically a beautiful woman. Rather, she is committed to seeing her novel as a tragedy of class and to placing the blame for Lily's fate on the erosion of values in upperclass New York, on the failure of that culture to link spirit and matter and to provide a framework which could support and give meaning to the lives of its members. Yet Lily's experience is not simply the result of her being a member of a particular socioeconomic class at a particular point in time; it is equally the result of her being a member of a sexual class. The tragedy of Lily Bart is peculiarly the tragedy of an upperclass woman faced with "the temptation to be a beautiful object"[8] which such a society presents to its women and destroyed by the consequences of that temptation. In her realization of Lily Bart as the only figure capable of redeeming her subject matter from triviality, Wharton has recorded a major truth: social waste is female. Lily's fate is the result of a complex system of double standards and double binds, "lines of force" as Walter B. Rideout would call them,[9] directed against her because she is a woman. *The House of Mirth* is, however unconsciously, a powerful denunciation of patriarchal culture.

In his reading of *The House of Mirth*, Blake Nevius defines the theme of the novel as "the victimizing effect of a particular environment on one of its more helplessly characteristic products."[10] Since his analysis does not include sexual class as an aspect of environment, his focus is on Lily as a universal symbol of "the expense of spirit that a program of material self-conquest entailed," analogous in this respect to Lawrence Selden.[11] Yet the concept of sexual class is clearly central to an understanding of the particular nature of Lily's victimization:

> Only one thought consoled her [Mrs. Bart], and that was the contemplation of Lily's beauty. She studied it with a kind of passion, as though it were some weapon she had slowly fashioned for her vengeance. It was

the last asset in their fortunes, the nucleus around which their life was to be rebuilt. She watched it jealously, as though it were her own property and Lily its mere custodian; and she tried to instill into the latter a sense of the responsibility that such a charge involved. (pp. 39-40)

This is the environment which shapes Lily's character and fate: the cult of woman as beautiful object. The multiple ways in which Lily's beauty is objectified emerge clearly from Mrs. Bart's "consolation": her beauty is a weapon, an asset, a property, a charge; above all, an "it" in relation to which Lily is perhaps possessor, perhaps only curator. The movement from her mother's indoctrination to Lily's presentation of herself in the Wellington Brys tableaux as a living art object is as inevitable as it is frightening.

The objectification of her physical beauty has a large effect on Lily. First, making a separate entity of her beauty creates a schism between what might be called Lily's "real self" and her cultural identity as beautiful object; it creates the conditions which make it possible for Lily to have what Howe terms a "core of personal being"[12] and leads directly to that pattern of ambivalences and consequent indecisions which mark her character and action. In addition, it creates the framework for her thoroughgoing self-hatred. Second, locating Lily's value in her beauty, something which she acquired by fluke, and over whose duration she has so little control, fixes in her an abiding sense of powerlessness, of fragility and impermanence, which weakens her will to survive and adds to her self-hatred. Finally, the language Mrs. Bart invokes to describe Lily's beauty implicitly reveals the ultimate destiny of the beautiful object: purchase. The view of herself as a piece of property available for purchase by the highest bidder is as central in shaping Lily's character and self-image as is the corollary mystique of beauty, the view of herself as the ultimate flowering of civilization which justifies the sordid fact of money and casts an aura of spiritual refinement and good taste over all it touches. Indeed, the heart of Lily's character, fate, and tragedy lies in the paradox embodied in her name—the Lily is up for barter—and the heart of Wharton's novel lies in her complex exploration of the multiple facets of this paradox.

Wharton's choice of the hat industry as an exemplar of one of the stages of Lily's inexorable social and economic descent is significant, for the structure of a hat is itself emblematic of the situation Wharton is describing just as Lily's relation to the industry provides the sharpest possible definition of the paradoxical realities of her existence. While the ornamentation which goes on hats as the finishing touch is what ultimately gives them their unique style and value, this value is made possible only by virtue of the dull, drab, undifferentiated base upon which the ornamentation can be placed. In her efforts to find some mode of supporting herself, Lily thinks instinctively of capitalizing upon her obvious talent for ornamentation, the ability, which she once boasted of to Selden as a potential economic asset, to trim her own hats, to exquisitely place a flower or a ribbon as a finishing touch upon an already prepared base. Lily soon discovers, however, that her talents can not be converted into capital and that the ornamental function is not in itself economically viable but is rather a fringe benefit supported by a base of money acquired for other services. The women who have succeeded in the hat business have done so not because of their ornamental abilities but because they have had capital behind them. Without such an economic base, Lily is helpless to make her way in the world. She can not exist without a framework like the hat supporting its spangles, nor is she able to create such a framework for herself.

The beautiful object, presumably so valuable, is in fact peculiarly valueless. As a result, Lily's existence is precarious. Like those rootless lilies that float upon surfaces and move in response to the movements of that which supports them, Lily has no place she can call her own; she is as much a temporary lodger in the massive and ugly rooms she inhabits at Mrs. Peniston's as she is in the airy and elegant quarters of the Trenors' Bellomont. Her efforts to impress her personality upon her succession of surroundings has merely the effect of emphasizing her transience, her impermanence. Lily's place in the system which has fashioned her is as fragile as the box of pansies perched on the windowsill of her last temporary habitation.

The paradoxes involved in Lily's definition as beautiful object are made sharper if one looks more closely at the economic vise which tightens around her. The ornamental cannot exist without a solid economic base; yet all Lily's attempts to acquire such a base are blocked and blocked precisely because of her nature as a beautiful object. As an upper-class woman, Lily has, of course, been in no way prepared for economic independence; her attempts to turn her ornamental talents into realizable economic value fail; nor can she hope to compete in the more menial work of the business with the women who have been trained to it from youth. However, while these women do achieve some mode of economic survival, they do so as a result of long hours spent in stifling conditions for minimal wages and as a consequence they have prematurely lost all health and youth and beauty. Had Lily the physical stamina of the working-class girl instead of the culturally induced delicacy of the upper-class, she might possibly make a go of it in the hat business, but she could do so only at the cost of everything for which she is presumably valuable and valued, her ornamentality. This point is a large part of the function of Gerty Farish in the novel, a character who in some ways raises the most difficult questions about Wharton's value system and moral position in *The House of Mirth.* Nevertheless, Gerty demonstrates that poverty and ornamentality are mutually exclusive. One might wish Lily to follow Gerty's example, though Lily's fixed income is not even so large as Gerty's pittance, but she could do so only at the cost of being a lily.

If Lily is effectively cut off from the possibility of economic independence, there presumably exists the possibility that she might turn to family or friends for economic assistance:

> Mrs. Peniston, under ordinary circumstances, was as much bored by her excellent cousin as the recipient of such services usually is by the person who performs them. She greatly preferred the brilliant and unreliable Lily, who did not know one end of a crochet-needle from the other. . .
> (p. 117)

Nevertheless, though Aunt Peniston is more pleasured by and prefers the ornamental Lily to the useful Grace, she is not finally willing to give an economic value to this pleasure nor to put her cash where her preference is. She assumes no financial responsibility for Lily beyond the sporadic dispensing of checks and an occasional willingness to assume the bills of her dressmaker. And when the chips are down, she quite comfortably disinherits beautiful ambiguity in favor of colorless rectitude. Similarly, while Lily's "best friend," Judy Trenor, is so in part because she gives Lily clothes and money from time to time, that friendship is abruptly and irreversibly terminated when Judy discovers that Lily has touched her husband's, and thus her own, pocketbook. Certainly none of Lily's other moneyed female friends even remotely considers the possibility of assisting Lily financially. Thus once again one is confronted with the disparity between what Lily's culture claims to value and what it is in fact willing to support. In these instances, however, the cause is a result of the fact that relationships between "beautiful objects" are hostile and competitive rather than supportive. Indeed, the patterns of hostility between women in *The House of Mirth* is a subject deserving of an essay in itself; suffice it to say that Wharton could have chosen no more appropriate metaphor for Lily's sense of doom than that of the Eumenides.

If women provide little or no support for Lily, there are some of her male moneyed friends who would appear to offer help. Yet Lily's connection with Gus Trenor proves to be a major trap: far from assisting her to economic independence, he reduces her to even greater poverty and even more humiliating dependence. The real nature of Lily's transaction with Trenor is implied by the disguises she invokes to cover it and is symbolized by the pressure of his beefy red hand upon hers. Indeed, were Lily to ask herself with any rigor why Gus is willing to help her financially when Judy is not, she would have had to confront the implications of the arrangement he makes with her, implications which Rosedale in his own blustering way exposes when, toward the end of the novel, he makes the heroic and preposterous offer to Lily of "a plain business arrangement, such as one man would make with another" (p. 348). That Rosedale must go to such lengths to establish his good faith makes clear, of course, that a financial transaction between a man and a woman is anything but plain and involves a great deal more than business. The realities of such a relationship are not good faith but exploitation in which the woman pays the price of her reputation. And since the economic survival of the beautiful object finally depends as much upon her reputation as it does upon her looks, the end result of such apparent assistance is ruin.

Thus all things conspire to make marriage Lily's sole significant option: the beautiful object must be bought. Yet Wharton's presentation of this option is hardly pleasant. Her description of the types of males available to Lily for marriage (Percy Gryce, George Dorset, Gus Trenor, Sim Rosedale) underscores its unpleasantness. *The House of Mirth* is pervaded by a sense of male flesh as repulsive and by a vision of men as gross dull beasts. There is beefy Gus Trenor, "his heavy carnivorous head sunk between his shoulders, as he preyed on a jellied plover," "his jeweled rings. . .wedged in the creases of his fat red fingers," his "small dull eyes" inflamed with liquor; there is George Dorset with his sallow gaunted dyspeptic look, totally given over to the quirks of his stomach and the manipulations of his wife, who feeds off Lily for weeks and then stands stupidly by while his wife humiliates her in public; there is glossy, greasy Rosedale with "a pink fold of skin above his collar," whose vulgarity is tempered only by the perception that he would be kind "in his gross, unscrupulous, rapacious way, the way of the predatory creature with his mate"; and there is Percy Gryce, whose resemblance to a "baffled beetle" is only one of a series of comparisons to which Lily is moved on observing him and whose dullness stretches out a bulk as vast as that of Trenor's beef and equally repulsive (pp. 64, 179, 346, 289, 78). When Wharton relates that a considerable portion of the Gryce fortune has been built upon the discovery and patenting of a device "for excluding fresh air from hotels," she equally provides an image of Lily's future were she to marry someone like Percy; she does not need to enter the Gryce mansion, that "appalling house, all brown stone without and black walnut within," to know that being Mrs. Percy Gryce would be equivalent to being buried alive (pp. 26, 25). Lily could no more survive and flower in such an atmosphere than she can do in the hat factory.

What makes marriage deadly, however, is not simply the character of the men who are the potential partners nor even the vision of what life with one of them would be like. Marriage is deadly because it is an economic transaction in which the beautiful object becomes the possession of that man who has money enough to buy her. Lily's distaste for marriage is clear, for while she bends all her talents and energies toward the goal of getting married, she equally exhibits a resistance to this fate. Her real attitude toward marriage emerges in an early conversation with Selden, who reflects her view when he queries, "And so why not take the plunge and have it over?" (p. 11). Marriage is imagined not as a delightful opportunity but rather as a grim necessity analogous to suicide. The violence of Lily's self-hatred when she discovers the implications of her connection with Gus Trenor is similar to the revulsion she feels when she contemplates marriage for the two transactions are in all essentials the same. Thus Lily can project herself imaginatively only as a bride, "the mystically veiled figure occupying the center of attention" (p. 102); she can not project herself as a wife, she can not imagine life after the plunge because she can not finally face the price she would have to pay for it: acceptance of a system which makes of her an object and treats her as a possession. When Lawrence Selden speaks to Lily of the "republic of the spirit," he evokes, however unwittingly, the multiple paradoxes of her situation, for what makes it possible for him to represent such a vision for her is precisely that which makes it impossible for her to ever achieve it: he does not have money enough to buy her.

Lily's situation can best be described as a complex set of double binds the end result of which is powerlessness, paralysis, and death. A major element in this set of double binds is the pattern of the double standard which pervades her world and which is central to the paradoxes defining her destiny. Lily knows that her life is structured and her conduct judged differently from that of men and from that of married women whose relative freedom is purchased by the fact that they act as adjuncts of men and that the question of approval or disapproval has been transferred from society at large to the individual male whose possession a woman is. This perception is demonstrated in the first chapter of the novel when Lily visits Selden's rooms and realizes that his life represents an option not available to her. Selden, as is his wont, denies the validity of Lily's assessment of reality and assures her that girls can have flats too. When the apartment Selden holds up to Lily as comparable to his own is finally seen, the sophistry behind his insistent myopia is even more sharply underlined. It is not for nothing that "Benedick" is "an old word for bachelor," as Rosedale so meaningfully puts it when he catches Lily leaving the building which he owns and in which Selden lives (p. 17). Indeed, the double standard which surrounds Lily at every step is sharply documented by the difference between the encounter which opens the first chapter and the encounter which closes it: Selden's chance meeting with Lily has none of the ominous implications or consequences for him which Lily's chance meeting with Rosedale has for her.

When Lily is at work trying to get Percy Gryce to do her the honor of boring her for life, she is struck by the parallels between her situation and that of her cousin, Jack Stepney. While she sees in Jack's courting of Gwen Van Osburgh a caricature of the activity which she herself is engaged in, one which clearly reveals to her its essential elements and thus accentuates her distaste for it, she is also struck by how much easier it is for Jack to accomplish his end than for her:

> "How impatient men are!" Lily reflected. "All Jack has to do to get everything he wants is to keep quiet and let that girl marry him; whereas I have to calculate and contrive, and retreat and advance, as if I were going through an intricate dance, when one misstep would throw me hopelessly out of time." (p. 56)

A moneyed marriage is relatively easy for Jack and relatively difficult for Lily because, as her similes indicate, he operates from a position of power and she does not. The roots of Jack's power are in the double standard: men are valued differently from women and money is valued differently in relation to them. Thus Jack's marriage strategy is seen as an understandable, perhaps even admirable, plan for self-advancement, while Lily bears the burden of a reputation for being on the hunt for a rich husband. There is, however, an aspect to Lily's powerlessness in this situation which provides an even sharper sense of how the double standard becomes a double bind. Lily's disgust for a proceeding which Jack takes in his stride is, of course, a tribute to her greater sensitivity; yet this greater sensitivity is itself a reflection of that double standard which expects women to be repulsed by situations considered natural for men and which faults them if they are not. Once again, there is the paradox: those qualities for which Lily is valued make her survival more difficult; that option to which she is restricted is almost impossible to achieve, "an intricate dance," indeed.

In her brief association with Norma Hatch, Lily has the experience of being on the other side of the social tapestry, the side from which one can discover the true nature of the design and its construction. In the figure of Freddy Van Osburgh, the slim heir of the Van Osburgh millions, Wharton creates, just as she did earlier with Jack Stepney, a parallel for Lily since both Lily and Freddy are from the same social milieu and both find themselves in the Hatch "Emporium." Once again, however, the differences between the two situations are crucial. Freddy is having a fling; Lily is compromising herself beyond repair. Just as Paul Morpeth, the painter, who does not want to go to the effort of relating to the Van Osburgh set, can associate with people like the Gormers and still retain his professional reputation, clientele, and social mobility, so Freddy is free after his fling to go home. Lily, on the other hand, after her contact with Norma Hatch, can only sink further in the socio-economic scale because her presence in the "Emporium" is itself presumptive of guilt. And it is Freddy, with all the power that his family and his money and his maleness represent, who is viewed by his world as the innocent victim of Lily's machinations. Assumed to be guiltless, Freddy is provided with a timely rescue by family and friends while Lily takes the blame. Thus she emerges from the experience doubly tainted, and this in turn makes her future even more precarious and provides further justification for those around her to cease to care about what happens to her. Again, double standard becomes double bind: women are more subject to taint than men and at the same time such taint has far more serious consequences for them. Lily's access to economic independence through setting up a hat shop is blocked not simply by a lack of capital but by the very real question of whether or not society will patronize her because of the suspicions surrounding her character. Similarly, Lily's marriageability is affected by the current estimates of her character. Lily's ability to survive economically is intimately connected to her reputation, yet her reputation is continually endangered by her efforts to survive.

The sexual politics of "morality" in the society which is the subject of *The House of Mirth* can be most clearly grasped by comparing Lily's career with Rosedale's, for the novel is to a considerable extent structured upon the inverse parallelism of his rise and her decline. Rosedale is admired and ultimately accepted by the world which condemns Lily, for his "success," his ability to amass a fortune slowly and steadily and to pursue with equal firmness and consistency the cultivation of the society which he aspires to be part of. The only thing that finally counts is that he has made the necessary money; no questions are asked about how because in his case morality is irrelevant. Yet Lily's relation to money is at every stage hedged round by questions of morality. It is not all right for Lily to make money by working for Norma Hatch, no matter how desperate her situation. Similarly, while it is all right for Gus Trenor to make money on a tip from Rosedale, it is not all right for Lily. When she jokingly suggests that in return for talking to Rosedale in the public crush of the Van Osburgh wedding, she might get a tip out of him for herself, Gus Trenor turns on her "with a look that made her change color": "I say, you know—you'll please remember he's a blooming bounder" (p. 109). The sexual politics of morality could hardly be put more sharply.

Thus Lily, born and bred to be the creature of wealth, to flower in an ambience of money which will support and float her, is blocked at every point in her efforts to realize the destiny for which she has been designed. And she is blocked not simply by fate, the failure to inherit a fortune or to encounter a man who has both money and soul, but by the internal contradictions in the design itself. For the ultimate expression of the double standard as double bind lies in the fact that Lily can survive only at the cost of those qualities for which she is valued: or, to put the point in its legitimately tautological form, Lily can be what she is supposed to be only at the cost of being what she is supposed to be. It is this tautology which produces the atmosphere described by Nevius as an absence of genuine conflict: "The action of *The House of Mirth* is in a sense all denouement, for Lily's conflict with her environment—no more than the feeble and intermittent beating of her wings against the bars of 'the great gilt cage'—is mortgaged to defeat."[13]

But Lily, of course, is not really in conflict with her environment; the waverings and ambivalences so characteristic of her are not the result of a conflict between herself and her environment but are rather the result of her response to the signals which her environment gives her. In the comparison between Lily and Rosedale, his success is not simply the result of his different relation to money; it is equally the result of the persistence of his will, the immense and unshakeable consistency of his purpose. And this strength of will and purpose derives from Rosedale's recognition of the fact that history is with him, that he is a man "whose personal will [is] synonymous with the will of history."[14] On the other hand, Lily's destruction is obviously tied to her endless waverings, her fatal ambivalence, her failure of purpose and her lack of will. And this weakness has its roots in Lily's perception, however unconscious, that the force of history is against the survival of the "lady" because the temptation to be a beautiful object is a culturally induced death trip. There is an anecdote, a little memory of history with which Rosedale at one point favors Lily, which provides a sharp image of the animus against the woman as beautiful object, the golden girl which the culture creates and then destroys, which is so large a part of the experience of *The House of Mirth*: "There was a girl in some history book who wanted gold shields, or something, and the fellows threw'em at her, and she was crushed under'em: they killed her" (p. 204).

Lily has obviously internalized the hostility toward her which this anecdote reflects and her self-destructive impulses are an acting out of her culture's attitudes toward her. Lily's self-hatred emerges as clearly in her violent reaction to the scene with Gus Trenor as it does in her despising Rosedale for daring to admire her. The self-loathing to which she is prone is so vastly in excess of any of the specific causes which elicit it that it can only be understood as the result of a radical and persistent vision of the self. And it is from this self that Lily is forever trying to escape. At first she is seeking society in order to avoid being alone with her thoughts; at the end she is taking an extra dose of chloral in order to gain one more night of oblivion, one more night of freedom from the self.

Lily's self-hatred is also expressed in what can finally only be called her contempt for her own survival. After her visit to Nettie Struther, Lily is struck by the implications of Nettie's "nest": "It was a meager enough life, on the grim edge of poverty, with scant margin for possibilities of sickness or mischance, but it had the frail audacious permanence of a bird's nest built on the edge of a cliff—a mere wisp of leaves and straw, yet so put together that the lives entrusted to it may hang safely over the abyss" (p. 372). It is precisely this capacity for and commitment to survival which Lily lacks; and it is this lack of commitment to survival which finally clarifies the contradictions of her character and explains her "sliding" nature, her immense adaptability to ambiguous situations, and the sporadic pattern of moral reactions which is its corollary, the scruple, so in contrast to other acts of confrontation and disregard, which she invokes to avoid taking a job modelling hats and to accept instead a job in the workroom where she is bound to fail; the excessive sensibility which leads her to return the money she got from Gus Trenor even though she can hardly be said to owe it to him and he doesn't need it and the act leaves her destitute. Lily's morality is characterized by a whimsy which can only be understood as the expression of her acquiescence in her own destruction and her unwillingness to make any real effort to save herself.

Yet Lily's value ultimately derives from her self-hatred; her beauty is finally located in her unwillingness to survive. Lily's relation to the letters of Bertha Dorset makes this point. In possessing these letters, Lily equally possesses the means of survival; the letters are her ticket back into society, security, and economic viability. Yet Lily's value lies in her refusal to use the letters. Similarly, for Lily to pay off her "debt" to Gus Trenor, even though it leaves her face to face with death, is noble, a final revelation of the "real" Lily Bart. The paradoxes of Lily's position, the internal contradictions of the design on which she is modelled, are clearly apparent in this double bind.

One might raise here, however, the question of the degree to which Wharton herself is complicit in the double binds which destroy Lily. To ennoble Lily for those acts which reject the means of survival carries with it overtones of a romanticization of female masochism. Similarly, in her treatment of Lawrence Selden, Wharton indicates that moral "superiority" is a result of sexual class and economic security; it is a luxury purchased by the possession of male prerogatives. Yet Lily is measured against a moral standard which seemingly takes no account of sexual politics and economic reality. In judging Lily, Wharton invokes a special standard, and in so doing becomes, in effect, one of the "fellows" throwing shields at and killing her heroine.

CHAPTER 5

The Forgotten Reaping-Hook: Sex in *My Antonia*

Blanche H. Gelfant

Our persistent misreading of Willa Cather's *My Antonia* rises from a belief that Jim Burden is a reliable narrator. Because we trust his unequivocal narrative manner, we see the novel as a splendid celebration of American frontier life. This is the view reiterated in a current critique of *My Antonia*[1] and in a recent comprehensive study of Cather's work: "*My Antonia* shows fertility of both the soil and human beings. Thus, in a profound sense *My Antonia* is the most affirmative book Willa Cather ever wrote. Perhaps that is why it was her favorite."[2] Critics also elect it their favorite Cather novel: however, they regret its inconclusive structure, as did Cather when she declared it fragmented and unsatisfactory in form.[3] David Daiches's complaint of twenty years ago prevails: that the work is "flawed" by "irrelevant" episodes and material of "uncertain" meaning.[4] Both critical positions—that *My Antonia* is a glorious celebration of American life and a defective work of art—must be reversed once we challenge Jim Burden's vision of the past. I believe we have reason to do so, particularly now, when we are making many reversals in our thinking. As soon as we question Jim's seemingly explicit statements, we see beyond them myriad confusions which can be resolved only by a totally new reading. This would impel us to reexamine Jim's testimony, to discover him a more disingenuous and self-deluded narrator than we supposed. Once we redefine his role, *My Antonia* begins to resonate to new and rather shocking meanings which implicate us all. We may lose our chief affirmative novel, only to find one far more exciting—complex, subtle, aberrant.

Jim Burden belongs to a remarkable gallery of characters for whom Cather consistently invalidates sex. Her priests, pioneers, and artists invest all energy elsewhere. Her idealistic young men die prematurely; her bachelors, children, and old folk remain "neutral" observers. Since she wrote within a prohibitive genteel tradition, this reluctance to portray sexuality is hardly surprising. What should intrigue us is the strange involuted nature of her avoidance. She masks sexual ambivalence by certainty of manner, and displays sexual disturbance, even the macabre, with peculiar insouciance. Though the tenor of her writing is normality, normal sex stands barred from her fictional world. Her characters avoid sexual union with significant and sometimes bizarre ingenuity, or achieve it only in dreams. Alexandra Bergson, the heroine of *O Pioneers!*, finds in recurrent reveries the strong transporting arms of a lover; and Jim Burden in *My Antonia* allows a half-nude woman to smother him with kisses only in unguarded moments of fantasy. Their dreams suggest the typical solipsism of Cather's heroes, who yield to a lover when they are most solitary, most inverted, encaptured by their own imaginations. As Alexandra dispels such reveries by a brisk cold shower, their inferential meaning becomes almost comically clear. Whenever sex enters the real world (as for Emil and Marie in *O Pioneers!*),[5] it becomes destructive, leading almost axiomatically to death. No wonder, then, that Cather's heroes have a strong intuitive aversion to sex which they reveal furtively though enigmatic gestures. In *A Lost Lady*, when young Niel Herbert, who idealizes the Forresters' sexless marriage, discovers Mrs. Forrester's love affair, he vents his infantile jealousy and rage the only way he can—symbolically. While the lovers are on the phone, he takes his "big shears" and cuts the wires, ostensibly to prevent gossip, but also to sever a relationship he cannot abide. Ingenious in rationalizing their actions, Cather's heroes do not entirely conceal an underlying fear of physical love; and the connection between love and death, long undiscerned in Cather's work, can be seen as its inextricable motif. Even in her first novel, *Alexander's Bridge*, the hero's gratuitous death—generally thought to flaw the work—fulfills the inherent thematic demand to show physical passion as disastrous. Here, as in *O Pioneers!*, a later work, illicitness is merely a distracting irrelevance which helps conceal the fear of sexuality in all relationships. *O Pioneers!* reduces the interval between love and death until they almost coincide. At three o'clock, Emil races "like an arrow shot from the bow" to Marie; for the first time they make love; by evening, they are dead, murdered by the half-demented husband.

In *My Antonia*, Jim Burden grows up with an intuitive fear of sex, never acknowledged, and in fact, denied: yet it is a determining force in his story. By deflecting attention from himself to Antonia, of whom he can speak with utter assurance, he manages to conceal his muddied sexual attitudes. His narrative voice, reinforced by Cather's, emerges firm and certain; and it convinces. We tend to believe with Jim that his authoritative recitation of childhood memories validates the past and gives meaning to the present even though his mature years stream before him emptied of love, intimacy, and purpose. Memory transports him to richer and happier days spent with Antonia, the young Bohemian girl who signifies *"the country, the conditions, the whole adventure of. . . childhood."*[6] Because a changing landscape brilliantly illumines his childhood—with copper-red prairies transformed to rich wheatfields and corn—his personal story seems to epitomize this larger historical drama. Jim uses the coincidence of his life-span with a historical era to imply that as the country changed and grew, so did he, and moreover, as his memoirs contained historical facts, so did they hold the truth about himself. Critics support Jim's bid for validity, pointing out that *"My Antonia* exemplifies superbly [Frederick Jackson] Turner's concept of the recurring cultural evolution on the frontier."[7]

Jim's account of both history and himself seems to me disingenuous, indeed, suspect; yet it is for this very reason highly pertinent to an understanding of our own uses of the past. In the introduction, Jim presents his memoirs as a spontaneous expression—unselected, unarranged, and uncontrolled by ulterior purpose:

> *From time to time, I've been writing down what I remember. . .about Antonia. . .and I didn't take time to arrange it; I simply wrote down pretty much all that her name recalls to me. I suppose it hasn't any form,. . .any title, either"* (p. 2).

Obviously, Jim's memory cannot be as autonomous or disinterested as he implies. His plastic powers reshape his experience, selecting and omitting in response to unconscious desires and the will. Ultimately, Jim forgets as much as he remembers, as his mind sifts through the years to retrieve what he most needs—a purified past in which he can find safety from sex and disorder. Of "a romantic disposition," Jim substitutes wish for reality in celebrating the past. His flight from sexuality parallels a flight from historical truth, and in this respect, he becomes an emblematic American figure, like Jay Gatsby and Clyde Griffiths. Jim romanticizes the American past as Gatsby romanticizes love, and Clyde money. Affirming the common, the prototypical, American dream of fruition, all three, ironically, are devastated—Gatsby and Clyde die violently, while Jim succumbs to immobilizing regressive needs. Their relationship to the dream they could not survive must strike us oddly, for we have reversed their situation by surviving to see the dream shattered and the Golden Age of American history impunged. Out of the past that Jim idealized comes our present stunning disorder, though Jim would deny such continuity, as Cather did. Her much-quoted statement that the world *broke* in 1922 reveals historical blindness mistaken for acuity.[8] She denied that "the beautiful past" transmitted the crassness, disorder, and violence which "ruined" the present for her and drove her to hermitic withdrawal. She blamed villainous men, such as Ivy Peters in *A Lost Lady,* for the decline of a heroic age. Like her, Jim Burden warded off broad historical insight. His mythopoeic memory patterned the past into an affecting creation story, with Antonia a central fertility figure, "a rich mine of life, like the founders of early races." Jim, however, stalks through his myth a wasteland figure who finds in the present nothing to compensate him for the loss of the past, and in the outer world nothing to violate the inner sanctum of memory. "Some memories are realities, are better than anything that can ever happen to one again"—Jim's nostalgic conclusion rationalizes his inanition. He remains finally fixated on the past, returning to the vast and ineffaceable image that dominates his memoirs—the Nebraska prairie yielding to railroad and plough. Since this is an impersonal image of the growth of a nation, and yet it seems so personally crucial to Jim, we must be alerted to the special significance it holds for him. At the very beginning of the novel, we are told that Jim *"loves with a personal passion the great country through which his railway runs"* (p. 2). The symbolism of the railroad penetrating virgin fields is such an embarrassingly obvious example of emotional displacement, it seems extraordinary that it has been so long unnoted.

Like Captain Forrester, the unsexed husband of *A Lost Lady,* Jim sublimates by traversing the country, laying it open by rail; and because he sees the land grow fertile and the people prosper, he believes his story to be a celebration.

But neither history's purely material achievement, nor Cather's aesthetic conquest of childhood material, can rightfully give Jim Burden personal cause to celebrate. Retrospection, a superbly creative act for Cather, becomes for Jim a negative gesture. His recapitulation of the past seems to me a final surrender to sexual fears. He was afraid of growing up, afraid of women, afraid of the nexus of love and death. He could love only that which time had made safe and irrefragable—his memories. They revolve not, as he says, about the image of Antonia, but about himself as a child. When he finds love, it seems to him the safest kind—the narcissistic love of the man for himself as a boy. Such love is not unique to Jim Burden. It obsesses many Cather protagonists from early novels to late: from Bartley Alexander in *Alexander's Bridge* to Godfrey St. Peter in *The Professor's House.* Narcissism focuses Cather's vision of life. She valued above all the inviolability of the self. Romantically, she saw in the child the original and real self; and in her novels she created adult characters who sought a seemingly impossible reunion with this authentic being—who were willing to die if only they could reach somehow back to childhood. Regression becomes thus an equivocal moral victory in which the self denies change and establishes its immutability. But regression is also a sign of defeat. *My Antonia*, superficially so simple and clear a novel, resonates to themes of ultimate importance—the theme of identity, of its relationship to time, and of its contest with death. All these are subsumed in the more immediate issue of physical love. Reinterpreted along these lines, *My Antonia* emerges as a brilliantly tortuous novel, its statements working contrapuntally against its meanings, its apparently random vignettes falling together to form a pattern of sexual aversion into which each detail fits—even the reaping-hook of Jim's dream:

> One dream I dreamed a great many times, and it was always the same. I was in a harvest-field full of shocks, and I was lying against one of them. Lena Lingard came across the stubble barefoot, in a short skirt, with a curved reaping-hook in her hand, and she was flushed like the dawn, with a kind of luminous rosiness all about her. She sat down beside me, turned to me with a soft sigh and said, "Now they are all gone, and I can kiss you as much as I like." (p. 147)

In Jim's dream of Lena, desire and fear clearly contend with one another. With the dreamer's infallibility, Jim contains his ambivalence in a surreal image of Aurora and the Grim Reaper as one. This collaged figure of Lena advances against an ordinary but ominous landscape. Background and forefigure first contrast and then coalesce in meaning. Lena's voluptuous aspects—her luminous glow of sexual arousal, her flesh bared by a short skirt, her soft sighs and kisses— are displayed against shocks and stubbles, a barren field when the reaping-hook has done its work. This landscape of harvest and desolation is not unfamiliar; nor is the apparitional woman who moves across it, sighing and making soft moan; nor the supine young man whom she kisses and transports. It is the archetypal landscape of ballad, myth, and drama, setting for *la belle dame sans merci* who enchants and satisfies, but then lulls and destroys. She comes, as Lena does, when the male is alone and unguarded. "Now they are all gone," Lena whispers, meaning Antonia, his threshold guardian. Keeping parental watch, Antonia limits Jim's boundaries ("You know you ain't right to kiss me like that") and attempts to bar him from the dark unexplored country beyond boyhood with threats ("If I see you hanging around with Lena much, I'll go tell your grandmother"). Jim has the insight to reply, "You'll always treat me like a kid"; but his dream of past childhood games with Antonia suggests that the prospect of perpetual play attracts him, offering release from anxiety. Already in search of safety, he looks to childhood, for adolescence confronts him with the possibility of danger in women. Characteristically, his statement that he will prove himself unafraid belies the drift of his unconscious feelings. His dream of Lena and the reaping-hook depicts his ambivalence toward the cycle of growth, maturation, and death. The wheat ripens to be cut; maturity invites death.

Though Jim has declared his dream "always the same," it changes significantly. When it recurs in Lincoln, where he goes as a university student, it has been censored and condensed, and transmuted from reverie to remembrance:

> As I sat down to my book at last, my old dream about Lena coming across the harvest-field in her short skirt seemed to me like the memory of an actual experience. It floated before me on the page like a picture, and underneath it stood the mournful line: "*Optima dies. . .prima fugit.*" (p. 175)

Now his memory can deal with fantasy as with experience: convert it to an image, frame it, and restore it to him retouched and redeemed. Revised, the dream loses its frightening details. Memory retains the harvest-field but represses the shocks and stubbles; keeps Lena in her short skirt, but replaces the sexual ambience of the vision. Originally inspired by the insinuative "hired girls," the dream recurs under the tranquilizing spell of Gaston Cleric, Jim's poetry teacher. As his name implies, Cleric's function is to guide Jim to renunciation of Lena, to offer instead the example of desire sublimated to art. Voluptuous excitement yields to a pensive mood, and poetry rather than passion engages Jim: "It came over me, as it had never done before, the relation between girls like those [Lena and "the hired girls"] and the poetry of Virgil. If there were no girls like them in the world, there would be no poetry" (p. 175). In his study, among his books, Lena's image floats before him on a page of the *Georgics*, transferred from a landscape of death to Virgil's bucolic countryside; and it arouses not sensual desire but a safer and more characteristic mood: nostalgia—"melancholy reflection" upon the past. The reaping-hook is forgotten. Lena changes from the rosy goddess of dawn to an apparition of evening, of the dimly lit study and the darkened theater, where she glows with "lamplight" rather than sexual luminosity.

This preliminary sublimation makes it possible for Jim to have an affair with Lena. It is brief and peculiar, somehow appropriating from the theaters they frequent an unreal quality, the aspect of play. In contrast to the tragic stage-lovers who feel exquisitely, intone passionately, and love enduringly, they seem mere engaged children, thrilled by make-believe people more than each other. "It all wrung my heart"; "there wasn't a nerve left in my body that hadn't been twisted"—Jim's histrionic (and rather feminine) outbursts pertain not to Lena but to *Marguerite Gauthier* as impersonated by "an infirm old actress." Camille's "dazzling loveliness," her gaiety and glitter—though illusory—impassion him far more than the real woman's sensuality. With Lena, he creates a mock-drama, casting himself in the stock role of callow lover pitted against Lena's older suitors. In this innocuous triangle, he "drifts" and "plays"—and play, like struggle, emerges as his memoirs' motif. Far from being random, his play is directed toward the avoidance of future responsibilities. He tests the role of lover in the security of a make-believe world where his mistress is gentle and undemanding, his adversaries ineffectual, and his guardian spirit, Cleric, supportive. Cleric wants him to stop "playing with this handsome Norwegian," and so he does, leaving Lena forever and without regret. Though the separation of the stage-lovers Armand and Camille wracks them—"Lena wept unceasingly" —their own parting is vapid. Jim leaves to follow Cleric to Boston, there to study, and pursue a career. His period of enchantment has not proved one of permanent thrall and does not leave him, like Keats's knight, haggard and woebegone.

Nevertheless, the interim in Lincoln has serious consequences, for Jim's trial run into manhood remains abortive. He has not been able to bypass his circular "road of Destiny," that "predetermined" route which carries him back finally to Antonia and childhood. With Lena, Jim seems divertible, at a crossroad. His alternatives are defined in two symbolic titles symbolically apposed: "Lena Lingard" and "Cuzak's Boys." Lena, the archetypal Woman, beckons him to full sexuality. Antonia, the eternal Mother, lures him back through her children, Cuzak's boys, to perennial childhood.

If Jim cannot avoid his destiny, neither can he escape the "tyrannical" social code of his small town, Black Hawk, which permits its young men to play with "hired girls" but not to marry them. The pusillanimous "clerks and book-keepers" of Black Hawk dance with the country girls, follow them forlornly, kiss them behind bushes—and run. "Respect for respectability" shunts them into loveless marriages with women of money or "refinement" who are sexless and safe. "Physically a race apart," the country girls are charged with sensuality, some of them considered "dangerous as high explosives." Through an empty conformist marriage, Jim avoids danger. He takes a woman who is independent and masculine, like Antonia, who cannot threaten him as Lena does by her sheer femininity. Though Lena may be "the most beautiful, the most innocently sensuous of all the women in Willa Cather's works,"[9] Jim is locked into his fantasy of the reaping-hook.

Jim's glorification of Lena as the timeless muse of poetry and the unattainable heroine of romance requires a closer look. For while he seems to exalt her, typically, he works at cross-purposes to demean her—in his own involuted way. He sets her etherealized image afloat on pages of poetry that deal with the breeding of cattle (his memoirs quote only the last line here):

So, while the herd rejoices in its youth
Release the males and breed the cattle early,
Supply one generation from another.
For mortal kind, the best day passes first.
   (*Georgics,* Book III)

As usual, Jim remembers selectively—only the last phrase, the novel's epigraph—while he deletes what must have seemed devastating counsel: "Release the males." Moreover, the *Georgics* has only factitious relevance to Lena (though I might point out that it undoubtedly inspired Cather by suggesting the use of regional material and the seasonal patterning of Book I of *My Antonia*). If anything, the allusion is downright inappropriate, for Virgil's poem extols pastoral life, but Lena, tired of drudgery, wants to get away from the farm. Interested in fashion and sensuous pleasure, settling finally in San Francisco, she is not really the muse for Virgil.

Jim's allusion does have a subtle strategic value: by relegating Lena to the ideal but unreachable world of art, it assures their separation. Mismatched lovers because of social class, they remain irreconcilable as dream and reality. A real person, Jim must stop drifting and study; he can leave the woman while possessing Lena the dream in remembered reverie. Though motivated by fear and expediency (as much as Sylvester Lovett, Lena's fearful suitor in Black Hawk), he romanticizes his actions, eluding the possibility of painful self-confrontation. He veils his escape by identifying secretly with the hero Armand Duval, also a mismatched lover, blameless, whose fervid affair was doomed from the first. But as a lover, Jim belongs as much to comedy as to melodrama. His affair fits perfectly within the conventions of the comedy of manners: the sitting-room, Lena's "stiff little parlour"; the serving of tea; the idle talk of clothes and fashion; the nuisance pet dog Prince; the minor crises when the fatuous elder lovers intrude—the triviality. Engaged with Lena in this playacting, Jim has much at stake—nothing less than his sexuality. Through the more serious drama of a first affair, he creates his existential self: an adult male who fears a sexual woman. Through his trivial small-town comedy of manners, he keeps from introspection. He is drifting but busy, too much preoccupied with dinner parties and theater dates to catch the meaning of his drift. His mock romance recalls the words he had used years earlier to describe a childhood "mock adventure": "the game was fixed." The odds are against his growing up, and the two mock episodes fall together as pseudo-initiations which fail to make him a man.

Jim's mock adventure occurs years back as he and Antonia explore a series of interconnected burrows in prairie-dog-town. Crouched with his back to Antonia, he hears her unintelligible screams in a foreign tongue. He whirls to discover a huge rattler coiling and erecting to spring. "Of disgusting vitality," the snake induces fear and nausea: "His abominable muscularity, his loathsome, fluid motion, somehow made me sick" (p. 32). Jim strikes violently and with revulsion, recognizing even then an irrational hatred stronger than the impulse for protection. The episode—typically ignored or misunderstood—combines elements of myth and dream. As a dragon-slaying, it conforms to the monomyth of initiation. It has a characteristic "call to adventure" (Antonia's impulsive suggestion); a magic weapon (Peter's spade); a descent into a land of unearthly creatures (prairie-dog-town); the perilous battle (killing the snake); the protective tutelary spirit (Antonia); and the passage through the rites to manhood ("You now a big mans"). As a test of courage, Jim's ordeal seems authentic, and critical opinion declares it so: "Jim Burden discovers his own hidden courage and becomes a man in the snake-killing incident."[10] But even Jim realizes that his initiation, like his romance later, is specious, and his accolade unearned: "it was a mock adventure; the game...fixed...by chance, as...for many a dragon-slayer."

As Jim accepts Antonia's praise, his tone becomes wry and ironic, communicating a unique awareness of the duplicity in which he is involved. Antonia's effect upon Jim seems to me here invidious because her admiration of his manhood helps undermine it. Pronouncing him a man, she keeps him a boy. False to her role as tutelary spirit, she betrays him from first to last. She leads him into danger, fails to warn him properly, and finally, by validating the contest, closes off the road to authentic initiation and maturity.

Jim's exploration "below the surface" of prairie-dog-town strikes me as a significant mimetic act, a burrowing into his unconscious. Who is he "below the surface"? In which direction do his buried impulses lead? He acts out his quest for self-knowledge symbolically: if he could dig deep enough he would find a way through this labyrinth and learn the course of its hidden channels—whether "they ran straight down, or were horizontal...whether they had underground connections." Projecting upon the physical scene his adolescent concern with self, he speaks an analytic and rational language—but the experience turns into nightmare. Archetypal symbol of "the ancient, eldest Evil," the snake forces him to confront deeply repressed images, to acknowledge for the only time the effect of "horrible unconscious memories."

The sexual connotations of the snake incident are implicit. Later in Black Hawk they become overt through another mis-adventure—Wick Cutter's attempted rape of Jim, whom he mistakes for Antonia. This time the sexual attack is literal. Wick Cutter, an old lecher, returns in the middle of the night to assault Antonia, but meanwhile, persuaded by Antonia's suspicions, Jim has taken her place in bed. He becomes an innocent victim of Cutter's lust and fury at deception. Threatened by unleashed male sex—the ultimate threat—he fights with primordial violence, though again sickened with disgust. Vile as the Cutter incident is—and it is also highly farcical—Jim's nausea seems an over-reaction, intensified by his shrill rhetoric and unmodulated tone. Unlike the snake episode, this encounter offers no rewards. It simply reduces him to "a battered object," his body pommeled, his face swollen. His only recognition will be the laughter of the lubricious "old men at the drugstore." Again Antonia has lured him into danger and exposed him to assault. Again he is furious:

> I felt that I never wanted to see her again. I hated her almost as much as I hated Cutter. She had let me in for all this disgustingness. (p. 162)

Through Wick Cutter, the sexual urge seems depraved, and more damning, ludicrous. No male in the novel rescues sex from indignity or gives it even the interest of sheer malevolence (as, for example, Ivy Peters does in *A Lost Lady*).

Also unexempt from the dangers of sex, Antonia is seduced, exploited, and left with an illegitimate child. When finally she marries, she takes not a lover but a friend. To his relief, Jim finds husband and wife "on terms of easy friendliness, touched with humour" (p. 231). Marriage as an extension of friendship is Cather's recurrent formula, defined clearly, if idiosyncratically, by Alexandra in *O Pioneers!*: "I think when friends marry, they are safe." Turning words to action, Alexandra marries her childhood friend, as does Cecile in *Shadows on the Rock*—an older man whose passion has been expended on another woman. At best, marriage has dubious value in Cather's fiction. It succeeds when it seems least like marriage, when it remains sexless, or when sex is only instrumental to procreation. Jim accepts Antonia's marriage for its "special mission" to bring forth children.

Why doesn't he take on this mission? He celebrates the myth of creation but fails to participate. The question has been put bluntly by critics (though left unanswered): "Why had not Jim and Antonia loved and married?"[11] When Antonia, abandoned by Donovan, needs Jim most, he passionately avers, "You really are a part of me": "I'd have liked to have you for a sweetheart, or a wife, or my mother or my sister—anything that a woman can be to a man" (p. 208). Thereupon he leaves—not to return for twenty years. His failure to seize the palpable moment seems to one critic responsible for the emotional vacuum of Jim's life: "At the very center of his relation with Antonia there is an emptiness where the strongest emotion might have been expected to gather."[12] But love for a woman is not Jim's "strongest emotion," cannot mitigate fear, nostalgia, or even simple snobbery. Nothing in Jim's past prepares him for love or marriage, and he remains in effect a pseudobachelor (just as he is a pseudolover), free to design a future with Antonia's family that excludes his wife. In his childhood, his models for manhood are simple regressive characters, all bachelors, or patently unhappy married men struggling, like Mr. Shimerda, Chris Lingard, and Ole the Swede, for and against their families. Later in Black Hawk, the family men seem merely vapid, and prophetically suburban, pushing baby-carriages, sprinkling lawns, paying bills, and driving about on Sundays (p. 105). Mr. Harling, Antonia's employer in Black Hawk, seems different: yet he only further confuses Jim's already confused sense of sexual roles, for he indulges his son while he treats his daughter as a man, his business partner. With Antonia, his "hired girl," Mr. Harling is repressive, a kind of superego, objecting to her adolescent contacts with men—the dances at Vannis's tent, the evening walks, the kisses and scuffles on the back porch. "I want to have my fling, like the other girls," Antonia argues, but Harling insists she quit the dances or his house. Antonia leaves, goes to the notorious Cutter, and then to the seductive arms of Larry Donovan—with consequences that are highly instructive to Jim, that can only reinforce his inchoate fears. Either repression of sex or disaster: Jim sees these alternatives polarized in Black Hawk, and between them he cannot resolve his ambivalence. Though he would like Antonia to become a woman, he wants her also to remain asexual.

By switching her sexual roles, Antonia only adds to his confusion. As "hired girl" in Black Hawk and later as Cuzak's wife, she cooks, bakes, sews, and rears children. Intermittently, she shows off her strength and endurance in the fields competing with men. Even her name changes gender—no adventitious matter, I believe; it has its masculine variant, Tony, as Willa Cather had hers, Willie. Cather's prototype for Antonia, Annie Pavelka, was a simple Bohemian girl; though their experiences are similar, Antonia Shimerda is Cather's creation—an ultimately strange bisexual. She shares Cather's pride in masculinity and projects both her and Jim's ambivalent sexual attitudes. Cather recalled that "much of what I knew about Annie came from the talks I had with young men. She had a fascination for them."[13] In the novel, however, Lena fascinates men while Antonia toils alongside them. "I can work like mans now," she announces when she is only fifteen. In the fields, says Jim, "she kept her sleeves rolled up all day, and her arms and throat were burned as brown as a sailor's. Her neck came up strongly out of her shoulders, like the bole of a tree out of the turf. One sees that draught-horse neck among the peasant women in all old countries" (p. 80). Sailor, tree, draught-horse, peasant—hardly seductive comparisons, hardly conducive to fascination. Antonia's illegitimate pregnancy brutalizes her even more than heavy farm-work. Her punishment for sexual involvement—and for the breezy pleasure of courtship—is thoroughgoing masculinization. Wearing "a man's long overcoat and boots, and a man's felt hat," she does "the work of a man on the farm," plows, herds cattle. Years later, as Cuzak's wife, her "inner glow" must compensate for the loss of her youthful beauty, the loss, even, of her teeth. Jim describes her finally as "a stalwart, brown woman, flat-chested, her curly brown hair a little grizzled"—his every word denuding her of sensual appeal.

This is not to deny that at one time Jim found Antonia physically desirable. He hints that in Black Hawk he had kissed her in a more than friendly way—and had been rebuffed. But he is hardly heartbroken at their impasse, for his real and enduring love for her is based not on desire but on nostalgia. Childhood memories bind him more profoundly than passion, especially memories of Mr. Shimerda. In their picnic reunion before Jim departs for Lincoln, Antonia recounts her father's story of transgression, exile, and death. Her miniature tale devolves upon the essential theme of destructive sex. As a young man, her father succumbs to desire for the family's servant girl, makes her pregnant, marries her against his parents' wishes, and becomes thereby an outcast. His death on the distant prairie traces back to an initial sexual act which triggers inexorable consequences. It strips him of all he values: his happy irresponsible bachelor life with the trombone-player he "loves"; his family home in beautiful Bohemia; his vocation as violinist when he takes to homesteading in Nebraska; and his joy in life itself. For a while, a few desultory pleasures could rouse him from apathy and despair. But in the end, he finds the pattern of his adult life, as many Cather characters do, unbearable, and he longs for escape. Though Antonia implies that her poppa's mistake was to marry, especially outside his social class (as Jim is too prudent to do), the marriage comes about through his initial sexual involvement. Once Mr. Shimerda acts upon sexual impulse, he is committed to a woman who alienates him from himself; and it is loss of self, rather than the surmountable hardships of pioneer life, which induces his despair. Suicide is his final capitulation to destructive forces he could have escaped only by first abnegating sex.

Though this interpretation may sound extreme—that the real danger to man is woman, that his protection lies in avoiding or eliminating her—it seems to me the essence of the most macabre and otherwise unaccountable episode in *My Antonia*. I refer to that grisly acting out of male aversion, the flashback of Russian Pavel feeding the bride to the wolves. I cannot imagine a more graphic representation of underlying sentiments than we find here. Like most of the episodes in Jim's memoirs, this begins innocently, with the young bride drawing Peter, Pavel, and other guests to a nearby village for her wedding. But the happy evening culminates in horror; for the wolves are bad that year, starving, and when the guests head for home they find themselves rapidly pursued through a landscape of terror. Events take on the surreality of nightmare as black droves run like streaks of shadows after the panicking horses, as sledges overturn in the snow, and mauled and dying wedding guests shriek. Fast as Pavel drives his team, it cannot out run the relentless "black ground-shadows," images of death. Pavel's murderous strategy to save himself and Peter is almost too inhuman to imagine: to allay the wolves and lighten his load, he wrests the bride from the struggling groom, and throws her, living bait, to the wolves. Only then does his sledge arrive in safety at his village. The tale holds the paradigm for Mr. Shimerda's fate—driven from home because of a woman, struggling for survival against a brutal winter landscape, pursued by regret and despair to death. The narrative distance at which this episode is kept from Jim seems to me to signify its explosiveness, the need to handle with care. It is told to Jim by Antonia, who overhears Peter telling it to Mr. Shimerda. Though the vignette emerges from this distance—and through Jim's obscuring nostalgia—its gruesome meaning focuses the apparently disjunct parts of the novel, and I find it inconceivable that critics consider it "irrelevant."[14] The art of *My Antonia* lies in the subtle and inevitable relevance of its details, even the most trivial, like the picture Jim chooses to decorate a Christmas book for Antonia's little sister: "I took 'Napoleon Announcing the Divorce to Josephine' for my frontispiece" (p. 55). In one way or another, the woman must *go*.

To say that Jim Burden expresses castration fears would provide a facile conclusion: and indeed his memoirs multiply images of sharp instruments and painful cutting. The curved reaping-hook in Lena Lingard's hands centralizes an overall pattern that includes Peter's clasp-knife with which he cuts all his melons; Crazy Mary's corn-knife (she "made us feel how sharp her blade was, showing us very graphically just what she meant to do to Lena"); the suicidal tramp "cut to pieces" in the threshing machine; and wicked Wick *Cut*ter's sexual assault. When Lena, the essence of sex, appears suddenly in Black Hawk, she seems to precipitate a series of violent recollections. First Jim remembers Crazy Mary's pursuit of Lena with her sharpened corn-knife. Then Antonia recalls the story of the crazy tramp in details which seem to me unconsciously reverberating Jim's dream. Like Jim, Antonia is relaxed and leaning against a strawstack; similarly, she sees a figure approach "across the stubble"—significantly, his first words portend death. Offering to "cut bands," within minutes he throws himself into the threshing machine and is "cut to pieces." In his pockets the threshers find only "an old penknife" and the "wish-bone of a chicken." Jim follows this anecdote with a vignette of Blind d'Arnault, a black musician who, as we shall see, represents emasculation; Jim tells how children used to tease the little blind boy and try "to get his chicken-bone away." Such details, I think, should not be considered fortuitous or irrelevant; and critics who have persisted in overlooking them should note that they are stubbornly there, and in patterned sequence.

I do not wish to make a case history of Jim Burden or a psychological document of *My Antonia*, but to uncover an elusive underlying theme—one that informs the fragmentary parts of the novel and illuminates the obsession controlling Cather's art. For like most novelists, Cather writes out of an obsessive concern to which her art gives various and varied expression. In *My Antonia*, her consummate work, that obsession has its most private as well as its most widely shared meanings. At the same time that the novel is highly autobiographical, it is representatively American in its material, mood, and unconscious uses of the past. In it, as in other novels, we can discover that Cather's obsession had to do with the assertion of self. This is the preoccupation of her protagonists who in their various ways seek to assert their identity, in defiance, if necessary, of others, of convention, of nature, of life itself. Biographers imply that Cather's life represented a consistent pursuit of autonomy, essential, she believed, to her survival as an artist. Undoubtedly, she was right; had she given herself to marriage and children, assuming she could, she might have sacrificed her chance to write. Clearly, she identified writing with masculinity, though which of the two constituted her fundamental drive is a matter of psychological dynamics we can never really decide. Like Antonia, she displayed strong masculine traits, though she loved also feminine frilleries and the art of cuisine. All accounts of her refer to her "masculine personality"—her mannish dress, her deep voice, her energetic stride; and even as a child she affected boyish clothes and cropped hair. Too numerous to document, such references are a running motif throughout the accounts of Mildred Bennett, Elizabeth Sergeant, and E.K. Brown. Their significance is complex and perhaps inescapable, but whatever else they mean, they surely demonstrate Cather's self-assertion; she would create her own role in life, and if being a woman meant sacrificing her art, then she would lead a private and inviolate life in defiance of convention.

Her image of inviolability was the *child*. She sought quaintly, perhaps foolishly, to refract this image through her person when she wore a schoolgirl costume. The Steichen photograph of her in middy blouse is a familiar frontispiece to volumes of her work; and she has been described as characteristically "at the typewriter, dressed in a childlike costume, a middy blouse with navy bands and tie and a duck skirt."[15] In life, she tried to hold on to childhood through dress; in art, through a recurrent cycle of childhood, maturity, and childhood again: the return effected usually through memory. Sometimes the regressive pattern signalized a longing for death, as in *The Professor's House* and *Death Comes for the Archbishop*; always it revealed a quest for reunion with an original authentic self. In *My Antonia*, the prologue introduces Antonia and the motif of childhood simultaneously, for her name is linked with "*the country, the conditions, the whole adventure of. . .childhood.*" The memoirs proper open with the children's journey into pristine country where men are childlike or project into life characters of the child's imagination: like Jake who "might have stepped out of the pages of 'Jesse James.'" The years of maturity comprise merely an interim period—and in fact, are hardly dealt with. For Jim, as for Cather, the real meaning of time is cyclical, its purpose to effect a return to the beginning. Once Jim finds again "the first road" he traveled as a wondering child, his story ends. Hardly discernible, this road returns him to Antonia, and through her, to his real goal, the enduring though elusive image of his original self which Cather represents by his childhood shadow. Walking to Antonia's house with her boys—feeling himself almost a boy again—Jim merges with his shadow, the visible elongation of self. At last, his narcissistic dream comes to fulfillment: "It seemed, after all, so natural to be walking along a barbed-wire fence beside the sunset, toward a red pond, and to see my shadow moving along at my right, over the close-cropped grass" (p. 224). Just as the magnified shadow of plow against sky—a blazing key image—projects his romantic notion of the West, so "two long shadows [that] flitted before or followed after" symbolize his ideal of perennial children running through, imaged against, and made one with the prairie grass.

Jim's return "home" has him planning a future with Cuzak's boys that will recapitulate the past: once more he will sleep in haylofts, hunt "up the Niobrara," and travel the "Bad Lands." Play reenters as his serious concern, not the sexual play of imminent manhood, but regressive child's play. In a remarkable statement, Jim says: "There were enough Cuzaks to play with for a long while yet. Even after the boys grew up, there would always be Cuzak himself!" (p. 239). A current article on *My Antonia* misreads this conclusion: "[though] Jim feels like a boy again. . .he does not *wish* that he were a boy again. . . . He has no more need to cling to the past, for the past has been transfigured like the autumn prairie of old."[16] Such reasoning falls in naively with Jim's self-deception, that the transformation of the land to country somehow validates his personal life. Jim's need to reenter childhood never relents, becomes even more urgent as he feels adult life vacuous. The years have not enriched him, except with a wealth of memories—"images in the mind that did not fade—that grew stronger with time." Most precious in his treasury of remembered images is that of a boy of ten crossing the prairie under "the complete dome of heaven" and finding sublimity in the union of self with earth and sky. An unforgettable consummation, never matched by physical union, he seeks to recreate it through memory. Jim's ineffable desire for a child more alive to him than his immediate being vibrates to a pathetic sense of loss. I believe that we may find this irretrievable boy in a photograph of young *Willie Cather*, another child who took life from imagination and desire.[17]

In a later novel, *The Professor's House*,[18] Cather rationalizes her cathexis on childhood through the protagonist's musings, at which we might glance briefly. Toward the end of his life, Professor Godfrey St. Peter discovers he has two identities: that of his "original" self, the child; and of his "secondary" self, the man in love. To fulfill himself, "the lover" creates a meretricious "design" of marriage, children, and career, now, after thirty years, suddenly meaningless. The Professor's cyclic return to his real and original self begins with solitary retrospection. All he wants is to "be alone"—to repossess himself. For, having yielded through love to another, he has lost "the person he was in the beginning." Now before he dies, he longs for his original image as a child, an image that returns to him in moments of "vivid consciousness" or of remembrance. Looking back, the Professor sees the only escape from a false secondary life to be through premature death: death of the sexual man before he realizes his sexuality and becomes involved in the relationships it demands. This is the happy fate of his student Tom Outland, who dies young, remaining inviolate, pure, and most important, self-possessed: "He seemed to know. . .he was solitary and must always be so; he had never married, never been a father. He was earth, and would return to earth" (p. 263).

This Romantic mystique of childhood illuminates the fear of sex in Cather's world. Sex unites one with another. Its ultimate threat is loss of self. In Cather's construct, naively and of course falsely, the child is asexual, his love inverted, his identity thus intact. Only Antonia manages to grow older and retain her original integrity. Like Tom Outland, her affinity is for the earth. She "belongs" to the farm, is one with the trees, the flowers, the rye and wheat she plants. Though she marries, Cuzak is only "the instrument of Antonia's special mission." Through him she finds a self-fulfillment that excludes him. Through her, Jim hopes to be restored to himself.

The supreme value Jim and other Cather characters attribute to "old friendships" reflects a concern with self. Old friends know the child immanent in the man. Only they can have communion without causing self-estrangement, can marry "safely." They share "the precious, the incommunicable past"—as Jim says in his famous final words. But to keep the past so precious, they must romanticize it; and to validate childhood, they must let memory filter its experiences through the screen of nostalgia. Critics have wondered whether Jim Burden is finally the most suitable narrator for *My Antonia*. I submit that Cather's choice is utterly strategic. For Jim, better than any other character, could control his memories, since only he knows of but does not experience the suffering and violence inherent in his story. And ultimately, he is not dealing with a story as such, but with residual "images in the mind." *My Antonia* is a magnificent and warped testimony to the mind's image-making power, an implicit commentary on how that creative power serves the mind's need to ignore and deny whatever is reprehensible in whatever one loves. Cather's friend and biographer said of her, "There was so much she did not want to see and saw not."[19] We must say the same of Jim Burden, who held painful and violent aspects of early American life at safe distance, where finally he could not see them.

Jim's vignette of Blind d'Arnault, the black piano player who entertains at Black Hawk, is paradigmatic of his way of viewing the past. Its factual scaffolding (whether Cather's prototype was Blind Boon, Blind Tom, or a "composite of Negro musicians") seems to me less important than its tone. I find the vignette a work of unconscious irony as Jim paints d'Arnault's portrait but meanwhile delineates himself. The motif of blindness compounds the irony. D'Arnault's is physical, as though it is merely futile for him to see a world he cannot enter. Jim's is moral: an unawareness of his stereotyped, condescending, and ultimately invidious vision. Here, in his description of the black man, son of a slave, Jim's emblematic significance emerges as shamefully he speaks for himself, for Cather, and for most of us:

> [His voice] was the soft, amiable Negro voice, like those I remembered from early childhood, with the note of docile subservience in it. He had the Negro head, too; almost no head at all, nothing behind the ears but the folds of neck under close-cropped wool. He would have been repulsive if his face had not been so kindly and happy. It was the happiest face I had seen since I left Virginia. (p. 122)

Soft, amiable, docile, subservient, kindly, happy—Jim's image, as usual, projects his wish-fulfillment; his diction suggests an unconscious assuagement of anxiety, also. His phrase of astounding insult and innocence—"almost no head at all"—assures him that the black man should not frighten, being an incomplete creature, possessed, as we would like to believe, of instinct and rhythm, but deprived of intellect. Jim's final hyperbole registers his fear of this alien black face saved from repulsiveness only by a toothy servile smile (it might someday lose). To attenuate his portrait of d'Arnault, Jim introduced innuendoes of sexual incompetence. He recognizes d'Arnault's sensuality but impugns it by his image of sublimation: "all the agreeable sensations possible to creatures of flesh and blood were heaped up on those black-and-white keys, and he [was] gloating over them and trickling them through his yellow fingers" (p. 126). Jim's genteel opening phrase connotes male sexuality, which he must sublimate, displace from the man to the music, reduce to a *trickle*. D'Arnault "looks like some glistening African god of pleasure, full of strong, savage blood"; but superimposed is our familiar Uncle Tom "all grinning," "bowing to everyone, docile and happy."

Similarly, consider Jim's entrancing image of the four Danish girls who stand all day in the laundry ironing the townspeople's clothes. How charming they are: flushed and happy; how fatherly the laundryman offering water—no swollen ankles; no boredom or rancor; no exploitation: a cameo image from "the beautiful past." Peter and Pavel, dreadful to any ordinary mind for their murderous deed, ostracized by everyone, now disease-ridden and mindless, are to Jim picturesque outcasts: Pavel spitting blood; Peter spitting seeds as he desperately eats all his melons after kissing his cow goodbye, the only creature for him to love. And Mr. Shimerda's suicide. Jim reconciles himself to the horror of the mutilated body frozen in its own blood by imagining the spirit released and homeward bound to its beloved Bohemia. Only the evocative beauty of Cather's language—and the inevitable validation as childhood memory—can romanticize this sordid death and the squalor in which it takes place. Violence is as much the essence of prairie life as the growth of the wheat and blossoming of the corn. Violence appears suddenly and inexplicably, like the suicidal tramp. But Jim gives violence a cameo quality. He has the insistent need—and the strategy—to turn away from the very material he presents. He can forget the reaping-hook and reshape his dream. And as the novel reveals him doing this, it reveals our common usage of the past as a romance and refuge from the present. *My Antonia* engraves a view of the past which is at best partial; at worst, blind. But our present is continuous with the whole past, as it was, despite Jim Burden's attempt to deny this, and despite Cather's "sad little refrain": "Our present is ruined— but we had a beautiful past."[20] Beautiful to one who recreated it so; who desperately needed it so; who would deny the violence and the destructive attitudes toward race and sex immortalized in his very denial. We, however, have as desperate a need for clarity of vision as Jim had for nostalgia; and we must begin to look at *My Antonia*, long considered a representatively American Novel, not only for its beauty of art and for its affirmation of history, but also, and instructively, for its negations and evasions. Much as we would like to ignore them, for they bring painful confrontations, we must see what they would show us about ourselves—how we betray our past when we forget its most disquieting realities; how we begin to redeem it when we remember.

CHAPTER 6

Ida, A Great American Novel

Cynthia Secor

There are positively days when I think *Ida, A Novel,* is the great American novel we have all sought hither and yon. Like the unicorn, the great American novel has proven elusive. And recently it has also occurred to me that it may take virgin eyes to see it. Gertrude Stein herself was fond of quoting her mentor William James to the effect that one should "never reject anything. Nothing has been proved. If you reject anything, that is the beginning of the end as an intellectual."[1] It is with just such a mind, supple, intellectual, and open, that one wants to approach the works of Gertrude Stein. Her works are some of the best of the century in our language, and they have received very little attention— attention, that is, that is both informed and concerned. As a lesbian, a Jew, a woman, and an expatriate; as one who persisted in writing; as one who by the 1930s confidently called herself a genius and the major literary critic of the century, she attracted attention. In the thirties her name was a household word, and in the seventies it is impossible to find literate folk well on in years who cannot recall her fame. She is a legend, a legend the younger generation is reviving.

Ida is a novel about a woman, a woman whose presence excited comment. Critical allusions to the novel have for the most part limited themselves to Ida as a study of identity and entity, as a portrait of a publicity saint, as a study of the Duchess of Windsor, as a comment on the dilemma of Stein as a publicly celebrated author, and as the chronicling of her first real whore since Melanctha.[2] All of these conceptions have merit, and they are compatible. Ida is not Gertrude Stein, and it is important to sense the variety of interests at play in the novel. As Stein says, "I like a thing simple but it must be simple through complication. Everything must come into your scheme, otherwise you cannot achieve real simplicity."[3]

Closely related to Stein's intention to bring everything into her scheme is her gift for rendering significant that which is deemed ordinary. Ida is in most respects a very ordinary woman of her period. She is not really a whore, though she gets married rather more often than usual; she is not really a publicity saint, whatever Stein meant by that charming phrase, but she is one of those persons people do talk about. Ida is fundamentally a woman in search of marriage, a marriage in which she can become more herself. Ida moves from marriage to marriage, state to state, city to city, until she comes to rest in a relation that allows her to be herself more fully than has any previous relation or occupation. The relation is not enough, her resting is not enough, but then what ever is? Life continues. One is maturing, aging, slowing down. Ida and Andrew are together. For this their life we can thank them. It is of interest to us.

And what is an ordinary woman? In summing up the work of Gertrude Stein, one of her most continuingly perceptive critics, Donald Sutherland, puts it this way: "Her own work undeniably contains an extraordinary force, an ele- mental force of being, that holds many readers whether they understand it or not, and often in spite of themselves. That is after all a normal situation created by female forces."[4] His words call to mind Virginia Woolf's phrase, "that extremely complex force of femininity."[5] Together these two not so common readers challenge one to articulate that force, at once subtle, serious, playful, and complete in *Ida*. This late novel, a fine example of Stein's mature narrative style, answers with authority Joanna Russ's by now classic question: "What can a heroine do?"[6] She can do very well, thank you.

Ida is a woman, every woman, an American woman, a woman not defined by her relation to woman or man, but to herself. Ida is herself. She is in quest of herself, though quest is much too self-conscious a term for her travels. In her youth she says to a friend, ". . .I am never tired and I am never very fresh. I change all the time. I say to myself, Ida, and that startles me and then I sit still."[7] Later she dreams:

> . . .that now she was married, she was not Ida she was Virginia. . . .She dreamed that she often longed for water. She dreamed that she said. When I close my eyes I see water and when I close my eyes I do see water.
> What is water, said Virginia.
> And then suddenly she said. Ida. (pp. 364-65)

At both the conscious and unconscious levels, Ida already experiences herself as complete. There are in this *Bildungsroman* no conventional maturation and no crises of identity. On the eve of her final marriage, to Andrew the first, there is the perception that she is "Andrew's Ida," "more than Ida she was Ida itself" (p. 388). But even this moment of "identity" is short-lived. Only briefly is her essential self, her "entity," heightened and augmented by a relational role, by being the focus of Andrew's romantic interest. Almost immediately Stein tells us that "Andrew had changed Ida to be more Ida" (p. 388). She is herself, now, more complete than ever for the experience of having seen and been seen. It is here that the first half of the novel culminates—with themes of entity and mar- riage firmly entwined.

The idea of marriage, so frequent a theme in the first half of the novel, is scarcely mentioned again, as in slow motion Stein proceeds in the second half to portray the gradual coming together of Ida and Andrew. Their coming together might be called marriage, but it is not Stein's purpose to explore the patriarchal institution of marriage. It is her purpose to explore the process through time of two persons bringing into step their characteristic rhythms. They come into step, as Melanctha and Jeff did not. In traditional narratives and dramas focused on the female person, whether they be popular or serious literature, marriage is the proper culmination. Events and interactions may follow upon the marriage of the female person; but ritually and metaphorically the moment of completion for the female person, within patriarchal literature, written by women or men, is the moment of union with the male person, the taking of the hymen. We may decorate and elaborate the event with issues of dowry, morality, and whatnot, but the moment is relational. Her role, her identity, her entity, are one: she is the helpmate of her lord, the bearer of his progeny. Or worse, she is fallen, too many men making use of her. All of this is precisely what Stein is not saying. Stein is the harbinger of the articulate feminist literary community that is currently emerging, challenging all of the generic conventions that have sought to portray women as the other, the anonymous, the helpful. What can a heroine do? She can be herself, that's what she can do.

The self-actualization of the female person has been a favorite subject of the novel since early in the nineteenth century, a subject which the best women writers have pursued diligently, if often self-consciously. Sydney Janet Kaplan traces the emergence of the psychological novel as a form used by women writers of our century to explore the female mind in conflict.[8] The women writers she chronicles are women unwilling to give up a definition of themselves as feminine and who must therefore struggle internally against the whole misogynist tradition. Male writers of the same period more often than not, ignoring this historical struggle taking place around them and within their female colleagues, have obscured the issue by using the female person as a metaphor for their own struggling souls. *Main Street* is a case in point. And *An American Tragedy.* But none of these, in my estimation, male or female, has addressed as firmly, as confidently, and with such authority as Stein the final question—What is it to be a female person?

Stein's own experience as a lesbian gives her a critical distance that shapes her understanding of the struggle to be one's self. Her own identity is not shaped as she moves into relation with a man. She cannot play Juliet, she cannot play Cleopatra. She knows that Mrs. Lehntman is the romance in the life of the good Anna, as Andrew is the romance in the life of Ida. She knows that the relation between Adele and Helen (in *Q.E.D.*) can be explored a second time with new insights as the relation between Jeff and Melanctha. Her women thus come into the world complete, static, centered in their own space. They are not androgynous. There is in their lives no strenuous dialectic of gender. No man comes to provide for them the masculine qualities lacking in their own feminine natures. Their individual rhythms are distinct and complete from childhood. From *Q.E.D.* through *The Mother of Us All* Stein is constantly giving us interesting and ground-breaking portraits of women. The good Anna, Ada, Melanctha, Alice and Gertrude of "Lifting Belly," Saint Therese, Rose, Mrs. Reynolds—each expands our sense of what it is for a woman to do and be.

It can be argued that Stein's entire effort to create the continuous present, intensely experienced for itself without reference to ideas, traditional syntax, and familiar metaphors, is her solution to the problem of having been born a female artist whose only tradition is a patriarchal one. Her method forces one to look slowly and carefully at what is in front of one, without explaining it in terms of ritual, myth, or other cultural artifacts. James Joyce is an archetypal patriarchal artist. His Molly, marvelous and memorable as she is, cannot be perceived as other than an earth mother and a cunt. Her "yes" is a male fantasy. Within Joyce's tradition women do not exist as active figures, as embodiments of the Godhead, as definers of reality; they are vessels, handmaidens, and at their most exciting temptresses of gods and men. Stein, predictably, has no interest in excitement, except as an expression of the self.

> Saturday, Ida.
> Ida never said once upon a time. These words did not mean anything to Ida. This is what Ida said. Ida said yes, and then Ida said oh yes, and then Ida said, I said yes, and then Ida said, Yes.
> Once when Ida was excited she said I know what it is I do, I do know that it is, yes.
> That is what she said when she was excited. (p. 410)

Stein repeatedly rejects liveliness that she might embody life. Ida has life. Stein puts it succinctly:

> But a continent can always be changed and so that is not why Ida and Woodward did not always meet.
> Very likely Ida is not anxious nor is Woodward. Well said Ida, I have to have my life and Ida had her life and she has her life and she is having her life. (p. 384)

Stein's intense concentration on the present moment, her focus on the human mind composing an image of human nature, allows her to treat women as seriously as men have been treated in traditional literature. Hers is not a vision preempted by kings and ministers of state. Ida in her less literary way says all there is to be said on the subject of patriarchy in response to her first husband.

> He met her on the road one day and he began to walk next to her and they managed to make their feet keep step. It was just like a walking marathon.
> He began to talk. He said, All the world is crying about it all. They all want a king.
> She looked at him and then she did not. Everybody might want a king but anybody did not want a queen. (p. 358)

Stein is clear enough. Yet even the best and most sympathetic of her critics have been loath to see her subject matter—when that subject matter is women— and to understand what it means that hers is a lesbian perspective. So good a critic as Donald Sutherland seems almost unaware of the metaphysical, erotic, even political content of *Tender Buttons*, and so fine a collaborator as Virgil Thomson finds "Patriarchal Poetry" hermetic. The first is a celebration of the domestic and sensual aspects of her relation with Toklas, and the latter is a brilliant and witty comment on the political nature of the traditional masculine literary establishment. Neither work is without meaning if one is interested in sharing with Stein her understanding of love, identity, and power. Both are good preparation for *Ida*, which asks her reader to look at a contemporary American woman moving from birth into her golden years, realizing as she goes the opportunities open to her. What do identity and entity mean for an American woman living in America in the twentieth century? The Stein of *Everybody's Autobiography, Paris France, Wars I Have Seen,* and *Brewsie and Willie* is a social commentator. No less the Stein of *Ida.*

It is impossible to read *Ida* with anything approaching a complete understanding of Stein's accomplishment without sensing her own acceptance of herself as a complete physical and intellectual human being and her understanding of just how pervasive and dysfunctional is the patriarchal understanding of the human mind and human nature. She understands that marriage, romance, and the roles of husband and wife are patriarchal institutions. It is out of this understanding that she creates the marriage of Ida and Andrew. Their union, while not denying their individual natures, has them meet on a plane that is truly the function of the human mind and not human nature.

> Slowly Ida knew everything about that. It was the first thing Ida had ever known really the first thing.
>
> . . . .
>
> Andrew was there, and it was not very long, it was long but not very long before Ida often saw Andrew and Andrew saw her. He even came to see her. (pp. 386-88)

It is Stein's genius to couch in the traditional setting of their courtship Ida's emergence as a more and more present person. Marriage is not the beginning of her real life as traditionalists would have it, nor the end of her real life as some would have it. This marriage is a deepening of her actual life. The same is true for Andrew. As Stein says in *The Geographical History of America:*

> I think nothing about men and women because that has nothing to do with anything.
> Anybody who is an American can know anything about this thing.[9]

Entitling her work *Ida, A Novel,* Stein signals that it is meant to be read as an example of the form. Novels in Stein's understanding focus on character, a subject of concern for her from her youth. In *Everybody's Autobiography* she tells us, "Lloyd Lewis said his mother told him when he told her that I said the novel as a form of writing is dead, I think she is right, characters in books do not count in the life of the reader the way they used to do and if they do not the novel as a form is dead."[10] In writing *Ida,* Stein rises to the challenge of creating a character with sufficient life to count in the life of the reader. That is why she so prominently labels it a novel. It was her own endless ruminations about publicity, reputations, identity, and entity that led her to the form of narration that gives to Ida the life that in the twentieth century is commonly reserved for movie stars, famous artists, war generals, and psychotic killers. Ida is food for the imagination.

Elsewhere in *Everybody's Autobiography* she outlines the technical problem.

> It is funny about novels and the way novels now cannot be written. They cannot be written because actually all the things that are being said about any one is what is remembered about that one or decided about that one. And since there is so much publicity so many characters are being created every minute of every day that nobody is really interested in personality enough to dream about personalities. In the old days when they wrote novels they made up the personality of the things they had seen in people and the things that were the people as if they were a dream.[11]

A character must capture the imagination, be familiar as a dream, but as elusive.

Stein's short novel *The Superstitions of Fred Anneday, Annday, Anday: A Novel of Real Life* discusses the craft of the novel as dream and in Fred himself provides an excellent example of a figure fit to be the focus of a novel:

> When two or three or ten people are together and you ask them what are they talking about they say oh about Fred Anday and some people are like that. They just naturally are the subject of discussion although everybody has said everything about that one and yet once again everybody begins again. What is the mystery of Fred Anday. Any conversation about him is a conversation about him. That is the way it is. Does he know it. Well I do not know that he does.[12]

Their interest in Fred is steady until "once he loved the only woman he ever loved,"[13] which for him is related to his interest in superstition. For Ida the attention soon focuses on her being together—she is either with a man or thought to be—and on her sudden, astonishing departures. Somehow she does it just a little bit differently, that's why they all talk about her, as they all talk about Fred.

And the novel as Stein is defining it is a way of composing everything in terms of the little difference that evokes comment. It is the discarding of all the events that do not clarify that little difference:

> It is not at all confusing to live every day and to meet everyone not at all confusing but to tell any one yes it is confusing even if only telling it to any one how you lived any one day and met everybody all of that day. And now what more can one do than that.
> And doing more than that is this.[14]

And "this" is to compose the novel itself. Identity is what is remarked upon, and entity is what is experienced. When people talk about Ida or Fred, they are responding to identities, to their own ideas of Ida and Fred. Their entity is what emerges for the reader as the reader experiences the ordering created by the writer as the writer sees and records Ida and Fred. What the human mind of the writer must grasp completely and uniformly is that which is the essential rhythm of the character being seen, the rhythm that through all variations remains constant. Ida is seen as striving to cease to be alone. The activity is not conscious, it is constant.

Stein, so little interested in or influenced by her contemporaries Freud and Jung, comes, nonetheless, to define the novel as a dream. Her definition grows out of her own understanding of the time sense that is necessary for a serious writer: "You can have a historical time but for you the time does not exist and if you are writing about the present the time element must cease to exist. . . . There should not be a sense of time but an existence suspended in time."[15] The character at the center of the novel then must be both food for the imagination and an existence suspended in time. *Ida* accomplishes this end by using a mode of narration so concrete and spare that the reader comes to feel that she is dreaming through Ida's mind the dream that is Ida. The intention of the novel is surely to provide an extended portrait of a woman, a woman whose human mind is the subject. The prose must embody her perception of successive moments in time—each frame as complete and accurate as the successive frames of a strip of celluloid movie film. Each paragraph is a frame; viewed successively they provide a portrait over time of reality as Ida sees it. Stein is not meant to be present; she is the camera.

This mode of narration is a solution to the problem of identity and entity as literary subject matter. The totality of the novel is the entity of Ida, whereas the successive frames—sometime vignettes or anecdotes as well as straightforward accounts of activity—record successive identities. Ida's memory of Frank, the Lurline Baths, and the wild onions is typical. The episode is neither gratuitous nor randomly placed. *Ida* is a distillation of all that is Ida, not a loosely ordered chronicle of her travels and loves. In each successive frame she repeats her essential self. The dreams, memories, and impressions recorded are the ones that impinge deeply on Ida, that sink deeply into her, as Wordsworth's stone into the lake. They are the scenes her perception sees and retains. The Lurline Baths episode confirms that the girl and the woman are the same person. Their anxiety is the same anxiety. When "Ida was also married to Andrew" (p. 398), she recalls the Lurline Baths in San Francisco and a youth named Frank teaching her to swim:

> . . .he leaned over and he said kick he was holding her under the chin and he was standing beside her, it was not deep water, and he said kick and she did and he walked along beside her holding her chin, and he said kick and she kicked again and he was standing very close to her and she kicked him. He let her go he called out Jesus Christ my balls and he went under and she went under they were neither of them drowned but they might have been. (p. 399)

The moment is recalled forcefully. She continues thinking: "Strangely enough she never thought about Frank, that was his name, Frank, she could not remember his other name, but once when she smelled wild onion she remembered going under and that neither were drowned" (p. 399). The incident is recalled because: "Any ball has to look like the moon. Ida just had to know what was going to be happening soon" (p. 399). Immediately after the incident is recalled, the narrative continues: "And now it was suddenly happening, well not suddenly but it was happening, Andrew was almost Andrew the first. It was not sudden" (p. 399). Her anxiety during the process of their coming together is the anxiety of her youth when during the process of being supported in the water she kicked her mentor unexpectedly and accidentally. It is just this anxiety that causes her so often throughout her life unexpectedly and seemingly without cause to pick up and leave. It is just this anxiety that the girl child experienced in her "nice family" that "did easily lose each other" (p. 339). It is the anxiety of the child who "the first time she saw anything it frightened her" (p. 339). It is the anxiety associated with romance as she becomes at once both more herself and less herself; it is the anxiety connected with sex and love. The presence of the episode does not argue for causation. The adult anxiety does not stem from the youthful event. It simply demonstrates that the adult woman coming together with the adult man is the same person who came into the world as Ida-Ida, held back by her mother, and who one more time "will get up suddenly once and leave but not just now" (p. 417).

A novel, then, is just like a dream. "And some dreams are just what any one would do only a little different always just a little different and that is what a novel is."[16] Like a dream, a novel ends when there is no more interest in it. Ida's story ends with marriage. What more can happen? Ida's quest for entity within marriage is achieved. What can happen to Ida by virtue of marriage has happened, and any further exploration of entity would turn out to be another novel, a novel about aging: "If Ida goes on, does she go on even when she does not go on any more" (p. 432). Ida rests in her marriage as Rose rests on her blue chair. Rose ends her climb, solitary, but not alone, watching the searchlight on the distant hill. In a more domestic, familiar fashion Andrew and Ida live ordinary lives "and Andrew is in, and they go in and that is where they are" (p. 423). They are as commonplace a couple as Mr. and Mrs. Reynolds. There is no more story to tell. The novel is over.

Clearly much of the force of this novel, that "complex force of femininity" which Woolf celebrates, comes from the fact that in creating the life of Ida, Stein does draw on her own past for emotional content. During the years preceding her writing the novel, she seems preoccupied with the relation of the child to the adult, ruminating on this theme in *The Geographical History of America, Everybody's Autobiography,* and *What Are Masterpieces?* In a wonderful turn on Wordsworth's idea that the boy is father to the man, Stein inquires: "What is the use of being a little boy if you are growing up to be a man."[17] And she continues, in a sentence, wryly universalizing the discussion: "And yet everybody does so unless it is a little girl going to grow up to be a woman."[18] What is the use of having been the youthful Gertrude involved with May Bookstaver and Leo Stein if she was to become the companion of Alice Toklas, to have lived so many places if she was to settle in Paris for most of her adult life?

Ida, then, which at the first reading seems so technically curious in the apparent break in tempo and focus between the first and second halves, reenacts the watershed in Stein's own life when after *Three Lives* and during *The Making of Americans* Alice arrived in her life. Her marriage to Alice was clearly the central emotional event in her own life. It both limited her options and freedom (Alice manipulated both her personal and her literary friendships, as Linda Simon notes), and it created the domestic and critical support that sustained her over the decades that marked the gradual recognition of her stature. This novel is not meant as a fictionalized autobiography, but it does bring into conjunction the two themes which would surely have been prominent had Stein written the autobiography of Gertrude Stein—entity and marriage. Such careful critics as Richard Bridgman and Michael J. Hoffman have found the novel tedious with the departure of Winnie, but surely this is because they focused on the theme of publicity rather than of marriage among Americans.

The rapid movement of Ida from place to place and from marriage to marriage is crucial to the portrait of her as a twentieth-century American woman. This restlessness and rootlessness, her lack of enduring connection with place or family, for Stein characterizes her as American:

> And then as it is to have these human nature and the human mind and the little boy and he has to grow up to be a man and is there any use in all of these then there is a geographical history of all these, you do feel that as it is where it is.
>
> I can just see the way the land lies as all of these are there. And so can you. And so can you.[19]

It is this mobility, this gift for abstraction, which Ida embodies, that makes it possible for any American to know anything about men and women, and so to understand the coming together of Ida and Andrew as that of two persons, to be experienced directly, unmediated by traditional conceptions of husband and wife, identities that the traditional culture of an earlier century would have taken as reality.

As Stein's geographical history of Ida concludes, the curious two-part structure of the novel takes on meaning. It is a curious blending of picaresque and epithalamium. Ida has traveled and now she rests much as Leopold Bloom does, but with the difference that her geography is meant to be literal geography, states crossed and recrossed, not mythical regions. In turn Ida and Andrew's motion is meant to be the stately and joyous rhythm of the epithalamium, not to recall it:

> Poetry and prose is not interesting.
> What is necessary now is not form but content.
> That is why in this epoch a woman does the literary thinking.
> Kindly learn everything please.[20]

The novel as Stein writes it understands these forms and their origins in patriarchal culture. And it is her genius as a critic and a writer that she creates for Ida a contemporaneous vehicle suited to her reality. "Ida did not get married so that never again would she be alone" (p. 363). At first Ida experiences reality by herself, then upon maturity in the company of another person. Stein's own marriage with Toklas was by the writing of *Ida* in its fourth decade, and it had given her to understand well the nature of marriage, the spaces within it, its mythology, rituals, and processes. Gertrude in relation to Alice became over the years both more Gertrude and less Gertrude. In the beginning before she met Alice she was Gertrude. In the end she was Gertrude.

The thrice rewritten novel rewards the labor Stein put into it. The Ida-Ida of the first page is a cypher, an abstraction, whereas the Ida of the final page is a fully seen person. Through the successive relations—Love, Winnie, the three men she loved, and Andrew—that mark her passage from place to place, Ida gains intensity, density, and finally luminosity. At the novel's end the abandoned child of nineteenth-century fiction has emerged as a woman of common substance, at once fragile and majestic, complete in herself, and in enduring balance with another of her kind. When all is said and done, she rests before us an aging woman. "Not too much not too much Ida. . . .And not enough Ida" (p. 423). Stein intends Ida to join the invisible choir of those who have gone before—Moll Flanders, Dorothea Brooke, Madame Bovary, and Isabel Archer.

CHAPTER 7

Winning:
Katherine Anne Porter's Women

Barbara Harrell Carson

In Katherine Anne Porter's "Old Mortality," Miranda Rhea watches her uncle's horse, Miss Lucy, win a race in a hundred-to-one long shot. Seeing the animal's bleeding nose, her wild eyes and trembling knees, Miranda thinks in anguish, "That was winning, too."[1] In many ways, the painful victory of the old mare (including the odds against it) epitomizes the victories of the human females in Porter's Miranda stories. For them, too, triumph and defeat are virtually indistinguishable. As if to underline the significance of the metaphorical race, Porter often presents her women on horseback, galloping for all they are worth toward Mexico or away from death or just around the farm, to convince themselves of their undiminished vigor. But whether they are involved only in symbolic contests or in literal races as well, her women—Miranda, Miranda's Grandmother (Sophia Jane Rhea), her Aunt Amy, her cousin Eva, and even, in her own way, the Grandmother's old servant, Nannie—all, with varying degrees of awareness, seek the same prize. We would call it, in the worn phraseology of our day, a valid selfhood. Porter herself speaks of it as entry "into. . .an honest life" (p. 336). If the words are vague, the concept is not. At its center are the recognition and use of one's own powers and abilities even in the face of custom, the discovery of truth for oneself (including the truth of one's own desires), and the strength to face that truth and act from that basis. It is, in short, the creation of an essence for oneself through self-initiated actions, rather than the passive acceptance of a role assigned by others.

Porter deals with the struggle for literal self-possession by the women of the Rhea family in nine stories: the seven sketches gathered under the title "The Old Order" in *The Collected Stories* and the two longer works, "Old Mortality" and "Pale Horse, Pale Rider." Although the stories (except for "Pale Horse, Pale Rider") are set in the South, the problems faced by these women apply beyond those geographical limits. The region that had, with such a hyperbole of lofty sentiments, elevated woman to a pedestal, convinced her of her own sacredness, and walled her in a crinoline prison, offered to the writer a perfect crucible for the study of what happens in general when the lady decides to abdicate her throne—or at least gets the feeling that it is not, after all, a very comfortable seat.

The black servant Nannie did not, of course, occupy the feminine pedestal (although as "Mammy" she did share in the "matriarchal tyranny" exercised by the Grandmother [p. 351]). Nevertheless, she is important to Porter's treatment of women for several reasons. For one, Nannie suggests Porter's view of woman's true condition. Although different in complexion and status, the other women in the Miranda stories are, at least at some time in their lives, as surely bound as Nannie to their society, to tradition, and to family. Porter makes Nannie's symbolic role explicit when she emphasizes that the slave Nannie and Miss Sophia Jane had been "married off" within days of each other—the passivity implied is chilling—and had started simultaneously "their grim and terrible race of procreation" (pp. 334-335). And the implication is clear when Porter says that even after Nannie was legally emancipated, she continued her life of service to the Grandmother, to her white "children," to her own offspring, and, during her childbearing years, to her husband.

However, Nannie does not serve Porter merely as a symbol. A realistic character in her own right, she is also a woman who manages to break her bonds and assert her honest self. In "The Last Leaf," the Grandmother dead, Nannie leaves the family she has served all her life, retreats to a cabin in the woods, takes off her neat servant's cap, dons the kerchief of her ancestral tribe, and sits on her doorstep, smoking, like "an aged Bantu woman of independent means. . .breathing the free air" (p. 349). The identity that she finds most satisfying in the end is one that antedates her lifetime of slavery. Her children, black and white, had thought of her only in terms of their needs. Now she begins to reveal a self they had never suspected, and they are astonished "to discover that Nannie had always liked and hoped to own certain things, she had seemed so contented and wantless" (p. 349). Her final rejection of servitude and sacrifice takes place when Uncle Jim-billy, the husband whom she had long ago stopped living with, hints that he would like to share her cabin with her. She tells him pointedly, "I don' aim to pass my las' days waitin on no man. . .I've served my time, I've done my do, and dat's all" (p. 351).

But Nannie's spirited self-emancipation is not unequivocal. Her coming to her "honest self" is late; it is limited; and even in her total emotional self-sufficiency there is great irony. Others had always meant burdens for Nannie; now in rejecting those externally imposed burdens she rejects too, their sources. She does not care, we are told, whether her children loved her or not; she wants only to be alone; she "wasn't afraid of anything" (p. 351). She is left finally only with herself. This reduction to the core of self—this recognition of one's ability to survive alone and of the validity of one's own desires—is a good starting point (it is the one Miranda discovers in "Pale Horse, Pale Rider"). But as a conclusion it is nihilistic, grim in its lack of connection with others, barren of emotions and of productivity. All Nannie has left to look forward to is restful night, both the immediate and the final one.

Death as liberator—perhaps the only one for those who can fight things as they are on no other terms—is also a theme in "Old Mortality" in the story of Amy Rhea Breaux. Owner of the original mare Miss Lucy (of which Miranda's bleeding winner is, significantly, only one in a long line of avatars), Amy has been dead over a decade at the beginning of "Old Mortality." In life she had been the victim of the weakness of her strengths. Had she been less perceptive she would, no doubt, have been happy as the belle of her day; had she been more perceptive she would have known what to do about her unhappiness. As it was, she sensed the emptiness of her life, but she had neither the understanding to define clearly what troubled her, the vision to see how she could successfully oppose it, nor the will or ability to effect that opposition, except fitfully. She cried out, "Mammy, I'm so sick of this world. I don't like anything in it. It's so *dull...*" (p. 188). But she possessed only the tools of the coquette to fight that dullness with: she had dangled the boring, spoiled Gabriel whom her family had chosen as her suitor; when he praised her long black hair, she snipped it off; after her father reprimanded her for her daring dress at a costume ball, she returned showing more ankle and bosom than before. Only once did her rejection of her empty life reach a serious level. After her brother Harry shot a man to save her "honor," she galloped off with him to the Mexican border in the one great self-willed horse ride of her life. But Amy had not the strength to sustain her defiance. Passivity soon replaced action, literally and psychologically. She returned home in a state of collapse, nearly immobilized, unable even to dismount by herself.

Although Amy was unaware of it, a good part of what she struggled against so vainly and inarticulately was represented in the brotherly defense that occasioned her ride. Her great enemy was the monolithic family, the family as viceroy of society and tradition, which determines how the individual will act and which, indeed, squeezes individuality out and makes the person (and particularly the women—Harry could, after all, ride to Mexico with impunity) just a unit expressing the larger whole. Porter's description of the Rheas' reaction to Amy's ride suggests a great spiderweb: "The rest of the family had to receive visitors, write letters, go to churches, return calls, and bear the whole brunt, as they expressed it. They sat in the twilight of scandal in their little world, holding themselves very rigidly, in a shared tension as if all their nerves began at a common center. This center had received a blow, and family nerves shuddered, even into the farthest reaches of Kentucky" (p. 189).

After the scandal had subsided, Amy married Gabriel, whom she had been alternately enticing and rejecting for years. But that act itself, like almost all of her confused life, was at once an acquiesence to social pressure and a flaunting of it. She accepted Gabriel only after he had been disinherited and thus placed, in some measure, outside the familial pale. Her wedding, too, had the same strange combination of rebellion and surrender, of assertion of an independent selfhood and denial of it: " 'She would not wear white, nor a veil,' said Grandmother. 'I couldn't oppose her, for I had said my daughters would each have exactly the wedding dress they wanted. But Amy surprised me..."I shall wear mourning if I like," she said, "it is *my* funeral, you know" ' " (p. 182).

Even in marriage she struggled (without real understanding of what she wanted) to preserve something of her individual identity. In the first days of her honeymoon, the letter to her mother beginning with a playful description of herself as "a staid old married woman," moved quickly to the plaintive announcement, "I'm going to put on a domino and take to the streets with Gabriel sometime during Mardi Gras. I'm tired of watching the show from a balcony" (p. 192). Except for her dash to Mexico, that was of course where she spent most of her life. The parties, the dancing, the flirtations—all had been only extensions of the balcony, because all had been essentially passive, not satisfying personal needs, but rather placating the demands and training of society. Marriage, she discovered, was only more of the same. She had planned after her marriage to follow the races in dizzying succession from New Orleans to Saratoga. Perhaps she realized now that this would have been merely another artificial escape, a substitute for the race she could not run herself.

Years later, her cousin Eva reminisced bitterly of Amy: "She rode too hard, and she danced too freely, and she talked too much. . .I don't mean she was loud or vulgar, she wasn't, but she was *too free*" (p. 215). The truth, of course, is just the opposite: Amy had not been free at all, except in things that mattered little. Finally, unwilling to live on other people's terms and unequipped to alter the emptiness of her existence, she chose simply to make that emptiness final. There is little question that her death from an overdose of drugs was suicide. Only in taking her life could she condemn the life she had been meted. William Nance has pointed out in *Katherine Anne Porter and the Art of Rejection* how right Gabriel was, without realizing it, in the epigraph he wrote for Amy: she "who suffered life," it read, was "now set free. . ." (p. 181).[2]

Forgetting Amy's rebellion, her cries of boredom, the hints of a suicide motivated by a deep dissatisfaction with their kind of life, the family transformed her in their memories into the ideal belle. But there is more here. The family was involved in an ancient protective ritual. Like primitive people who worship what they fear and so regulate its powers, Amy's family reasserted its control over the woman who challenged it, by declaring her an "angel." They negated what her life and death really meant by worshiping what they said she stood for. By mythologizing her, they restored the woman to her "proper" place. The rebellious one was reintegrated; the spider web was whole once more—and Amy now became the pattern by which future generations of young girls could measure themselves and be measured.

If Amy's acquiescense to family and social pressure cloaked an inner defiance and desire for independence, the life of Cousin Eva Parrington reveals the reverse: that assertions of independence can just as easily hide real psychological bondage. Eva, the woman who accused Amy of having been too free, the old-maid without a chin who had endured in humiliation her mother's middle-aged flirtations while *she* sat a wallflower at all the parties—ugly Eva is the emancipated woman. She has taught Latin at a female seminary, fought for the franchise for women, and suffered imprisonment and loss of her job because of her stand. In terms of political action and professional and economic independence, Eva's emancipation is real. She speaks truly when she tells Miranda, "You'll live in a better world because we worked for it" (p. 210).

But like the victories of all Porter's women, Eva's is ambiguous. Her problem is that she has never faced a source of restrictions on her liberty far more basic than being denied the right to vote. She does not perceive that what really bars her discovery of her honest self is her failure to achieve psychological freedom from her family. She is irrevocably bound to it by a strange mixture of hatred and need. In her work for women's rights she unconsciously transfers her fight for freedom from the area of family—where she can never win because of her masochistic dependency on it—to that of society in general. Her lack of awareness of her motivations diminishes both the freedom and the personal validity of her libertarian activities. Their underpinning is self-delusion, not self-awareness. Eva can criticize the familial and social pressures which, she says, had turned the Amys of her time into sex-ridden, festering bodies; she can hiss, "Ah, the family. . .the whole hideous institution should be wiped from the face of the earth. It is the root of all human wrongs. . ." (p. 217). But she does not see that it has turned her into something festering, too. The very violence and exaggeration with which she avows her hatred show how strongly she still feels the family's influence and how severely it has warped her view of reality. And even while denouncing it, Eva is on a train, riding to the funeral of Amy's widower, Gabriel—that act itself a profession of the efficacy of family ties.

In Nannie, Amy, and Eva, Porter presents the terms of woman's fight for an independent and honest life. The opponents she faces are delineated: family, tradition, her own vacillation between desire for independence and need for others, her lack of preparation—philosophical, psychological, and practical—for establishing any relationship with others except the traditional ones requiring sacrifice of her own selfhood. The usual outcome of the fight has also been adumbrated: the emotional negativism, the defeat, the pain, and the delusion that are involved in even the smallest victories. These themes are repeated and elaborated in the stories about the Grandmother and Miranda.

In their youths both of these women suffered from what Simone de Beauvoir in *The Second Sex* has called being made other than self. Family, society, romantic mythology (including, for the Grandmother, the idealistic literature she was brought up on, and, for Miranda, the idealization of Amy)—all conspire to shape their attitudes, goals, and actions. But both Sophia Jane and Miranda manage somehow to preserve a secret self, an area of honesty within. For both women the process of moving toward an authentic life is one of unmasking that secret self and acting on the basis of inner rather than external motivations.

The double life from which the Grandmother emerged is described, largely in flashbacks, in the first two stories of "The Old Order." As a young girl, she appeared to be the belle of Southern stereotypes, "gay and sweet and decorous, full of vanity and incredibly exalted daydreams. . ." (p. 335). But in the rest of this sentence, in the rhetorical irony so typical of her, Porter reveals the hidden self of Sophia Jane. Those "incredibly exalted daydreams. . .threatened now and again to cast her over the edge of some mysterious frenzy." Dreams of loss of her virginity, envy of "the delicious, the free, the wonderful, the mysterious and terrible life of men," visions of the "manly indulgences" of her "wild" cousin—and future husband—Stephen: all these had filled her thoughts, giving evidence of her sense of the inadequacies of her life and offering compensations for its dullness. She had protected herself from her family's censure by memorizing high-minded poetry or bits of music to have on hand when they offered pennies for her thoughts. "She lived her whole youth so," Porter writes, "without once giving herself away. . ." (p. 336).

Her marriage to the dashing cousin had been, no doubt, motivated at least in part by the hope that it would grant access to the mysterious, exciting world that seemed to be his. Instead, marriage had revealed that the "wild" Stephen was spineless and self-indulgent, having neither ambition nor adhesiveness. Sophia Jane's true character began to develop as she tried to change his, her strength growing, for the most part secretly, in proportion to his weakness. To compensate for the sensual pleasure denied her in her marriage bed, she had begun, with her fourth child, to nurse her own children (and when Nannie was sick, her black foster child, too) in defiance of custom and her shocked husband and mother.

Yet except for this one overtly defiant act, Sophia Jane seems, on the whole, to have accepted the passive role in marriage. Even while despising her husband, she had been ruled by him. In fact, this must have been at least a partial cause for her hatred: her being forced by the conventions of marriage to submit to his decisions, while recognizing her own superiority. Many critics have pointed out the failure of love in Porter's women, overlooking the very good reasons for that failure. How can real love exist between people who know each other only by their false, public masks? How can a woman love when she is on all sides being forced to sacrifice that honest self from which, alone, love can come? How can she love when according to her training, love, for a woman, means exactly that sacrifice? Of Sophia Jane we are told: "She could not help it, she despised him. . .Her husband threw away her dowry and her property in wild investments in strange territories: Louisiana, Texas; and without protest she watched him play away her substance like a gambler. She felt that she could have managed her affairs profitably. But her natural activities lay elsewhere, it was the business of a man to make all decisions and dispose of all financial matters" (p. 337).

However, just as the Grandmother's symbolic counterpart, the literally enslaved Nannie, won one type of emancipation during the war, so, after her fashion, did Sophia Jane. She found herself in one of the "epochs of social disintegration" during which, according to de Beauvoir, "woman is set free." It was in the war that Sophia Jane's husband received the wound from which he would afterwards die, allowing her "finally [to] emerge into something like an honest life. . ." Then "with all the responsibilities of a man but with none of the privileges," she had made her secret self (assertive, willful, self-conscious in the basic sense of the term) her public self (p. 336). She took charge not only of her own existence, but of all her family, both black and white. Her sense of responsibility extended finally to the fate of Nannie's soul and the color of the children born in the black quarters. And it is precisely this assumption of responsibility that indicates the true measure of the Grandmother's triumph. To take, by an act of will, the burden of one's world on one's own shoulders, to create obligations for oneself—that is the mark of the traditional hero. It is also the mark of the authentic self, which can be defined only in process, never in stasis.

Porter continually emphasizes the importance of action in the Grandmother's new life. Before her husband's death, her contact with the world of decision-making, planning, working—outside of her genteel wifely labors at home—had come only in her daydreams and in her usually unspoken criticism of her husband's failures in these areas. As a widow, however, she had set out for Louisiana with her nine children, repaired a house, planted an orchard, sold the house, moved on to Texas, built a house, had the fields fenced and crops planted, all the while driving herself as she drove her children and servants and horses.

But if she had achieved much, she had also suffered and lost a great deal. Independence had come to her only in what seemed an utter life-or-death dilemma. In such extremities, the one involved can scarcely appreciate the victory that results. For the hero the triumph is often only grim and ugly toil. For the Grandmother it meant realizing that she had driven her own children too hard and fed them too little. It meant that her very strength had hardened her to enable her to endure: "griefs never again lasted with her so long as they had before" (p. 339). And it had meant weakening her children, probably because, feeling guilty about her own strength, she had begun to vacillate between firmness and indulgence, spoiling particularly her sons and making them unfit for effective living.

Nevertheless, the action to which she had been freed continued to characterize her life. Even in old age, when the reader first sees her, she cannot rest from her habit of doing. "The Source," a description of her yearly visit to the family farm, is dominated by the whirlwind of her activity: the flurry surrounding her arrival, her brisk supervisory walk through the house and yards, the uproar created by the soapmaking and washing and painting and dusting and sewing under her direction. Yet, to read this story is to see that something is wrong. The Grandmother's descriptions of what she plans to do do not jibe with what really takes place. She proposes going to the farm for "change and relaxation" instead of for work; she takes with her an elegant shepherdess hat "woven for herself just after the War"; she imagines "walking at leisure in the shade of the orchards watching the peaches ripen"; she speaks "with longing of clipping the rosebushes, or of tying up the trellised honeysuckle with her own hands" (pp. 321-322). But she never wears the hat; she puts on instead a sensible chambray bonnet; and her work is more likely to be in the Negroes' cabins than among the fruit trees and flowers. Her vigor on horseback is also, significantly, diminished, but she does not speak of that either.

What we see happening to the Grandmother here is a reversion in mind, if not in fact, to the stereotype of the Southern lady. (Her actions are of a piece with those of other women of the postwar South one reads of, who, bereft of servants, rose before dawn to scrub their floors and do their laundry in secret, in order to maintain their society's myth of its ladies' delicate, indulged lives.) It is precisely in this self-deception that the Grandmother becomes a threat to Miranda and her generation. In spite of her own repression under it, she chooses to keep alive the myth that had contributed to the limitations of her selfhood in youth. The spider web of family, society, and tradition that made Amy its own after her death begins to ensnare the Grandmother as her life draws to a close.

"The Journey" (originally called "The Old Order") also deals with the Grandmother's retreat, in her last years, from significant action into a romantic evasion of reality. Even though the story makes clear that the Grandmother keeps busy literally until the day of her death (when she is working on moving a fifty-foot adobe wall), its imagistic emphasis is on lack of action. This apparent contradiction is resolved if one sees the imagery of stasis as underscoring the philosophical and psychological change that has taken place in the Grandmother in her old age. Her real passivity now lies in accepting the values and beliefs of the order she once chafed under. She and Nannie sit fingering the "material" of the past; making patchwork quilts of it; "gilding" each piece (with edgings of lemon-colored thread and linings of yellow silk); covering heirlooms with velvet and removing them—as she has, in effect, removed herself—from useful life. In re-ordering the past (or "carefully disordering" it, as she does the pieces in the quilts), the Grandmother idealizes it in spite of its bitterness, dreaming of a cessation of change and a return to the old ways. She overlooks her own life of hard work and censures her new daughter-in-law for "unsexing herself." (Porter suggests the daughter-in-law's participation in the race for integrity—the Grandmother describes her as "self-possessed"—by noting that her idea of a perfect honeymoon would have been riding on a cattle roundup.) She was, the Grandmother decides, "altogether too Western, too modern, something like the 'new' woman who was beginning to run wild, asking for the vote, leaving her home and going out in the world to earn her own living. . ." (p. 333).

How can we account for the Grandmother's forgetting the price of her own liberation and reverting to the prison of custom? The guilt the Grandmother felt toward her sons, with its suggestion of her early ambivalence concerning her strength, could itself have forced her back into the solace of traditional life patterns. Here at least there would be authority to blame if things went wrong; the other way, there was only self. Or maybe the Grandmother's reversion is more simply explained. Perhaps it is merely that freedom for women, in her time, could come only in moments of cultural chaos. When the talents that enabled her to survive and flourish were no longer so much in demand, after the re-establishment of the *status quo ante bellum*, society itself could have re-claimed her simply by no longer offering arenas for the exercise of her selfhood.

Whatever the reasons, by the time of "The Journey" she has fallen back upon a belief in "authority," and in "the utter rightness and justice of the basic laws of human existence, founded as they were on God's plans. . ." (pp. 328-329). So the cycle has come round full. The Grandmother, who, with Nannie, had wished that "a series of changes might bring them, blessedly, back full-circle to the old ways they had known" has, as in fairy tales, been granted the wish unwittingly asked for (p. 327). She has returned to her original dichotomized psychological state; she is once again playing a role; her secret self is once more hidden by the mask of her public face. It is as if Porter is suggesting that liberation is a non-transferable commodity and must be won anew by each individual.

But Porter's point is not so simple as that, for in sacrificing her real self—with its doubts, hesitancies, and social heresies—the Grandmother does give something of value to the next generation. We are told that the children "loved their Grandmother; she was the only reality to them in a world that seemed otherwise without fixed authority or refuge. . ." (p. 324). Porter's irony in all this is multi-layered, quite properly posing more questions than it answers. Must the freed woman of one generation inevitably become the oppressor of the next? Can order be established only at the expense of freedom? Is one—order or freedom—

more valuable than the other? Or do they always exist in a dynamic relationship, one rising cyclically from the other? It is surely the Grandmother's very role as defender of order that, at least in part, makes possible Miranda's fight for freedom, by giving her a strong adversary to exercise her selfhood against.

Porter's awareness of the dialectic inevitably involved in establishing an identity, is suggested in her essay on Willa Cather. She quotes approvingly Cather's comments on "the many kinds of personal relations which exist in any everyday 'happy family' who are merely going on with their daily lives, with no crises or shocks or bewildering complications. . ." Even in such a stable household, Cather says, "every individual. . .(even the children) is clinging passionately to his individual soul, is in terror of losing it in the general family flavor. . .the mere struggle to have anything of one's own, to be oneself at all, creates an element of strain which keeps everybody almost at breaking point."[3] Miranda's own early struggle against family control is presented symbolically in the opening of "The Fig Tree," where we see Miranda squirming as old Aunt Nannie grips the child tightly with her knees, brushes her hair back firmly, snaps a rubber band around it, and jams a freshly starched bonnet over her ears—a bonnet Miranda does not want to wear. Already, the story also reveals, Miranda wants to know where she is going and hates being taken some place by the family as a surprise.

A major part of what Miranda has to fight against in her attempts to save her "individual soul" is the romantic vision of reality represented by the Grandmother's mythology and perpetuated by all of her family. This is the problem she faces in "Old Mortality." Here Miranda finds previous generations' versions of reality contradicted on all sides by the evidence offered by her own senses. The picture of "lovely" Amy seems to Miranda not romantic, but "merely most terribly out of fashion. . ." (p. 173). Her father declares, "There were never any fat women in the family, thank God," in face of the plain fact of mountainous Great-aunt Kesiah (p. 174). And the dashing, impetuous Gabriel, Amy's "handsome romantic beau," turns out to be "a shabby fat man with bloodshot blue eyes, sad beaten eyes, and a big melancholy laugh, like a groan" (p. 197). But even as Miranda frets about the family's habit of making their own past into "love stories against a bright blank heavenly blue sky," she is beginning to gild her life in the same way (p. 175). She speaks with her sister Maria of being "immured" in their convent school, because "it gave a romantic glint to what was otherwise a very dull life for them. . ." (p. 194). Already her chances of discovering reality, exterior and interior, are threatened.

The problem reaches its climax in the final section of "Old Mortality," where Miranda, now eighteen and a year married, is confronted with two versions of the Amy story. As devil's advocate, she voices the family's romantic legend, while Cousin Eva Parrington gives the sordid, "Freudian," and ostensibly more realistic side. It is to Miranda's credit that she sees that Eva's tale is as romantic in its own way as the family's version. This awareness leaves her, however, with little certainty about what the truth really is. Her immediate reaction to this confusion is itself romantic and naive:

> She was not going to stay in any place, with any one, that threatened to forbid her making her own discoveries. . .Oh, what is life, she asked

herself in desperate seriousness, in those childish unanswerable words, and what shall I do with it?...She did not know that she asked herself this because all her earliest training had argued that life was a substance, a material to be used, it took shape and direction and meaning only as the possessor guided and worked it; living was a progress of continuous and varied acts of the will directed toward a definite end. (p. 220)

Miranda will never be able to escape the past completely. But there is strength in it as surely as there is weakness. From it had come the essentially Existentialist precept behind her question about life, the idea that life is a process defined by actions directed toward a goal. If she works from this premise given her by the past, while still acting, as she resolves here, from the basis of her own will and her own vision of reality, Miranda will be able to establish an authentic selfhood and avoid passively accepting a role or a view of reality created by others. She will, in Existentialist terms, become subject rather than object, and if she can sustain this identity derived from willed action, she will find all the freedom possible to her in this world.

At the end of "Old Mortality," Miranda's plans are vague, but she has at least decided to stop being like her Shakespearean namesake, watching in awe the phantom shows created by her forebears. Her name implies not only "the wonderer," but also "the seeing one."[4] True to the second implication, she has determined to discover reality for herself. Her mind, we are told, "closed stubbornly against remembering, not the past but the legend of the past, other people's memory of the past, at which she had spent her life peering in wonder like a child at a magic-lantern show" (p. 221). Since this is her determination, we are not surprised to learn in "Pale Horse, Pale Rider" that she has left her home and family and started a career. It may seem ironical, however, that she is still watching shows created by others, now as theater critic for a western newspaper (a "female job" to which she was relegated after compassion allowed her to suppress a news item about a scandalous elopement). By the end of the story, however, Miranda has become a critic of the *theatrum mundi*, a reviewer of reality, who will be, not just a passive "wonderer," but a creator. She is on her way to becoming, as Mark Schorer has said, Katherine Anne Porter herself, "the artist, who will proceed to write these stories and others with that ultimate clarity—clairvoyance—that only the true artist possesses."[5]

Perhaps the best internal evidence that the way Miranda will claim her "honest self" is through art lies in the title "Pale Horse, Pale Rider." It comes from the song that Miranda, sick with influenza, sings with Adam, the man she has known for ten days and is falling in love with. In the old spiritual, Miranda says, the pale horse of death takes away lover, mother, father, brother, sister, the whole family, but is always implored to "leave one singer to mourn." Miranda is left, after multiple remembered deaths of family members and after the death of Adam, as the one who will sing of the others. As she once wrote about the theater of the stage, she will now write of the theater of life. This interpretation is supported by the frequent comparisons of life to plays or to movies, occurring throughout the story. Bill, the city editor of the Blue Mountain *News*, behaves "exactly like city editors in the moving pictures, even to the chewed cigar" (p.

287); Chuck, the tubercular sportswriter, dresses his part from turtlenecked sweater to tan hobnailed boots; the restaurant next door to the newspaper, like all its cinematic counterparts, it seems, is nicknamed "The Greasy Spoon"; Miranda finds Liberty Bond salesmen in her office and on the stage of the theater; she and Adam talk to each other in the prescribed flippancies of the day as if they are role-playing; even the vision that comes to her when she is near death is couched in imagery of the theater: she sees that "words like oblivion and eternity are curtains hung before nothing at all" (p. 310).

Just as it took a war to release the Grandmother's true, subjective self in action, so it takes a war to free Miranda's to art. In her case, however, the war is clearly internal as well as external. As surely as Miranda fights against death from influenza at the end of World War I, she also fights—as a woman struggling for psychological and creative independence—against the death that comes from intellectual passivity, from the failure to act or to create, from the surrender of one's honest self. The story opens, significantly, with a description of an almost totally motionless Miranda, just beginning to feel the symptoms of her disease. She is half in a coma; "her heart was a stone lying upon her breast outside of her; her pulses lagged and paused. . ." (p. 269). It is not really very mysterious that, in this state, her mind should turn to her family, the cause of another kind of inertia in her life. She thinks: "Too many have died in this bed already, there are far too many ancestral bones propped up on the mantelpieces, there have been too damned many antimacassars in this house. . .and oh, what accumulation of storied dust never allowed to settle in peace for one moment" (p. 269). Only through a stubborn act of will, conscious refusal to die, will Miranda make it to the other side. In "Old Mortality" the child Miranda dreamed of being a jockey when she grew up, envisioning the day "she would ride out. . . and win a great race, and surprise everybody, her family most of all" (p. 196). Her victory will, like Miss Lucy's, be filled with suffering, but this is her day to ride. Although her pulse lags and her heart is almost lifeless, in her mind there is still action: she dreams of mounting her horse and riding to escape death—physical death and that other death, that sacrifice of self, associated with the spider web, or tangled fishing lines, of family.

But if the family was, in her past, the major source of temptations to passivity, other lures have presented themselves in her new life, calling on her to deny her integrity. Even though she believes the war "filthy," it takes all the strength she can muster to resist the intimidations of the men selling Liberty Bonds (the pun is perfect), who assert that she is the lone holdout in all the businesses in the entire city. She surrenders at least momentarily to social pressure when she puts in her time visiting hospitalized soldiers. And when an irate performer whom she has panned assails her, she is once again tempted to retreat from commitment. She wails: "There's too much of everything in this world just now. I'd like to sit down here on the curb, Chuck, and die, and never again see—I wish I could lose my memory and forget my own name. . ." (p. 289). In treating Amy and Eva, Porter was concerned with the near impossibility of a woman's finding her true self under all the debris of psychological determinism, social pressures, acculturation. In Miranda's case, Porter turns—as she did by indirection in the story of the Grandmother—to the problems faced by the woman who, having discovered her own version of truth and the kind of life she wants to lead, must fight tooth and toenail to keep from denying them. Never again to see would be for Miranda, "the seeing one," the ultimate denying of self; it would be truly to forget her name. To lose her memory would be to abandon the very source of her art. Even Adam and the love she feels for him seem a threat to her free will—Adam who keeps her "on the inside of the walk in good American style," who helps her "across street corners as if she were a cripple," who would have carried her over mud puddles had they come across any, and whom she does not want to love, not now, but whom she feels forced to love *now,* because their time seems so short (p. 295).

There are, of course, more important reasons symbolically and thematically for Adam's death than just the fact that he would limit Miranda's independence. Described as "like a fine healthy apple," Adam is Miranda's Edenic self. He has "never had a pain in his life"—a "monstrous uniqueness" in Adam and, by symbolic transfer, in Miranda's own untested self. What pains she has suffered so far have given her, Porter says, only the "illusion of maturity and experience" (p. 280). The Biblical Eve invited Adam to partake of the tree of knowledge; Miranda's Adam, in effect, offers her escape from that knowledge. Perhaps there is a suggestion here of the archetypal offer of the male to "protect" the female, that protection, as it often turns out, effectively blocking creative participation in life, except on the biological level. It is significant that Adam "confessed that he simply could not get through a book" except for technical works, which deal with facts, but not with the truths that interest the artist (p. 285). And it is appropriate that Adam should stop Miranda in her prayer to Apollo, to god of poets—and of seers. Had Adam lived—or, on the symbolic level, had she accepted the kind of life he represented, the life of innocence, of avoidance of pain and reality—Miranda could never become the "singer" who would mourn for human suffering and loss. Adam becomes the "pure. . .sacrificial lamb" given in exchange for her new life (p. 295).

With Adam's death and her own delirious vision of oblivion, Miranda gives up all illusions, all hopes, all love. She is left with what Nannie had found only at the end of her life: that reduction to the very core of selfhood, that "hard unwinking angry point of light" that Miranda saw in her death sleep and heard say, "Trust me. I stay." She is left with the awareness of the power of her own will (strong enough to conquer death); of her ability to survive alone; and of an identity, a reality that is hers without dependence on any one else. But unlike Nannie, Miranda has the time and the emotional and practical equipment to make this center a starting point instead of a final station. As she returns from her race with death, she is not only a Lazarus come forth, but a "seer" in another sense now, a *vates,* who has looked into the depths and will, no doubt, be compelled to tell about it in certain seasons to come, when Pegasus replaces that other pale horse. "The Grave" in "The Old Order" had revealed to Miranda that treasure can come from a tomb; her art will be another proof of the truth of this promise.

The likelihood that Miranda will express her selfhood in art may also suggest her superiority to her Grandmother in Porter's view. Porter once indicated her agreement with E.M. Forster's belief that "there are only two possibilities for any real order: art and religion."[6] The essential difference is significant: religion, the Grandmother's source of order in old age, has its anchor outside the self, in institutions, rules, dogmas. Art, on the other hand, has an interior source; the self becomes creator. Religion, as the Grandmother practiced it, means limitation of the self; art, expression of the self. For Porter it is the center that will hold. As she wrote in her introduction to *Flowering Judas and Other Stories*: "[The arts] cannot be destroyed altogether because they represent the substance of faith and the only reality. They are what we find again when the ruins are cleared away. And even the smallest and most incomplete offering at this time can be a proud act in defense of that faith."

And that is winning, too.

CHAPTER 8

The Visionary Art of Flannery O'Connor

Joyce Carol Oates

> . . .something is developing in the world by means of us, perhaps at
> our expense.
>
> *—Teilhard de Chardin*

The greatest of Flannery O'Connor's books is her last, posthumously-published collection of stories, *Everything That Rises Must Converge.* Though it is customary to interpret O'Connor's allusion to the philosophy of Teilhard de Chardin as ironic, it seems to me that there is no irony involved. There are many small ironies in these nine stories, certainly, and they are comic-grotesque and flamboyant and heartbreaking—but no ultimate irony is intended and the book is not a tragic one. It is a collection of revelations; like all revelations, it points to a dimension of experiential truth that lies outside the sphere of the questing, speculative mind, but which is nevertheless available to all.

The "psychic interpenetrability" of which Teilhard speaks in *The Phenomenon of Man* determines that man, in "rising" to a higher consciousness, will of necessity coalesce into a unity that is basically a phenomenon of mind (hence of man, since only man possesses self-consciousness). It is misleading to emphasize Teilhard's optimism at the expense of his cautious consideration of what he calls the "doctrine by isolation"[1] and the "cynical and brutal theories" of the contemporary world; O'Connor has dramatized the tragic consequences of the locked-in ego in earlier fiction, but in *Everything That Rises Must Converge* nearly every story addresses itself to the problem of bringing to consciousness the latent horror, making manifest the Dream of Reason—which is of course a nightmare. It is a measure of her genius that she can so easily and so skillfully evoke the spiritual while dealing in a very concrete, very secular world of fragmentary people.

Despite her rituals of baptism-by-violence, and her apparently merciless subjecting of ordinary "good" people to extraordinary fates, O'Connor sees the world as an incarnation of spirit; she has stated that the art of fiction itself is "very much an incarnational art."[2] In a way she shares the burdens of her fanatical preachers Motes and Tarwater: she sees herself as writing from a prophetic vision, as a "realist of distances."[3] Her people are not quite whole until violence makes them whole. They must suffer amazing initiations, revela-

tions nearly as physically brutal as those in Kafka—one might explore the similarities between Parker of "Parker's Back" and the heroic, doomed officer of
"In The Penal Colony"—because their way into the spiritual is through the
physical; the way into O'Connor's dimension of the sacred is through the secular
or vulgar. Teilhard's rising of consciousness into a mysterious Super-Life, in
which the multiplicity of the world's fragments are driven to seek one another
through love assumes a mystical "gravity of bodies"[4] that must have appealed to
O'Connor's sacramental imagination. Fundamental to the schoolteacher Rayber's insistence upon rationality is his quite justified terror of the Unconscious—
he must act out of his thinking, calculating, mechanical ego simply in order to
resist the gravity that threatens to carry him out of himself; otherwise, he will
become another "fanatic," another victim of that love that is hidden in the
blood, in this specific instance in terms of Christ. The local, human tragedy is,
then, the highly conscious resisting of the Incarnation. As human beings (who
are fragments) resist the gravity that should bring them into a unity, they
emphasize their isolation, their helplessness, and can be delivered from the
trance of Self only by violence.

Paradoxically, the way into O'Connor's vision that is least ambiguous is
through a story that has not received much attention, "The Lame Shall Enter
First." This fifty-seven page story is a reworking of the nuclear fable of *The
Violent Bear It Away* and, since O'Connor explored the tensions between the
personalities of the Rationalist-Liberal and the object of his charity at such
length in the novel, she is free to move swiftly and bluntly here. "We are accustomed to consider," says Teilhard in a discussion of the energies of love "Beyond the Collective," "only the sentimental face of love...."[5] In "The Lame
Shall Enter First" it is this sentimental love that brings disaster to the would-be
Savior, Sheppard. He is a young, white-haired City Recreational Director who,
on Saturdays, works as a counselor at a boys' reformatory; since his wife's
death he has moved out of their bedroom and lives an ascetic, repressed life,
refusing even to fully acknowledge his love for his son. Befriending the crippled,
exasperating Rufus Johnson, Sheppard further neglects his own son, Norton,
and is forced to realize that his entire conception of himself has been hypocrit-
ical. O'Connor underscores the religious nature of his experience by calling it a
revelation. Sheppard hears his own voice "as if it were the voice of his accuser."
Though he closes his eyes against the revelation, he cannot elude it:

> His heart contracted with a repulsion for himself so clear and so intense
> that he gasped for breath. He had stuffed his own emptiness with good
> works like a glutton. He had ignored his own child to feed his vision of
> himself. He saw the clear-eyed Devil, the sounder of hearts, leering at
> him....His image of himself shrivelled until everything was black before
> him. He sat there paralyzed, aghast.

Sheppard then wakes from his trance and runs to his son, but, even as he
hurries to the boy, he imagines Norton's face "transformed; the image of his
salvation; all light," and the reader sees that even at this dramatic point Sheppard is deluded. It is still *his* salvation he desires, *his* experience of the trans-

formation of his son's misery into joy. Therefore it is poetically just that his change of heart leads to nothing, to no joyous reconciliation. He rushes up to the boy's room and discovers that Norton has hanged himself.

The boy's soul has been "launched. . .into space"; like Bishop of *The Violent Bear It Away* he is a victim of the tensions between two ways of life, two warring visions. In the image of Christ there is something "mad" and "stinking" and catastrophic, at least in a secularized civilization; in the liberal, manipulative humanitarianism of the modern world there is that "clear-eyed Devil" that cuts through all bonds, all mystery, all "psychical convergence" that cannot be reduced to simplistic sociological formulas. It is innocence that is destroyed. The well-intentioned Savior, Sheppard, has acted only to fill his own vacuity; his failure as a true father results in his son's suicide.

He had stuffed his own emptiness with good works like a glutton.

Perhaps this is O'Connor's judgment, blunt and final, upon our civilization. Surely she is sympathetic with Teilhard's rejection of egoism, as the last desperate attempt of the world of matter—in its fragmentary forms, "individuals"—to persist in its own limited being. In discussing the evolutionary process of love, the rising-to-consciousness of individuals through love, Teilhard analyzes the motives for "the fervour and impotence" that accompany every egoistic solution of life:

> In trying to separate itself as much as possible from others, the element individualises itself; but in so doing it becomes retrograde and seeks to drag the world backwards toward plurality and into matter. In fact it diminishes itself and loses itself. . . .The peak of ourselves, the acme of our originality, is not our individuality but our person; and according to the evolutionary structure of the world, we can only find our person by uniting together.[6]

What is difficult, perhaps, is to see how the humanitarian impulse—when it is not spiritual—is an egoistic activity. O'Connor's imagination is like Dostoyevsky's: politically reactionary, but spiritually fierce, combative, revolutionary. If the liberal, atheistic, man-centered society of modern times is dedicated to manipulating others in order to "save" them, to transform them into flattering images of their own egos, then there is no love involved—there is no true merging of selves, but only a manipulative aggression. This kind of love is deadly, because it believes itself to be selfless; it is the sudden joy of the intellectual Julian, in the story "Everything That Rises Must Converge," when he sees that his mother is about to be humiliated by a black woman who is wearing the same outrageously ugly hat his mother has bought—"His grin hardened until it said to her as plainly as if he were saying aloud: Your punishment exactly fits your pettiness. This should teach you a permanent lesson." The lession his mother gets, however, is fatal: the permanence of death.

"He thinks he's Jesus Christ!" the club-footed juvenile delinquent, Rufus Johnson, exclaims of Sheppard. He thinks he is divine, when in fact he is empty;

he tries to stuff himself with what he believes to be good works, in order to disguise the terrifying fact of his own emptiness. For O'Connor *this* is the gravest sin. Her madmen, thieves, misfits, and murderers commit crimes of a secular nature, against other men; they are not so sinful as the criminals who attempt to usurp the role of the divine. In Kafka's words, "They. . .attempted to realize the happiness of mankind without the aid of grace."[7] It is an erecting of the Tower of Babel upon the finite, earthly Wall of China: a ludicrous act of folly.

O'Connor's writing is stark and, for many readers, difficult to absorb into a recognizable world, because it insists upon a brutal distinction between what Augustine would call the City of Man and the City of God. One can reject O'Connor's fierce insistence upon this separation—as I must admit I do—and yet sympathize with the terror that must be experienced when these two "realms" of being are imagined as distinct. For, given the essentially Manichean dualism of the Secular and the Sacred, man is forced to choose between them: he cannot comfortably live in both "cities." Yet his body, especially if it is a diseased and obviously, immediately, *perpetually* mortal body, forces him to realize that he is existing in that City of Man, at every instant that he is not so spiritually chaste as to be in the City of God. Therefore life is a struggle; the natural, ordinary world is either sacramental (and ceremonial) or profane (and vulgar). And it follows from this that the diseased body is not only an affirmation, or a symbolic intensification of, the spiritual "disease" that attends physical processes; it becomes a matter of one's personal salvation—Jung would use the term 'individuation'—to interpret the accidents of the flesh in terms of the larger, unfathomable, but ultimately *no more abstract* pattern that links the Self to the Cosmos. This is a way of saying that for Flannery O'Connor (as for Kafka and for D.H. Lawrence) the betrayal of the body, its loss of normal health, must be seen as necessary; it must make sense. *Wise Blood*, ironically begun before O'Connor suffered her first attack of the disease that ultimately killed her, a disease inherited from her father, makes the point dramatically and lyrically that the "blood" is "wise". And rebellion is futile against it. Thus, the undulant fever suffered by the would-be writer, Asbury, is not only directly and medically attributable to *his* rash behavior (drinking unpasteurized milk, against his mother's rules of the dairy), but it becomes the means by which he realizes a revelation he would not otherwise have experienced. Here, O'Connor affirms a far more primitive and far more brutal sense of fate than Teilhard would affirm—at least as I understand Teilhard—for in the physical transformation of man into a higher consciousness and finally into a collective, god-like "synthesized state"[8] the transformation is experienced in terms of a space/time series of events, but is in fact (if it could be a demonstrable or measurable "fact") one single event: one phenomenon. Therefore, the "physical" is not really a lower form of the spiritual, but is experienced as being lower, or earlier in evolution, and the fear of or contempt for the body expressed by Augustine is simply a confusion. The physical *is* also spiritual; the physical only seems not to be "spiritual." Though this sounds perplexing, it is really a way of saying that Augustine (and perhaps O'Connor, who was very much influenced by Augustine and other Catholic theologians) prematurely denied the sacredness of the body, as if it were a hindrance and not the only means by which the spirit can attain its "salvation." Useless to rage against his body's deterioration, Lawrence says sadly, and nobly, because that body was the only means by which D.H. Lawrence could have appeared in the world. But this is not at all what O'Connor does, for in her necessary and rather defiant acceptance of her inherited disease in terms of its being, perhaps, a kind of Original Sin and therefore not an accident—somehow obscurely willed either by God or by O'Connor herself (if we read "The Enduring Chill" as a metaphor for O'Connor's predicament)—we are forced to affirm the disease-as-revelation:

> The boy [Asbury] fell back on his pillow and stared at the ceiling. His limbs that had been racked for so many weeks by fever and chill were numb now. The old life in him was exhausted. He awaited the coming of new. It was then that he felt the beginning of a chill, a chill so peculiar, so light, that it was like a warm ripple across a deeper sea of cold. . . . Asbury blanched and the last film of illusion was torn as if by a whirlwind from his eyes. He saw that for the rest of his days, frail, racked, but enduring, he would live in the face of a purifying terror. A feeble cry, a last impossible protest escaped him. But the Holy Ghost, emblazoned in ice instead of fire, continued, implacable, to descend.
>
> ("The Enduring Chill")

This particular story and its epiphany may not have the aesthetic power to move us that belong to O'Connor's more sharply-imagined works, but it is central to an understanding of all of her writing and, like Lawrence's "The Ship of Death", it has a beauty and a terrible dignity that carry it beyond criticism. For while Teilhard's monumental work stresses the uniqueness of the individual through his absorption in a larger, and ultimately divine, "ultimate earth," there cannot be in his work the dramatization of the real, living, bleeding, suffering, *existing* individual that O'Connor knows so well. She knows this existing individual from the inside and not from the outside; she knows that while the historical and sociological evolution causes one group of people to "rise" (the blacks; the haughty black woman in "Everything That Rises Must Converge"), it is also going to destroy others (both Julian and his mother, who evidently suffers a stroke when the black woman hits her), and she also knows—it is this point, I believe, missed by those critics who are forever stressing her 'irony'— that *the entire process is divine.* Hence her superficially reactionary attitude toward the secularized, liberal, Godless society, and her affirmation of the spontaneous, the irrational, the wisdom of the blood in which, for her, Christ somehow is revealed. Because she does believe and states clearly[9] that her writing is an expression of her religious commitment, and is itself a kind of divine distortion ("the kind that reveals, or should reveal," as she remarks in the essay "Novelist and Believer"), the immediate problem for most critics is *how* to wrench her work away from her, *how* to show that she didn't at all know herself, but must be subjected to a higher, wiser, more objective consciousness in order to be understood. But the amazing thing about O'Connor is that she seems to have known exactly what she was doing and how she might best accomplish it. There is no ultimate irony in her work, no ultimate despair or pessimism or tragedy, and certainly not a paradoxical sympathy for the Devil.[10] It is only when O'Connor is judged from a secular point of view, or from a "rational" point of view, that she seems unreasonable—a little mad—and must be chastely revised by the liberal imagination.

"Everything That Rises Must Converge" is a story in which someone appears to lose, and to lose mightily; but the "loss" is fragmentary, a necessary and minor part of the entire process of "converging" that is the entire universe—or God. The son, Julian, is then released to the same "entry into the world of guilt and sorrow" that is Rayber's, and Sheppard's, and his surrender to the emotions he has carefully refined into ironic, cynical, "rational" ideas is at the same time his death (as an enlightened Ego) and his birth (as a true adult). Many of the stories in this volume deal literally with the strained relationships between one generation and another, because this is a way of making explicit the psychological problem of ascending to a higher self. In *A Good Man Is Hard to Find* the tensions were mainly between strangers and in terms of very strange gods. The life you save *may* be your own, and if you cannot bear the realization that a freak is a Temple of the Holy Ghost, that is unfortunate for you. As Rufus Johnson says of the Bible, superbly and crazily, *Even if I didn't believe it, it would still be true*—a reply to infuriate the rationalist Sheppard, and no doubt most of us! But O'Connor's art is both an existential dramatization of what it means to suffer, and to suffer intelligently, coherently, and a deliberate series of parodies of that subjectivist philosphy loosely called "existentialism"—though it is the solipsistic, human-value-oriented existentialism she obviously despises, Sartrean and not Kierkegaardian. The Deist may say "Whatever is, is right," but the Deist cannot prove the truth of his statement, for such truths or revelations can only be experienced by an existing, suffering individual whom some violent shock has catapulted into the world of sorrow. When the intellectual Julian suffers the real loss of his mother, the real Julian emerges; his self-pitying depression vanishes at once; the faith he had somehow lost "in the midst of his martyrdom" is restored. So complex and so powerful a story cannot be reduced to any single meaning; but it is surely O'Connor's intention to show how the egoistic Julian is a spokesman for an entire civilization, and to demonstrate the way by which this civilization will—inevitably, horribly—be jolted out of its complacent, worldly cynicism. *By violence.* And by no other way, because the Ego cannot be destroyed except violently, it cannot be argued out of its egoism by words, by any logical argument, it cannot be instructed in anything except a physical manner. O'Connor would have felt a kinship with the officer of Kafka's "In the Penal Colony," who yearns for enlightenment that can only come through his own body, through a sentence tattooed on his body. As Christ suffered with his real, literal body, so O'Connor's people must suffer in order to realize Christ in them.

Yet is not finally necessary to share O'Connor's specific religious beliefs in order to appreciate her art. Though she would certainly refute me in saying this, the "Christ" experience itself may well be interpreted as a psychological event which is received by the individual according to his private expectations. No writer obsessively works and re-works a single theme that is without deep personal meaning, so it is quite likely that O'Connor experienced mystical "visions" or insights, which she interpreted according to her Catholicism; her imagination was visual and literal, and she is reported to have said of the Eucharist that if it were only a symbol, "I'd say the hell with it."[11] This child-like or primitive rejection of a psychic event—*only* a symbol!—as if it were somehow less real than a physical event gives to O'Connor's writing that curious sense of blunt, graphic impatience, the either/or of fanaticism and genius, that makes it difficult for even her most sympathetic critics to relate her to the dimension of psychological realism explored by the traditional novel. Small obscenities or cruelties in the work of John Updike, for instance, have a power to upset us in a way that gross fantastic acts of violence in O'Connor do not, for we read O'Connor as a writer of parables and Updike as an interpreter of the way we actually live. Yet, because she is impatient with the City of Man except as it contrasts with the City of God, she can relate her localized horrors to a larger harmony that makes everything, however exaggerated, somehow contained within a compact vision.

The triumph of "Revelation" is its apparently natural unfolding of a series of quite extraordinary events, so that the impossibly smug, self-righteous Mrs. Turpin not only experiences a visual revelation but is prepared for it, demands it, and is equal to it in spite of her own bigotry. Another extraordinary aspect of the story is the protagonist's assumption—an almost automatic assumption—that the vicious words spoken to her by a deranged girl in a doctor's waiting room ("Go back to hell where you came from, you old wart hog") are in fact the words of Christ, intended for her alone. Not only is the spiritual world a literal, palpable fact, but the physical world—of other people, of objects and events—becomes transparent, only a means by which the "higher" judgment is delivered. It is a world of meanings, naturalistic details crowded upon one another until they converge into a higher significance; an anti-naturalistic technique, perhaps, but one which is firmly based in the observed world. O'Connor is always writing about Original Sin and the ways we may be delivered from it, and therefore she does not—cannot—believe in the random innocence of naturalism, which states that all men are innocent and are victims of inner or outer accidents. The naturalistic novel, which attempts to render the "real" world in terms of its external events, must hypothesize an interior randomness that is a primal innocence, antithetical to the Judaeo-Christian culture. O'Connor uses many of the sharply-observed surfaces of the world, but her medieval sense of the *correspondentia* of the ancient "sympathy of all things" forces her to severely restrict her subject matter, compressing it to one or two physical settings and a few hours' duration. Since revelation can occur at any time and sums up, at the same time that it eradicates, all of a person's previous life, there is nothing claustrophobic about the doctor's waiting room, "which was very small," but which becomes a microcosm of an entire Godless society.

"Revelation" falls into two sections. The first takes place in the doctor's waiting room; the second takes place in a pig barn. Since so many who live now are diseased, it is significant that O'Connor chooses a doctor's waiting room for the first half of Mrs. Turpin's revelation, and it is significant that gospel hymns are being played over the radio, almost out of earshot, incorporated into the

98 / OATES

mechanical vacant listlessness of the situation: "When I looked up and He looked down. . .And wona these days I know I'll we-eara crown." Mrs. Turpin glances over the room, notices white-trashy people who are "worse than niggers any day," and begins a conversation with a well-dressed lady who is accompanying her daughter: the girl, on the verge of a breakdown, is reading a book called *Human Development*, and it is this book which will strike Mrs. Turpin in the forehead. Good Christian as she imagines herself, Mrs. Turpin cannot conceive of human beings except in terms of class, and is obsessed by a need to continually categorize others and speculate upon her position in regard to them. The effort is so exhausting that she often ends up dreaming "they were all crammed in together in a box car, being ridden off to be put in a gas oven." O'Connor's chilling indictment of Mrs. Turpin's kind of Christianity grows out of her conviction that the displacement of Christ will of necessity result in murder, but that the "murder" is a slow steady drifting rather than a conscious act of will.

The ugly girl, blue-faced with acne, explodes with rage at the inane biogtry expressed by Mrs. Turpin, and throws the textbook at her. She loses all control and attacks her; held down, subdued, her face "churning", she seems to Mrs. Turpin to know her "in some intense and personal way, beyond time and place and condition." And the girl's eyes lighten, as if a door that had been tightly closed was now open "to admit light and air." Mrs. Turpin steels herself, as if awaiting a revelation: and indeed the revelation comes. Mary Grace, used here by O'Connor as the instrument through which Christ speaks, bears some resemblance to other misfits in O'Connor's stories—not the rather stylish, shabby-glamorish men, but the pathetic over-educated physically unattractive girls like Joy/Hulga of "Good Country People." That O'Connor identifies with these girls is obvious: it is *she*, through Mary Grace, who throws that textbook on human development at all of us, striking us in the forehead, hopefully to bring about a change in our lives.

Mrs. Turpin is shocked, but strangely courageous. It is rare in O'Connor that an obtuse, unsympathetic character ascends to a higher level of self-awareness; indeed, she shows more courage than O'Connor's intellectual young men. She has been called a wart hog from hell and her vision comes to her in the pig barn, where she stands above the hogs that appear to "pant with a secret life." It is these hogs, the secret panting mystery of life itself, that finally allow Mrs. Turpin to realize her vision. She seems to absorb from them some "abysmal life-giving knowledge" and, at sunset, she stares into the sky where she sees

> . . .a vast swinging bridge extending upward from the earth through a field of living fire. Upon it a vast horde of souls were rumbling toward heaven. There were whole companies of white-trash, clean for the first time in their lives, and bands of black niggers in white robes, and battalions of freaks and lunatics shouting and clapping and leaping like frogs. And bringing up the end of the procession was a tribe of people whom she recognized at once as those who, like herself and Claude, had always had a little of everything. . . .They were marching behind the others with great dignity, accountable as they always had been for good order and common sense and respectable behavior. They alone were on key. Yet

she could see by their shocked and altered faces that even their virtues were being burned away. . . .

This is the most powerful of O'Connor's revelations, because it questions the very foundations of our assumptions of the ethical life. It is not simply our "virtues" that will be burned away, but our rational faculties as well, and perhaps even the illusion of our separate, isolated egos. There is no way in which the ego can confront Mrs. Turpin's vision, except as she does—"her eyes small but fixed unblinkingly on what lay ahead." Like Teilhard, O'Connor is ready to acquiesce to the evolution of a form of higher consciousness that may be forcing itself into the world *at our expense*; as old Tarwater says, after he is struck and silenced by fire, "even the mercy of the Lord burns." Man cannot remain what he is; he cannot exist without being transformed. We are confronted, says Teilhard, with two directions and only two: one upward and the other downward.

> Either nature is closed to our demands for futurity, in which case thought, the fruit of millions of years of effort, is stifled, still-born in a self-abortive and absurd universe. Or else an opening exists—that of the super-soul above our souls; but in that case the way out, if we are to agree to embark upon it, must open out freely onto limitless psychic spaces in a universe to which we can unhesitatingly entrust ourselves.[12]

O'Connor's people are forced into the upward direction, sometimes against their wills, sometimes because their wills have been burned clean and empty. Rayber (*The Violent Bear It Away*), who has concentrated his love for mankind into a possessive, exaggerated love for an idiot child, is forced to contemplate a future without the "raging pain, the intolerable hurt that was his due"; he is at the core of O'Connor's vision, a human being who has suffered a transformation but who survives. The wisdom of the body speaks in us, even when it reveals to us a terrifying knowledge of Original Sin, a perversion of the blood itself.

O'Connor's revelations concern the mystic origin of religious experience, absolutely immune to any familiar labels of "good" and "evil." Her perverted saints are Kierkegaardian knights of the "absurd" for whom ordinary human behavior is impossible. Like young Tarwater, horrified at having said an obscenity, they are "too fierce to brook impurities of such a nature"; they are, like O'Connor herself, "intolerant of unspiritual evils. . . ." There is no patience in O'Connor for a systematic, refined, rational acceptance of God; and of the gradual transformation of apocalyptic religious experience into dogma, she is strangely silent. Her world is that surreal primitive landscape in which the Unconscious is a determining quantity that the Conscious cannot defeat, because it cannot recognize. In fact, there is nothing to be recognized—there is only an experience to be suffered.[13]

CHAPTER 9

"A Ritual For Being Born Twice": Sylvia Plath's *The Bell Jar*

Marjorie G. Perloff

Now that Sylvia Plath has become the darling of those very ladies' magazines that she satirized so mercilessly in *The Bell Jar*, critics have begun to question her claims to literary eminence. Irving Howe, for example, in a recent reconsideration of Sylvia Plath's poetry, asks, "what illumination—moral, psychological, social—can be provided of. . .the general human condition by a writer so deeply rooted in the extremity of her plight? Suicide is an eternal possibility of our life and therefore always interesting; but what is the relation between a sensibility so deeply captive to the idea of suicide and the claims and possibilities of human existence in general?"[1]

These are by no means easy questions to answer, especially in the case of *The Bell Jar*, which was, after all, originally published under a pseudonym because Sylvia Plath herself regarded it as an "autobiographical apprenticework," a confession which, so she told A. Alvarez, she had to write in order to free herself from the past.[2] The novel's enormous popularity, it would seem, has less to do with any artistic merits it may have than with its inherently titillating subject matter. As the dust jacket of the Harper edition so melodramatically puts it, "this extraordinary work chronicles the crackup of Esther Greenwood: brilliant, beautiful, enormously talented, successful—but slowly going under, and maybe for the last time."

Yet surely novels that chronicle the mental breakdowns and suicide attempts of beautiful and talented girls are by now legion. One thinks of Scott Fitzgerald's Nicole Diver, of Julien Green's Adriènne Mésurat, or of J.R. Salamanca's Lilith as possible analogues for Esther, and an especially interesting parallel can be found in Virginia Woolf's *The Waves*: the despair and total isolation ("I have nothing. I have no face.") of the schizophrenic Rhoda, a character with whom Virginia Woolf explicitly identified,[3] recall Esther's sufferings, and in both of these novels written by women, suicide—real in Rhoda's case, abortive in Esther's—ominously foreshadows the suicide of the novelist herself.

I do not think, in short, that subject matter alone can account for *The Bell Jar*'s popular appeal. The novel's most enthusiastic admirers, after all, have been the young, who tend to take health, whether physical or mental, enormously for granted, and whose preoccupations, a decade after *The Bell Jar* was written and two decades after the period with which it deals, are far removed from the fashion world of the *Mademoiselle* College Board, the Barbizon Hotel for Women, the Yale Junior Prom, or even the particular conditions under which shock therapy is likely to benefit the schizophrenic. Yet, although it deals with the now hopelessly anachronistic college world of proms and petting, *The Bell Jar* has become for the young of the early seventies what *Catcher in the Rye* was to their counterparts of the fifties: the archetypal novel that mirrors, in however distorted a form, their own personal experience, their sense of what Irving Howe calls "the general human condition." How and why *The Bell Jar* succeeds in doing this is the topic of my essay.

In *The Divided Self*, R.D. Laing gives this description of the split between inner self and outer behavior that characterizes the schizoid personality: "The 'inner self' is occupied in phantasy and observation. It observes the processes of perception and action. Experience does not impinge...directly on this self, and the individual's acts are the provinces of a false-self system."[4] The condition Laing describes is precisely that of Esther at the beginning of the novel. For example, when Jay Cee, the *Ladies' Day* editor, asks Esther, "What do you have in mind after you graduate?" Esther's inner self observes her own external response with strange detachment; " 'I don't really know,' *I heard myself say. . . .* It sounded true, and I recognized it, the way you recognize some nondescript person that's been hanging around your door for ages and then suddenly comes up and introduces himself as your real father and looks exactly like you, so you know he really is your father, and the person you thought all your life was your father is a sham" (p. 35, italics mine). In a similarly detached way, Esther listens to the words of Elly Higginbottom, the name she has suddenly and inexplicably adopted in order to cope with the stranger who has picked her up on Times Square. But while Elly prattles on, Esther's real self becomes "a small dot" and finally "a hole in the ground" (p. 17).

If we take the division of Esther's self as the motive or starting point of the novel's plot, the central action of *The Bell Jar* may be described as the attempt to heal the fracture between inner self and false-self system so that a real and viable identity can come into existence. But because, as Laing reminds us, "everyone in some measure wears a mask,"[5] Esther's experience differs from that of so-called "normal" girls in degree rather than in kind. It is simply a stylized or heightened version of the young American girl's quest to forge her own identity, to be herself rather than what others expect her to be.

The dust jacket image of Esther as the brilliant, beautiful, successful girl who is somehow "going under" is, to begin with, wholly misleading. The Esther others see is, from the very first page of the novel, an elaborate contrivance, an empty shell: the fashionable Smith girl with her patent leather bag and matching pumps, the poised guest editor, brainy but no bookworm, equally at home on the dance floor or behind the typewriter. The novel's flashbacks make clear that Esther has always played those roles others have wanted her to play. For her mother, she has been the perfect *good girl*, "trained at a very early age and...no trouble whatsoever" (p. 228).[6] For Mr. Manzi, her physics professor, she is the ideal student, even though she secretly loathes the "hideous, cramped, scorpion-lettered formulas" with which he covers the blackboard (p. 38). For Buddy Willard, her one serious boyfriend, she is all sweetness and acquiescence. When, for example, Buddy disparages her literary aspirations with the profound remark that a poem is really only "a piece of dust," Esther masks her outrage and replies humbly, "I guess so" (p. 62). Or when, after their first kiss, Buddy says admiringly, "I guess you go out with a lot of boys," Esther, falling in line with his image of her as Popular Girl on Campus, answers, "Well, I guess I do" (p. 68). Even when Buddy has the ridiculous idea that it is time for the virginal Esther to "see a man" and suggests that he disrobe for her inspection, she answers, "Well, all right, I guess so" (p. 75). And the more the false self responds in this contrived and artificial way, the more Esther's inner self nurtures a hatred for Buddy.

The scenes in the present which lead up to Esther's breakdown reveal the same pattern. For Doreen, Esther wears the mask of tough cookie, willing to be picked up by strangers on downtown street corners. For Betsy from the Middle West, she is the fun girl who likes fur shows. For Constantin, the simultaneous interpreter at the UN, she is a no-nonsense type, preparing for a career as a war correspondent. Perhaps the final action committed by Esther's external self is the terrible forced smile she bestows on the *Ladies' Day* photographers (see the photograph on the dust jacket), a smile that suddenly dissolves in tears. Here the false-self system finally crumbles, and the old Esther must die before she can be reborn as a human being.

Recurrent mirror and light images measure Esther's descent into the stale air beneath the bell jar. In the first chapter, when Esther returns from Lenny's apartment and enters the mirrored elevator of the Amazon Hotel, she notices "a big, smudgy-eyed Chinese woman staring idiotically into my face. It was only me, of course. I was appalled to see how wrinkled and used up I looked" (pp. 19-20). As the self becomes increasingly disembodied, the reflection in the mirror gradually becomes a stranger. Having symbolically killed her false self by throwing her clothes to the winds from the hotel rooftop, Esther rides home on the train to the Boston suburbs and notes that "The face in the mirror looked like a sick Indian" (p. 125). But the "two diagonal lines of dried blood" on her cheeks (p. 126) do not perturb her, for her body no longer seems real. Appearances do not count—Esther no longer washes or changes clothes or puts on make-up—and yet she is constantly afraid of being recognized by others. "In a world full of dangers," writes Laing, "to be a potentially seeable object is to be constantly exposed to danger. . . .The obvious defence against such a danger is to make oneself invisible in one way or another."[7] Thus Esther, hiding behind the bedroom shutters, feels Dodo Conway's "gaze pierce through the white clapboard and pink wallpaper roses and uncover me" (p. 131); she finds the early morning light so oppressive that she crawls beneath the mattress to escape it, but it seems as if "the mattress was not heavy enough" (p. 138), and, after twenty-one sleepless nights, Esther thinks that "the most beautiful thing in the world must be shadow" (p. 165). Only by returning to the womb in the shape of the basement crawl space at her mother's house and then gulping down a bottle of sleeping pills, does she hope to find the "dark. . .thick as velvet," which is the darkness of death (p. 191).

Esther's body is recalled to life fairly easily, but the self that emerges from her suicide attempt is hopelessly disembodied. When she looks into the mirror the hospital nurse reluctantly brings her, Esther thinks, "It wasn't a mirror at all, but a picture. You couldn't tell whether the person in the picture was a man or a woman, because their hair was shaved off and sprouted in bristly chicken-feather tufts all over their head. One side of the person's face was purple. . . . The most startling thing about the face was its supernatural conglomeration of bright colors" (p. 197). It is only when she smiles at this funny face, and "the mouth in the mirror cracked into a grin," that Esther is reminded of her identity and sends the mirror crashing to the floor. It will take a long time to pick up the pieces.

But why is Esther's inner self so precarious, so disembodied in the first place? Why must she invent such an elaborate set of masks with which to face the world? To label Esther as "schizophrenic" and leave it at that does not take us very far. For Sylvia Plath's focus in *The Bell Jar* is not on mental illness per se, but on the relationship of Esther's private psychosis to her larger social situation. Indeed, her dilemma seems to have a great deal to do with being a woman in a society whose guidelines for women she can neither accept nor reject. It is beautifully ironic that Sylvia Plath, who never heard of Women's Liberation and would be unlikely to join The Movement were she alive today,[8] has written one of the most acute analyses of the feminist problem that we have in contemporary fiction. What makes *The Bell Jar* so moving—and often so marvelously funny—is that the heroine is just as innocent as she is frighteningly perceptive. Far from rejecting the stereotyped world which she inhabits—a world whose madness often seems much more intense than Esther's own—she is determined to conquer it. Fulfillment, the novel implies, must come here or not at all; there is no better world around the corner or across the ocean. Thus Esther's quest for identity centers around her repeated attempts—sometimes funny but always painful—to find both a female model whom she can emulate and a man whom she need not despise. If this quest does not lead to a Brave New World of happy liberated women, we need not be disappointed. Like Chekhov, Sylvia Plath knows that the novelist's job is not to solve problems but to diagnose them correctly.

New York is for Esther what Europe was for Isabel Archer—the Great Good Place where one's values are put to the test. Prior to her summer in New York, Esther's world has been safely circumscribed: like a racehorse, she has been "running after good marks and prizes and grants of one sort and another" (p. 31) for as long as she can remember. Now for the first time, she is presented with real alternatives. What does it mean to be a woman, she wonders, and which of the female roles she has studied by observing those around her should she play? Esther is particularly aware of this problem because the person who should be her model—her mother—cannot help her. Characterized in only a few brief flashes, Mrs. Greenwood is a terrifying presence in the novel, and one can hardly be surprised that Sylvia Plath's mother, recognizing herself in the portrait, tried to suppress the book's publication.[9] Here is Esther's first reference to her mother:

> My own mother wasn't much help. My mother had taught shorthand and typing to support us ever since my father died, and secretly she hated it and hated him for dying and leaving no money because he didn't trust life insurance salesmen. She was always on to me to learn shorthand after college, so I'd have a practical skill as well as a college degree. "Even the apostles were tentmakers," she'd say. "They had to live, just the way we do." (pp. 42-43)

The image is one of a hopelessly rigid, strong-willed, loveless person who has survived the battle of life only by reducing it to neat little proverbs and formulas. When her daughter becomes so overtly psychotic that she can neither eat, sleep, nor wash herself, this mother reasons with her sweetly and blandly. When Esther refuses to return to the frightening Dr. Gordon, her first psychiatrist, her mother replies triumphantly, "I *knew* you'd *decide* to be all right again" (p. 163, italics mine). At the end of the novel, when Esther contemplates her impending return to the world outside the asylum walls, she thinks: "My mother's face floated to mind, a pale reproachful moon, at her last and first visit to the asylum since my twentieth birthday. A daughter in an asylum! I had done that to her. Still, she had obviously decided to forgive me" (p. 267).

Whether or not this portrait of the mother as uncomprehending martyr is unfair to the real-life Aurelia Plath seems to me totally beside the point. What matters is that her daughter *sees* her in this light. Given such a mother image, she must clearly find her models elsewhere. But where? In the course of her quest, Esther is attracted by a bewildering variety of female roles: Dodo Conway, Catholic mother of 6½, whose face is perpetually lit up by a "serene, almost religious smile" (p. 129); Buddy Willard's mother, professor's wife and leading citizen, whose words of wisdom are regularly quoted by her brainwashed and adoring son; Doreen, the Southern blonde sex kitten who always knows how to get her man; Betsy, innocently happy and uncomplicated Midwestern fashion model; Jody, loyal friend, "practical and a sociology major" (p. 83), who instinctively knows how to spice up scrambled eggs; Philomena Guinea, best-selling novelist, whose endowed scholarship Esther holds at college; and finally, Jay Cee, the successful editor who "knew all the quality writers in the business" (p. 6). Even a Russian girl translator, whom Esther glimpses only briefly at the UN, becomes an object of envy: "I wished with all my heart I could crawl into her and spend the rest of my life barking out one idiom after another. . ." (p. 82).

But although she envies Dodo's placid contentment, Jay Cee's cleverness, and Betsy's innocence, Esther quickly discovers that each of these women is, despite her particular gift or talent, essentially a flawed human being. Doreen's intrinsic vulgarity and triviality are symbolized by her fluffy cotton candy blonde hair, which is, on close inspection, dark at the roots. Eternally pregnant Dodo is little more than a mindless misshapen animal. Refined and cultured Mrs. Willard lets her husband walk all over her as if she were one of the wool mats she makes as a hobby. Philomena Guinea's novels turn out to be endless soap operas, "crammed. . .with long suspenseful questions" like " 'Would Evelyn discern that Gladys knew Roger in her past?' wondered Hector feverishly" (p.

44). Jay Cee is a walking time clock, devouring manuscripts with mechanical regularity and reserving her emotional commitment for her potted plants. Betsy is "Pollyanna Cowgirl" (p. 125); the Russian translator is no more than a "little pebble of efficiency among all the other pebbles" (p. 82); and even Jody, the truly "nice" girl, seems to have a touch of Rosencrantz and Guildenstern in her when she plots with Mrs. Greenwood to distract Esther from her illness by taking her along on a double date.

It seems, in short, all but impossible for a woman to attain what Yeats called Unity of Being. In what I take to be the novel's key passage, Esther, sitting with Constantin "in one of those hushed plush auditoriums in the UN" (p. 82), has a vision of her life branching out like a green fig tree:

> From the tip of every branch, like a fat purple fig, a wonderful future beckoned and winked. One fig was a husband and a happy home and children and another fig was a famous poet and another fig was a brilliant professor, and another fig was Ee Gee, the amazing editor, and another fig was Europe and Africa and South America, and another fig was Constantin and Socrates and Attila and a pack of other lovers with queer names and offbeat professions, and another fig was an Olympic lady crew champion, and beyond and above these figs were many more figs I couldn't quite make out.
>
> I saw myself sitting in the crotch of this fig tree, starving to death, just because I couldn't make up my mind which of the figs I would choose. I wanted each and every one of them, but choosing one meant losing all the rest, and, as I sat there, unable to decide, the figs began to wrinkle and go black, and, one by one, they plopped to the ground at my feet. (pp. 84-85).

Esther's symbolic tree, appropriately bearing phallic figs, is the objectification of her central malaise, a malaise that is hardly confined to schizophrenics, however starkly and dramatically Sylvia Plath presents Esther's case. I would guess that every woman who reads this passage has felt, at one time or another, that "choosing one meant losing all the rest," that because female roles are no longer clearly defined, women are confronted by such a bewildering variety of seeming possibilities that choice itself becomes all but impossible.

But Sylvia Plath's feminism is never militant; Esther's diagnosis of her situation is totally devoid of self-pity or self-importance. Shortly after describing her vision of the fig tree, she beautifully undercuts her own high seriousness. The occasion is dinner in a Russian restaurant with Constantin; "I don't know what I ate, but I felt immensely better after the first mouthful. It occurred to me that my vision of the fig tree and all the fat figs that withered and fell to earth might well have arisen from the profound void of an empty stomach" (p. 86). So much, Plath sardonically implies, for the profound insights of the weaker sex!

Like her ambivalence to the women she meets, Esther's response to men is hopelessly divided. On the one hand, she is always looking for the perfect lover; on the other, experience repeatedly tells her that men are, however subtly, exploiters and hypocrites. Here, for example, is Esther observing the process of childbirth under the tutelage of her medical student boyfriend, Buddy Willard:

> The woman's stomach stuck up so high I couldn't see her face or the upper part of her body at all. She seemed to have nothing but an enormous spider-fat stomach and two little ugly spindly legs propped in the high stirrups, and all the time the baby was being born she never stopped making this unhuman whooing noise.
>
> Later Buddy told me the woman was on a drug that would make her forget she'd had any pain and that when she swore and groaned she really didn't know what she was doing because she was in a kind of twilight sleep.
>
> I thought it sounded just like the sort of drug a man would invent. Here was a woman in terrible pain, obviously feeling every bit of it or she wouldn't groan like that, and she would go straight home and start another baby, because the drug would make her forget how bad the pain had been, when all the time, in some secret part of her, that long, blind, doorless and windowless corridor of pain was waiting to open up and shut her in again.
>
> The head doctor...kept saying to the woman, "Push down, Mrs. Tomolillo, push down, that's a good girl, push down," and finally through the split, shaven place between her legs, lurid with disinfectant, I saw the dark fuzzy thing appear. (p. 72)

It is easy to dismiss Esther's reaction to the delivery as simply "sick"; here is a girl, one can argue, so full of self-loathing and insecurity that she cannot understand the beauty and wonder of a great "natural" event like childbirth. But then, who is it that has always told us of the wonders of childbirth if not men like Doctors Spock, Guttmacher, and the father of natural childbirth, Dr. Grantley Dick Read? Sylvia Plath forces us to forget all the usual clichés about incipient motherhood and to take a good hard look at the birth process itself; her technique is, as Robert Scholes has argued in his excellent review of *The Bell Jar*,[10] one of *defamiliarization*. The Russian critic Victor Shklovsky, who coined this term in 1917, held that "art removes object from the automatism of perception"; its aim is to make "the familiar seem strange by not naming the familiar object."[11] In this scene, for example, Sylvia Plath describes the delivery as if it were happening for the first time in history. From the point of view of the uninitiated observer, childbirth seems to be a frightening ritual in which a "dark fuzzy thing" finally emerges from "the split shaven place" between the woman's legs. In her state of heightened sensitivity, Esther shares the pain of Mrs. Tomolillo, with her "spider-fat stomach," "ugly, spindly legs propped in high stirrups," and "unhuman whooing noise." Only a man, Esther thinks, could conclude that when the woman "swore and groaned she really didn't know what she was doing." And, after witnessing the "sewing up of the woman's cut with a needle and long thread," Esther wonders, not irrationally, "if there were any other ways to have babies" (pp. 73-74).

While Esther wholly identifies with the woman in labor, Buddy, contemplating the birth from his male point of view, is proud of the expert and efficient treatment his colleagues give the patient. As he and Esther leave the delivery room, she notes his "satisfied expression" (p. 73). And no wonder. For beneath the surface of his charming manners and his evident respect for bright articulate girls, Buddy harbors a cynical contempt for women, a contempt that leads him to play off the virginal Esther against the "dirty" waitress he sleeps with. A staunch believer in the double standard, Buddy accepts as axiomatic his mother's wise words that "What a man wants is a mate and what a woman wants is infinite security," or "What a man is is an arrow into the future and what a woman is is the place the arrow shoots off from" (p. 79). It follows that Buddy takes a dim view of woman writers. Contemplating her future, Esther remembers "Buddy Willard saying in a sinister, knowing way that after I had children I would feel differently, I wouldn't want to write poems any more. So I began to think maybe it was true that when you were married and had children it was like being brainwashed, and afterward you went about numb as a slave in some private, totalitarian state" (p. 94).

Because Esther is, in one sense, an innocent and inexperienced small town girl who drinks out of finger bowls and never knows how much to tip, it takes her some time to realize that "The last thing I wanted was infinite security and to be the place an arrow shoots off from. I wanted change and excitement and to shoot off in all directions myself, like the colored arrows from a Fourth of July rocket" (p. 92). Typing and shorthand—her mother's domain—become the symbols of male oppression: she rejects her mother's practical notion that "an English major who knew shorthand. . .would be in demand among all the up-and-coming young men and she would transcribe letter after thrilling letter" (p. 83). "The trouble was," Esther thinks, "I hated the idea of serving men in any way. I wanted to dictate my own thrilling letters." Naturally, then, Esther cannot love Constantin, the pleasant, polite, but thoroughly conventional UN translator, or Marco, the Latin American woman hater who literally forces her down into the dirt, or Dr. Gordon, the sinister psychiatrist, whose silver-framed family photograph, conspicuously placed on his desk facing the patient, is a tacit reminder that he, at any rate, is a "normal" American male, dwelling in a world of suburban lawns, cute children, and golden retrievers. Esther's final sexual encounter is the most ludicrous of all: having won what she thinks is freedom with the help of birth control, she arranges to have herself seduced by Irwin, the bespectacled young math professor from Harvard, who takes girls to bed as thoughtlessly and mechanically as Jay Cee reads manuscripts. The outcome of this parody seduction is not passion but severe hemorrhage for Esther, a bloody wound emblematic of the spirit in which Irwin has made love to her—a spirit not of tenderness but of all-out war.

When one considers Irwin's strange unconcern about Esther's hemorrhage, one cannot help wondering who is "saner"—the girl who learns that losing her virginity is not, after all, a great and thrilling adventure, or the man who, ignoring the pain and fear of the girl he has just deflowered, gallantly kisses her hand and bids her goodnight. Whatever the extent of Esther's congenital predisposition to madness, the mad world she inhabits surely intensifies her condition. R.D. Laing's insistence that "the experience and behavior that gets labeled schizophrenic is a *special strategy that a person invents in order to live in an unlivable situation*,"[12] may sound extreme but it seems wholly relevant to *The Bell Jar.*

Take, for example, the superbly rendered scene in which Esther, on the verge of total mental collapse, is persuaded to take a volunteer job at the local hospital by her mother's argument that "the cure for thinking too much about yourself was helping somebody who was worse off than you" (p. 182). Esther's job is to take around the patients' flowers, but when she notices, not at all insensibly, that some are "droopy and brown at the edges," she discards the dead flowers and rearranges the bouquets as attractively as possible. Wheeling her trolley into the maternity ward, she finds that her "helpful smile" is greeted by a furious uproar:

> "Hey, where's my larkspur?" A large, flabby lady from across the ward raked me with an eagle eye.
> The sharp-faced blonde bent over the trolley. "Here are my yellow roses," she said, "but they're all mixed up with some lousy iris." (p. 184)

By the time the nurse has arrived on the scene to investigate the cause of the commotion, Esther is overcome by panic and bolts, a reaction that seems at least as sane as the righteous indignation of the women in curlers, "chattering like parrots in a parrot house" (p. 183), who occupy the hospital beds. By society's standards, however, Esther's emphasis on the aesthetics of flower arrangement rather than on its economics (the notion that every woman patient is *entitled* to the flowers bought for her) is dismissed as schizophrenic behavior.

Throughout the novel, Sylvia Plath emphasizes the curious similarity of physical and mental illness as if to say that both are symbolic of a larger condition which is our life today. *The Bell Jar* opens with the following sentence: "It was a queer, sultry summer, the summer they electrocuted the Rosenbergs, and I didn't know what I was doing in New York." This reference to electrocution sets the scene for everything that is to come: before the novel is over, Esther herself will know only too well what it feels like to be "burned alive all along your nerves" (p. 1). The terrible electric shock therapy that Dr. Gordon makes her undergo is a frightening counterpart of the Rosenbergs' punishment; "I wondered," Esther thinks as she goes under, "what terrible thing it was that I had done" (p. 161). Even the bare room in which the shock treatment is administered resembles the Rosenbergs' prison cell: the windows are barred, and "everything that opened or shut was fitted with a keyhole so it could be locked up" (p. 160).

From the start, when Esther contemplates the terrible fate of the Rosenbergs, sickness is everywhere around her; it begins when Esther finds the drunken Doreen lying on the floor of the hotel corridor: "A jet of brown vomit flew from her mouth and spread in a large puddle at my feet" (p. 24). Here, Sylvia Plath suggests, is the real picture of the desirable debutante, whose smiling photographs grace the pages of the fashion magazines. A similar deception motif occurs in the account of the banquet given by the *Ladies' Day* Food Testing kitchens, at which every girl lucky enough to attend gets ptomaine poisoning from the beautiful avocados stuffed with crabmeat. The irony here is that, although, in the case of the food poisoning, Esther is pitied by all for the terrible "accident" that has made her so ill and is treated with great respect, her own inner experience during the illness foreshadows that in the mental hospital. In both cases, the self seems to inhabit a dark underground region; voices come from "far above my head" (p. 50); and events seem totally beyond the patient's control. After receiving an injection from the hotel nurse, for example, Esther watches the door take the nurse's place "like a sheet of blank paper, and then a larger sheet of paper took the place of the door" (p. 51). Similarly, when Esther later receives shock therapy, she senses the darkness wiping out everything in the room "like chalk on a blackboard" (p. 241). Again, when Esther starts to recover from the ptomaine poisoning and receives broth to drink, she feels "purged and holy and ready for a new life" (p. 52), just as later, after her first successful shock treatment, she feels that "All the heat and fear had purged itself" (p. 242). The external situations are totally different, but to the self that experiences them, they seem almost indistinguishable.

In the world of *The Bell Jar*, no one is exempt from illness. Even Buddy Willard, the all-American boy who radiates good health, develops tuberculosis and has to spend a winter in a sanatorium. "TB," he writes Esther, "is like living with a bomb in your lung. . . . You just lie around very quietly hoping it won't go off" (p. 98). There are interesting parallels between Buddy's physical illness and Esther's mental one. Just as Mr. Willard cannot stand the sight of Buddy's sickness "because he thought all sickness was sickness of the will" (p. 101), so Esther's mother is unable to face the truth that her daughter's illness will not disappear by *willing* it to stop. Just as the reception room of Buddy's sanatorium contains "burnt-brown leather chairs, walls that might once have been white" and "a low coffee table, with circular and semicircular stains bitten into the dark veneer," on which lie "a few wilted numbers of *Time* and *Life*" (p. 98), so the lounge at the private mental hospital where Esther slowly recovers has "shabby furniture," a "threadbare rug," and "A girl with a round pasty face and short black hair [who] was sitting in an arm chair, reading a magazine" (p. 212). Again, both the TB patient and the mental patient engage in occupational therapy: Buddy makes clay pots while the girls at the asylum play the piano or badminton. "What was there about us, in Belsize," Esther wonders, "so different from the girls playing bridge and gossiping and studying in the college to which I would return? Those girls, too, sat under bell jars of a sort" (p. 268).

Sylvia Plath is no silly sentimentalist; she knows quite well that her heroine *is* different from most college girls, that her bell jar is less fragile, less easy to remove than theirs. But the external or official distinction between madness and sanity, she suggests in her linkage of physical and mental illness, is largely illusory. When, to take the novel's most striking example, Esther breaks her leg skiing, Buddy—and the world at large—regard her broken leg as the most normal of accidents. Yet Esther's account of her mental state as she plummets down the slope suggests that she is never closer to insanity than at this particular moment. A novice skier, she suddenly conceives an overwhelming desire to fly off into "the great, gray eye of the sky" (p. 107). Like the ecstatic speaker of "Ariel," who longs to make the "Suicidal" leap "Into the red/Eye, the cauldron of morning,"[13] Esther longs for the annihilation of death. "People and trees receded on either hand like the dark sides of a tunnel as I hurtled on to the still, bright point at the end of it, the pebble at the bottom of the well, the white sweet baby cradled in its mother's belly" (p. 108). Yet this suicidal leap earns Esther no more than a plaster cast, whereas her later, not unrelated suicide attempt precipitates her admission to the dangerous ward of the hospital.

The plot of *The Bell Jar* moves from physical sickness (the ptomaine poisoning) to mental illness and back to the physical, culminating in Esther's hemorrhage. The arrangement of incidents implies that all illness is to be viewed as part of the same spectrum: disease, whether mental or physical, is an index to the human inability to cope with an unlivable situation. For who can master a world where the Testing Kitchens of a leading women's magazine poison all of its guest editors, where a reputable psychiatrist asks a girl, on the verge of suicide, whether there is a WAC station at her college?

But Esther does come back to life. At the end of *The Bell Jar*, her external situation has not appreciably changed—she has found neither a lover nor her future vocation—but now she can view that situation differently. Having passed through death, she learns, with the help of Dr. Nolan, to forge a new identity. It is important to note that Dr. Nolan, the only wholly admirable woman in the novel, is also the only woman whom Esther never longs to imitate or resemble. The point is that Dr. Nolan serves not as model but as anti-model; she is the instrument whereby Esther learns to be, not some other woman, but herself. The new Esther takes off the mask: she openly rejects Joan's lesbian advances; she can cope with Irwin as well as with Buddy. Best of all, the world of nature, distorted and fragmented in the opening pages of the novel when Esther walks through the "granite canyons" of Manhattan, is no longer inaccessible. Shovelling Buddy's car out of the snow, Esther watches with pleasure as the sun emerges from the clouds: "Pausing in my work to overlook that pristine expanse, I felt the same profound thrill it gives me to see trees and grassland waist-high under flood water—as if the usual order of the world had shifted slightly, and entered a new phase" (p. 269).

As if the usual order of the world had shifted slightly. . . . When Esther pauses on the threshold of the room where the hospital board is waiting to pass final sentence on her, she still sees her future as a series of "question marks" (p. 275), but she has learned something very important. Isolation, Sylvia Plath suggests, the terrible isolation Esther feels when, one by one, her props crumble, is paradoxically the result of negating one's own separateness. The hardest thing in the world to do—and it is especially hard when one is young, female and highly gifted—is simply to be oneself. Only when Esther recognizes that she will never be a Jody, a Jay Cee, a Doreen, or a Mrs. Guinea, that she will never marry a Buddy Willard, a Constantin, or a Dr. Gordon, that she wants no lesbian affairs with a Joan or a Dee Dee—does the bell jar lift, letting Esther once again breathe "the circulating air" (p. 242). As a schizophrenic, Esther is, of course, a special case, but her intensity of purpose, her isolation, her suffering, and finally her ability to survive it all with a sense of humor, make her an authentic, indeed an exemplary heroine of the seventies.

When one compares Esther to Carson McCuller's Frankie Addams, the heroine of *The Member of the Wedding*, written in 1946, the contemporary appeal of *The Bell Jar*, especially for the young, is readily understood. Both Frankie and

Esther are sensitive young girls, isolated from friends and family and unable to express their most deep-seated feelings to anyone. But whereas Frankie "gets over" her difficult tom-boy stage as well as her brief incarnation as F. Jasmine, the vamp, and emerges at the end of the novel as a happy high school girl, who can share her new interest in Michelangelo and Tennyson with an ideal close friend, Esther can never forget what her mother so ludicrously calls "a bad dream." On the contrary, she remembers everything:

> I remembered the cadavers and Doreen and the story of the fig tree and Marco's diamond and the sailor on the Common and Doctor Gordon's wall-eyed nurse and the broken thermometers and the Negro with his two kinds of beans and the twenty pounds I gained on insulin and the rock that bulged between sky and sea like a gray skull.
> Maybe forgetfulness, like a kind of snow, should numb and cover them. But they were part of me. They were my landscape. (p. 267)

Esther's landscape, with its confusing assortment of cadavers and diamonds, thermometers and beans, is, in heightened form, *our* landscape. When Ibsen's Nora slammed the door of her doll's house and embarked on a new life, she nobly refused to take with her any of Torvald's property. The New Woman, I would posit, will not let men off that easily. Esther, having undergone emergency treatment for the hemorrhage induced by Irwin's lovemaking, calmly sends him the bill.

CHAPTER 10

Eruptions of Funk: Historicizing Toni Morrison

Susan Willis

"I begin to feel those little bits of color floating up into me–deep in me. That streak of green from the june-bug light, the purple from the berries trickling along my thighs. Mama's lemonade yellow runs sweet in me. Then I feel like I'm laughing between my legs, and the laughing gets all mixed up with the colors, and I'm afraid I'll come, and afraid I won't. But I know I will. And I do. And it be rainbow all inside."[1]

This is the way in which Polly Breedlove remembers the experience of orgasm–*remembers* it, because in the grim and shabby reality of her present, orgasm (which we might take as a metaphor for any deeply pleasurable experience) is no longer possible.[2] Living in a storefront, her husband fluctuating between brutality and apathy, her son estranged, her daughter just plain scared, Polly has no language to describe the memory of a past pleasure, except one drawn from her distant childhood.

The power of this passage is not just related to the fact that it evokes the most intense female experience possible. Much of its impact is produced by the way it describes. Morrison de-familiarizes the portrayal of sensual experience. Adjectives become substantives, giving taste to color and making it possible for colors to trickle and flow and, finally, be internalized like the semen of an orgasmic epiphany.

As often happens in Morrison's writing, sexuality converges with history and functions as a register for the experience of change, i.e., historical transition. Polly's remembrance of childhood sensuality coincides with her girlhood in the rural South. Both are metaphorically condensed and juxtaposed with the alienation she experiences as a black emigrant and social lumpen in a Northern industrial city. The author's metaphoric language produces an estrangement of alienation. While her metaphors are less bold in their form and content, they, nevertheless, achieve an effect very similar to that of the Negritude poets. Indeed, the image of an internal rainbow evokes the poetics of surrealism, but in a language less disjunctive because prose reveals the historical and artistic process through which the image is produced.[3]

When Polly Breedlove reminisces, her present collides with her past and spans her family's migration from the hills of Alabama to a small Kentucky town, and her own subsequent journey as the wife of one of the many black men who, in the late '30s and early '40s, sought factory jobs in the industrial North. The rural homeland is the source of the raw material of experience and praxis, which in the border-state small town is abstracted to colors, tastes, and tactile sensations. Ohio is, then, the site where images are produced out of the discontinuity between past and present.

If metaphor, and much of Morrison's writing in general represents a return to origins, it is not rooted in a nostalgia for the past. Rather, it represents a process for coming to grips with historical transition. Migration to the North signifies more than a confrontation with (and contagion of) the white world. It implies a transition in social class. Throughout Morrison's writing, the white world is equated with the bourgeois class—its ideology and lifestyle. This is true of *Song of Solomon* in which Macon Dead's attitudes toward rents and property make him more "white" than "black." This is true of *Tar Baby* in which notions of bourgeois morality and attitudes concerning the proper education and role of women have created a contemporary "tar baby," a black woman in cultural limbo. And it is made dramatically clear in *The Bluest Eye*, whose epigrammatic introduction and subsequent chapter headings are drawn from a white, middle-class Dick-and-Jane reader. In giving voice to the experience of growing up black in a society dominated by white, middle-class ideology, Morrison is writing against the privatized world of suburban house and nuclear family, whose social and psychological fragmentation does not need her authorial intervention, but is aptly portrayed in the language of the reader: "Here is the family. Mother, Father, Dick, and Jane live in the green-and-white house. They are very happy" (*TBE*, p. 7).

The problem at the center of Morrison's writing is how to maintain an Afro-American cultural heritage once the relationship to the black rural South has been stretched thin over distance and generations. While a number of black Americans will criticize her problematizing of Afro-American culture, seeing in it a symptom of Morrison's own relationship to white bourgeois society as a successful writer and editor, there are a number of social and historical factors that argue in support of her position. These include the dramatic social changes produced by recent wide-scale migration of industry to the South, which has transformed much of the rural population into wage laborers; the development, particularly in the Northern cities, of a black bourgeoisie; and the coming into being, under late capitalism, of a full-blown consumer society capable of homogenizing society by recouping cultural difference. The temporal focus of each of Morrison's novels pinpoints strategic moments in black American history during which social and cultural forms underwent disruption and transformation. Both *The Bluest Eye* and *Sula* focus on the '40s, a period of heavy black migration to the cities, when, particularly in the Midwest, black "neighborhoods" came into being in relation to towns which had never before had a sizable black population. *Sula* expands the period of the '40s by looking back to the First World War, when blacks as a social group were first incorporated in a modern capitalist system as soldiers; and it looks ahead to the '60s, when cultural identity seems to flatten out and, as Helene Sabat observes, all young people tend to look like the "Deweys." *Song of Solomon* focuses on the '60s, when neighborhoods are perceived from the outside and called ghettos, a time of urban black political activism and general counter-cultural awareness. And *Tar Baby*, Morrison's most recent book, is best characterized as a novel of the '80s, in which the route back to cultural origins is very long and tenuous, making many individuals cultural exiles.

With this as an outline of modern black history in the United States, Morrison develops the social and psychological aspects which characterize the lived experience of historical transition. For the black emigrant to the North, the first of these is alienation. As Morrison defines it, alienation is not simply the result of an individual's separation from his or her cultural center, although this is a contributory factor which reinforces the alienation produced by the transition to wage labor. For the black man incorporated into the wartime labor pool (as for many white Appalachians),[4] selling one's labor for the creation of surplus value was only half of alienation, whose brutal second half was the grim reality of unemployment once war production was no longer necessary. The situation for the black woman was somewhat different. Usually employed as a maid and therefore only marginally incorporated as a wage laborer, her alienation was the result of striving to achieve the white bourgeois social model (in which she worked but did not live), which is itself produced by the system of wage labor under capitalism. As housemaid in a prosperous lakeshore home, Polly Breedlove lives a form of schizophrenia, in which her marginality is constantly confronted with a world of Hollywood movies, white sheets, and tender blond children. When at work or at the movies, she separates herself from her own kinky hair and decayed tooth. The tragedy of a woman's alienation is its effect on her role as mother. Her emotions split, Polly showers tenderness and love on her employer's child, and rains violence and disdain on her own.

Morrison's aim in writing is very often to disrupt alienation with what she calls "eruptions of funk." Dismayed by the tremendous influence of bourgeois society on young black women newly arrived from deep South cities like "Meridian, Mobile, Aiken and Baton Rouge," Morrison decries the women's loss of spontaneity and sensuality. They learn "how to behave. The careful development of thrift, patience, high morals, and good manners. In short, how to get rid of the funkiness. The dreadful funkiness of passion, the funkiness of nature, the funkiness of the wide range of human emotions" (*TBE*, p. 68).

For Polly Breedlove, alienation is the inability to ever again experience pleasure—orgasm or otherwise—, whereas for the "thin brown girls from Mobile," whose husbands are more successful and, therefore, better assimilated into bourgeois society, alienation is the purposeful denial of pleasure. Once again Morrison translates the loss of history and culture into sexual terms and demonstrates the connection between bourgeois society and repression:

> He must enter her surreptitiously, lifting the hem of her nightgown only to her navel. He must rest his weight on his elbows when they make love, ostensibly to avoid hurting her breasts but actually to keep her from having to touch or feel too much of him.

While he moves inside her, she will wonder why they didn't put the necessary but private parts of the body in some more convenient place—like the armpit, for example, or the palm of the hand. Someplace one could get to easily, and quickly, without undressing. She stiffens when she feels one of her paper curlers coming undone from the activity of love; imprints in her mind which one it is that is coming loose so she can quickly secure it once he is through. She hopes he will not sweat—the damp may get into her hair; and that she will remain dry between her legs—she hates the glucking sound they make when she is moist. When she senses some spasm about to grip him, she will make rapid movements with her hips, press her fingernails into his back, suck in her breath, and pretend she is having an orgasm. (p. 69)

At a sexual level, alienation is the denial of the body, produced when sensuality is redefined as indecent. Sounds and tactile sensations which might otherwise have precipitated or highlighted pleasure provoke annoyance or disdain. Repression manifests itself in the fastidious attention given to tomorrow's Caucasian-inspired coiffure and the decathexis of erogenous stimulation. While repression inhibits sexual pleasure, it does not liberate a woman from sexuality. In faking an orgasm, the woman negates her pleasure for the sake of her husband's satisfaction, thus defining herself as a tool for his sexual gratification.

To break through repressed female sexuality, Morrison contrasts images of stifled womanhood with girlhood sensuality. In *The Bluest Eye*, the author's childhood alter ego, Claudia, is fascinated by all bodily functions and the physical residues of living in the world. She rebels at being washed, finding her scrubbed body obscene due to its "dreadful and humiliating absence of dirt" (*TBE*, p. 21). Even vomit is interesting for its color and consistency as it "swaddles down the pillow onto the sheet" (*TBE*, p. 13). In wondering how anything can be "so neat and nasty at the same time" (*TBE*, p. 13), Claudia shows a resistance toward the overdetermination of sensual experience, which, as Morrison sees it, is the first step toward repression. Openness to a full range of sensual experience may be equated with polymorphous sexuality, typified by the refusal of many young children to be thought of as either a boy or a girl. As my own four-year-old daughter sees it, "Little girls grow up to be big boys," and because there is no firm distinction between the sexes, her teddy is "both a boy and a girl." The refusal to categorize sensual experience—and likewise sex—captures the essence of unrepressed childhood, which Morrison evokes as a mode of existence prior to the individual's assimilation into bourgeois society.

The ultimate horror of bourgeois society against which Morrison writes, and the end result of both alienation and repression, is reification.[5] None of Morrison's black characters actually accedes to the upper reaches of bourgeois reification, but there are some who come close. They are saved only because they remain marginal to the bourgeois class and are imperfectly assimilated to bourgeois values. In *Song of Solomon*, Hagar offers a good example. Rejected by her lover, she falls into a state of near catatonia, oblivious to all around her. However, chancing to look in a mirror, she is horrified by her appearance and marvels that anyone could love a woman with her looks. Thus roused from her withdrawal, Hagar embarks on a day-long shopping spree, driven by the desire to be the delightful image promised by her brand-name purchases:

> She bought a Playtex garter belt, I. Miller No Color hose, Fruit of the Loom panties, and two nylon slips—one white, one pink—one pair of Joyce Fancy Free and one of Con Brio ("Thank heaven for little Joyce heels"). . . .
>
> The cosmetics department enfolded her in perfume, and she read hungrily the labels and the promise. Myrurgia for primeval woman who creates for him a world of tender privacy where the only occupant is you, mixed with Nina Ricci's L'Air du Temps. Yardley's Flair with Tuvaché's Nectaroma and D'Orsay's Intoxication.[6]

Hagar's shopping spree culminates in a drenching downpour. Her shopping bags soaked, everything—her "Sunny Glow" and "fawn-trimmed-in-sea-foam shortie nightgown"—her wished-for identity and future, falls into the wet and muddy street. Returning home, Hagar collapses with fever and dies after days of delirium.

Hagar's hysteria and death mark the limits of her assimilation to bourgeois culture. Neither through withdrawal nor through commodity consumption can Hagar transform herself into an object. Her marginality, by reason of race and lumpen background, is the basis for her inalienable human dimension. As Morrison might have put it, she is simply too black, too passionate, too human ever to become reified.

Reification, while never attained by any of Morrison's characters—not even those drawn from the white world[7]—is, instead, embodied in a number of figural images from *The Bluest Eye*. These are the celluloid images of Shirley Temple or her "cu-ute" face on a blue-and-white china cup, and the candy wrapper images of Mary Jane. Most of all, reification is evident in the plastic smile and moronic blue eyes of a white Christmas baby doll. When Claudia destroys these—dismembering the doll and poking its eyes out—her rebellion is not just aimed at the idea of beauty incarnated in a white model. She is also striking out against the horrifying dehumanization that acceptance of the model implies—both for the black who wears it as a mask and for the white who creates commodified images of the self.

If Morrison's highly sensual descriptions explode the effects of alienation and repression and stave off the advent of reification, they do so because sensuality is embedded in a past which is inaccessible to sexual repression and bourgeois culture. The retrieval of sensuality allows an alternative social mode and historical period to be envisioned. When, again in *The Bluest Eye*, the prostitute Marie remembers the succulent taste and crunch of fried fish, her memories bring forth tastes and textures which are not separate from the moment of their production, but integral with praxis. Her memory summons up her specific past—her boyfriend and free-spirited youth—and makes these concrete for the reader and for the child, Pecola, who in the depths of fearful alienation perceives a very different image of the world, in which adolescence, petty outlawry, and economic marginality constitute a form of freedom.

For Morrison, everything is historical. Even objects are embedded in history and are the bearers of the past. For those characters closest to the white bourgeois world, objects contain the residues of repressed and unrealized desires. For Ruth Foster in *Song of Solomon*, the daughter of the town's first black doctor and wife of the slumlord Macon Dead, a water mark on a table is the stubborn and ever-present reminder of her husband's remorseless rejection. The bowl of flowers around which their hatred crystallized is no longer present; only its sign remains, an opaque residue indelibly written into the table. If, for the bourgeois world, experience is capable of being abstracted to the level of sign, this is not the case for the world of the marginal characters. To cite an example from the same novel, Pilate, Ruth Foster's sister-in-law and in every way her antithesis, enjoys a special relationship to all levels of natural experience—including a specific shade of blue sky. Now, color does not function as a sign in the way that the water mark on the table does. While it bears a concrete relationship to a real object (the blue ribbons on Pilate's mother's hat), it is not an abstract relationship in the way that the water mark stands for the bowl of flowers. For Ruth Foster, the water mark is an "anchor" to the mental and sexual anguish imprisoned in the sign. In contrast, when Pilate points to a patch of sky and remarks that it is the same color as her mother's bonnet ribbons, she enables her nephew Milkman (Ruth Foster's overly sheltered son) to experience a unique moment of sensual perception. The experience is liberational because Pilate is not referring to a specific bonnet—or even to a specific mother—; rather, the color blue triggers the whole range of emotions associated with maternal love, which Pilate offers to anyone who will share the experience of color with her.

In contrast to the liberational aspect of *Song of Solomon*, Morrison's most recent novel, *Tar Baby*, registers a deep sense of pessimism. Here, cultural exiles—both white and black—come together on a Caribbean island where they live out their lives in a neatly compartmentalized bourgeois fashion: the candy magnate Valerian Street[8] in his stereophonic-equipped greenhouse; his wife, cloistered in her bedroom; and the servants, Ondine and Sydney, ensconced in their comfortable quarters. Daily life precludes "eruptions of funk," a lesson poignantly taught when Margaret Lenore discovers the bedraggled wild man, Son, in her closet. While Son's appearance suggests Rastafarianism and outlawry, any shock value stirred by his discovery is cancelled when he, too, proves to be just another exile. Except for one brief incident, when Ondine kills a chicken and in plucking it recalls a moment from her distant past when she worked for a poultry butcher, there are no smells, tastes, or tactile experiences to summon up the past. Rather, there is a surfeit of foods whose only quality is the calories they contain.

In contrast with Morrison's earlier novels, the past in *Tar Baby* is never brought to metaphoric juxtaposition with the present. Rather, it is held separate and bracketed by dream. When Valerian Street, sipping a brandy in his greenhouse, lapses into daydream, his recollection of the past, which in essence contrasts entrepreneurial capitalism to modern corporate capitalism, does not intrude upon his present retirement. The past is past, and the significant historical transition evoked is perceived as inaccessible and natural.

The past is made more remote when it informs a nighttime dream. This is the case for Sydney, who every night dreams of his boyhood in Baltimore. "It was a tiny dream he had each night that he would never recollect from morning to morning. So he never knew what it was exactly that refreshed him."[9] For the black man hanging to the coattails of the white upper bourgeoisie, who thinks of himself as a "Philadelphia Negro," the back streets of Baltimore are a social debit. His desire for assimilation to white bourgeois culture and the many years spent in service to the bourgeois class negate his ever experiencing the deep sensual and emotional pleasure that Pilate has whenever she beholds a blue sky or bites into a vine-ripened tomato.

With every dreamer dreaming a separate dream, there are no bridges to the past and no possibility of sharing an individual experience as part of a group's social history. While a reminiscence like Marie's account of eating fried fish can be communicated, a dream, as Son finds out, cannot be pressed into another dreamer's head. Son's dream of "yellow houses with white doors" and "fat black ladies in white dresses minding the pie table in the basement of the church" (*TB*, p. 119) is an image of wish fulfillment, rooted in private nostalgia. It bears no resemblance to his real past as we later come to understand it out of what the book shows us of Eloe, Florida, where tough black women with little time for pie tables have built their own rough-hewn, unpainted homes.

For the tar baby, Jadine, fashioned out of the rich white man's indulgence and the notions of culture most appealing to bourgeois America (European education and Paris "haute couture"), the past is irretrievable and no longer perceived as desirable. As the individual whose cultural exile is the most profound, Jadine is haunted by waking visions, born out of guilt and fear. In her most terrifying vision, a mob of black women—some familiar, some only known by their names—crowds into her room. Revealing, then waving their breasts at her, they condemn Jadine for having abandoned the traditional, maternal role of black women.

While Jadine lives her separation from the past and rejection of traditional cultural roles with tormented uncertainty and frenzied activity, Milkman, in Morrison's previous novel, experiences his alienation from black culture as a hollow daily monotony. Jadine, whose desire to find self and be free leads to jet hops between Paris, the Caribbean, and New York, has not had the benefit of a powerful culture mentor like Pilate, who awakens Milkman's desire to know his past. In contrast, all of Jadine's possible culture heroes are bracketed by her rupture with the past and her class position. Jadine rejects family—her Aunt Ondine, for her homey ways and maternal nature—and culture, the black islanders, so remote from Jadine's trajectory into the future that she never even bothers to learn their names.

Milkman, on the other hand, has been born and raised in the ghetto, albeit in the biggest house. He has never been to college, but he has had the benefit of teachers—both the "street-wise" Guitar and the "folk-wise" Pilate. If Milkman's present is a meaningless void of bourgeois alienation, the possibility of a past opens out to him like a great adventure. A quest for gold initiates Milkman's journey into the past—and into the self—, but gold is not the novel's real object. Imagining that gold will free him from his father's domination and his family's emotional blackmail, Milkman comes to realize that only by knowing the past can he hope to have a future.

There is a sense of urgency in Morrison's writing, produced by the realization that a great deal is at stake. The novels may focus on individual characters like Milkman and Jadine, but the salvation of individuals is not the point. Rather, these individuals, struggling to reclaim or redefine themselves, are portrayed as epiphenomenal to community and culture; and it is the strength and continuity of the black cultural heritage as a whole which is at stake and being tested.

As Morrison sees it, the most serious threat to black culture is the obliterating influence of social change. The opening line from *Sula* might well have been the novel's conclusion—so complete is the destruction it records: "In that place, where they tore the night shade and blackberry patches from their roots to make room for the Medallion City Golf Course, there was once a neighborhood."[10] This is the community Morrison is writing to reclaim. Its history, terminated and dramatically obliterated, is condensed in a single sentence whose content spans from rural South to urban redevelopment. Here, as throughout Morrison's writing, natural imagery refers to the past, the rural South, the reservoir of culture which has been uprooted—like the blackberry bushes—to make way for modernization. In contrast, the future is perceived of as an amorphous, institutionalized power embodied in the notion of "Medallion City," which suggests neither nature nor a people. Joining the past to the future is the neighborhood, which occupies a very different temporal moment (which history has shown to be transitional), and defines a very different social mode, as distinct from its rural origins as it is from the amorphous urban future.

It is impossible to read Morrison's four novels without coming to see the neighborhood as a concept crucial to her understanding of history. It defines a Northern social mode rather than a Southern one, for it describes the relationship of an economic satellite, contiguous to a larger metropolis rather than separate, subsistence economies like the Southern rural towns of Shalimar and Eloe. It is a Midwestern phenomenon rather than a Northeast, big-city category, because it defines the birth of principally first-generation, Northern, working-class black communities. It is a mode of the '40s rather than the '60s or the '80s, and it evokes the many locally specific black populations in the North before these became assimilated to a larger, more generalized, and less regionally specific sense of black culture which we today refer to as the "black community."

The fact that Milkman embarks on a quest for his past is itself symptomatic of the difference between the '40s' neighborhood and the '60s' community. In contrast with Milkman, the black youth of the '40s had no need to uncover and decipher the past simply because enough of it was still present, born on successive waves of Southern black immigrants. For Milkman the past is a riddle, a reality locked in the verses of a children's song (the song of Solomon) whose meaning is no longer explicit because time has separated the words from their historical content. Childhood and the way children perceive the world is again a figure for a mode of existence prior to the advent of capitalism and bourgeois society. And in *Song of Solomon*, it coincides with the function of song in all marginal cultures as the unwritten text of history and culture.

Milkman's quest is a journey through geographic space in which the juxtaposition of the city to the countryside represents the relationship of the present to the past. In tracing his roots from the Detroit ghetto, where he was familiar with Pilate's version of the Solomon song; to Danville, Pennsylvania, where his father grew up; and then to Shalimar, West Virginia, where his grandfather was born and children still sing of Solomon, Milkman deciphers the twin texts of history: song and genealogy. In so doing, he reconstructs a dialectic of historical transition, in which individual genealogy evokes the history of black migration and the chain of economic expropriation from hinterland to village, and village to metropolis. The end point of Milkman's journey is the starting point of his race's history in this country: slavery. The confrontation with the reality of slavery, coming at the end of Milkman's penetration into historical process, is liberational because slavery is not portrayed as the origin of history and culture. Instead, the novel opens out to Africa, the source, and takes flight on the wings of Milkman's great grandfather, the original Solomon. With the myth of the "flying Africans," Morrison transforms the moment of coming to grips with slavery as an allegory of liberation.

The fact that geographic space functions for history is symptomatic of a time when a people's past no longer forms a continuity with the present. It is one of the features which differentiates literary modernism from realism, in which people's lives are portrayed as integral to the flow of history. Because the past is perceived as problematical and historical transition is represented by the relationship among countryside, village, and city, Song of Solomon is very similar to the great modernist novels of the Latin American "Boom." In Morrison's novel, as in the Peruvian Mario Vargos Llosa's La Casa Verde, the synchronic relationship defined in geographic space stands for a diachronic relationship. The most interesting feature about these modernist texts is that, in reading them, the reader, like Milkman, restores diachrony to the text and, in so doing, realizes the historical dialectic which the text presents as inaccessible.

Milkman's journey into the past takes him out of consumer society, where he, Christmas shopping in the Rexall, practices the translation of human emotions into commodities, and thrusts him into the pre-industrial world of Shalimar, where for the first time in his life Milkman sees women with "nothing in their hands" (SOS, p. 262). Stunned, Milkman realizes that he "had never in his life seen a woman on the street without a purse slung over her shoulder, pressed under her arm, or dangling from her clenched fingers" (SOS, p. 262). The vision of women walking empty-handed produces an estrangement of Milkman's normal view of women who, conditioned by a market economy, haul about purses like grotesque bodily appendages.

The descent into the past means stepping out of reified and fetishized relationships. Milkman's sensitivities are abruptly awakened when, trudging through the woods, he is scratched by branches, bruised by rocks, and soaked in a stream. As all of his commodified possessions fall away—his watch, his Florsheim shoes, and his three-piece suit—he comes to realize a full range of sensual perceptions (along with some human social practices—like sharing) he had never before experienced. Entering Solomon's General Store, Milkman is struck by its dramatic antithesis to the big-city department store, in which money (rather than need or use) mediates the exchange of human identities for brand names.

For Macon Dead, Milkman's father, all human relationships have become fetishized by their being made equivalent to money. His wife is an acquisition; his son, an investment in the future; and his renters, dollar signs in the bank. The human sentiments he experienced as a boy have given way to the emotional blackmail he wages as an adult. Driven by the desire to own property, the basis of bourgeois class politics, Macon Dead uses property, like a true capitalist, for futher accumulation through the collection of rents. When Milkman, echoing his father's words, refers to money as "legal tender," he reveals how deeply fetishized and abstracted the concept of money itself has become. In this context, the search for gold takes on new meaning as a search for the only unfetishized form of value and, in an allegorical sense, as the retrieval of unfetishized human relationships.

However, Macon Dead is not so totally integrated into the bourgeois class that he cannot sense the impoverishment of his life—"his wife's narrow unyielding back; his daughters, boiled dry from years of yearning; his son, to whom he could speak only if his words held some command or criticism" (*SOS*, pp. 28-29). A phantom in search of some vision of human fulfillment, Macon wanders one evening into the Southside ghetto, his sister's neighborhood. There, drawn by her singing, he pauses to peer in her window. In every way Pilate is her brother's emotional and social antithesis. What Macon sees when he looks into her house is a totally alternative lifestyle, whose dramatic opposition to the spiritual impoverishment of Macon's world gives rise to a utopian moment:

> . . .he crept up to the side window where the candlelight flickered lowest, and peeped in. Reba was cutting her toenails with a kitchen knife or a switchblade, her long neck bent almost to her knees. The girl, Hagar, was braiding her hair, while Pilate, whose face he could not see because her back was to the window, was stirring something in a pot. Wine pulp, perhaps. Macon knew it was not food she was stirring, for she and her daughters ate like children. Whatever they had a taste for. No meal was ever planned or balanced or served. Nor was there any gathering at the table. Pilate might bake hot bread and each of them would eat it with butter whenever she felt like it. Or there might be grapes, left over from the winemaking, or peaches for days on end. If one of them bought a gallon of milk they drank it until it was gone. If another got a half bushel of tomatoes or a dozen ears of corn, they ate them until they were gone too. They ate what they had or came across or had a craving for. Profits from their wine-selling evaporated like sea water in a hot wind—going for junk jewelry for Hagar, Reba's gifts to men, and he didn't know what all. (*SOS*, p. 29).

In its journey back to rural origins, the novel demonstrates that Pilate's household is not, as this passage tends to suggest, structured in infantile desires and relationships, but that the world of childhood is rooted in rural society, where reciprocity and the unmediated response to desire determine social life. The utopian aspect of Pilate's household is not contained within it, but generated out of its abrupt juxtaposition to the bourgeois mode of her brother's household. In contrast to Macon's world, which is based on accumulation, Pilate's household is devoted in true "potlatch" fashion to non-accumulation. With everyone working to separate berries from thorns, winemaking is not a means for creating surplus value, but a communal social activity, whose natural raw material suggests, in Morrison's symbolic register, another link to rural agricultural society. Reba, who wins lotteries and department-store give-aways, enjoys a non-commodified relationship to objects, in which value is defined not by an object's monetary equivalent but by the gratuity of its possession and the pleasure it renders in the giving. Finally, Pilate's only pretense to property ownership is purely symbolic: a bag of bones, which turn out to be her father's, and rocks, one gathered from every state she has visited.

Throughout her writing Morrison defines and tests the limits of individual freedom. Unlike those characters who realize total freedom and, as a result, are incapable of living in society and maintaining human relationships, like Cholly Breedlove[11] and Sula, Pilate lives an unencumbered life which is the basis for a social form of freedom, rich in human understanding and love, which is neither sexual nor familial. In the text, Pilate's freedom, which makes her different from everybody else, has a very curious explanation: namely, the lack of a navel.

Now, it would be wrong simply to see Pilate's lack as just one more example of the mutilated, deformed, and stigmatized characters who tend to crop up in Morrison's writing. And it would be equally wrong to dismiss these forms of physical difference as nothing more than the author's obsession with freaks of nature. Rather, as Morrison herself indicates, Pilate's lack is to be read in social terms. It, like the other versions of physical deformity, functions as a metaphor which allows the reader to perceive a unique personal relationship to society as a whole.

Born without a navel, Pilate is a product of an "unnatural birth." In social terms, her father dead and having never known her mother, she is an orphan. Her smooth, unbroken abdominal skin causes her to be shunned by everyone who either befriends her or comes to be her lover. Consequently, she has "no people." Because no clan claims her, she is outside all the potentially limiting aspects of blood relationships and traditional forms of social behavior. Apparently without a past and a place, Pilate embodies the "mythic hero,"[12] first portrayed by Faulkner's Thomas Sutpen. The difference between Faulkner and Morrison, conditioned by the intervening years which have brought black civil rights, counter-cultural politics, and the feminist perspective, is that, while Morrison invests her "mythic hero" with utopian aspirations, Faulkner does not. In making Sutpen and his "design" for plantation and progeny the epitome of Southern class society, Faulkner negates the utopian potential that his mythic outsider first represents in opposition to the stifled, small-town sensibilities of Jefferson, Mississippi.

Another dimension which Pilate's lack of a navel allows the reader to experience is the child's discovery of sexual difference. The metaphor of lack articulates the relationship between the advent of adult sexuality and the way it transforms the individual's relationship to others. As a child, having seen only her brother's and father's stomachs, Pilate imagines that navels, like penises, are something men have and women lack. Later, when others point to her lack as a form of freakishness, Pilate achieves adult sexuality only to have it denied her. Deprived of sex because of her unique body and the superstitious fear it creates, Pilate's lack becomes the basis for her liberation from narrowly defined human relationships based on sexuality and the expansion of her social world to one based on human sensitivity. This is very different from the way Pilate's sister-in-law, Ruth Foster, lives her sexual deprivation. Shunned by her husband, she turns inward to necrophiliac fantasies of her father, a mildly obscene relationship with her son, and masturbation. Ruth, like many of Morrison's female characters dependent on a possessive and closed heterosexual relationship, never comes to see human relationships as anything but sexual. For her, the denial of sex simply means a more narrowly defined sexuality and the closure of her social world.

The only aspect of lack as a metaphor for social relationships which is not explicit but does, nevertheless, inform Morrison's treatment of Pilate is its function as a figure for the experience of racial otherness. This is not the case for other instances of lack, which, like Pecola's lack of blue eyes and Hagar's lack of copper-colored hair, capture the horror of seeing oneself as "other" and inferior. While Pilate, like many of Morrison's other characters, does undergo a moment of looking at (and into) the self, during which she recognizes her lack (or difference) and, as a consequence, determines to live her life according to a very different set of values, her moment of self-recognition (unlike many of theirs) is not couched in racial terms. Because lack in every other instance is a figure for the experience of race, it would seem to be implicit—if not explicit—in the characterization of Pilate. There is just no need for Pilate to affirm herself through race as the shell-shocked Shadrack does in *Sula* when, amnesiac and terrified by his own body, he glimpses the reflection of his face and sees in it the bold reality of his "unequivocal" blackness. For Pilate, blackness is already unequivocal. And pastlessness does not endanger identity, or separate her from society, as it does for Shadrack. Rather, it liberates the self into society.

As a literary figure for examining the lived experience of social difference, and testing the human potential for liberation, lack has its opposite in a full term: bodily stigma. In contrast to Pilate, who has no mark, Sula possesses a striking birthmark above her eye. A patch of skin unlike that found on any other human, Sula's birthmark is thought to represent a tadpole, a flower, or a snake depending on the mood of the beholder. Stigma is the figural equivalent of Sula's role in the community. As a social pariah branded as different, she is the freedom against which others define themselves.

Bodily deformity is another metaphor for the experience of social difference. When Shadrack awakes in a hospital bed, he comes into a world so totally fragmented and sundered that he is unsure where his own hands might be, after all "anything could be anywhere" (*S*, p. 8). When he finally does behold his hands, he imagines that they are monstrously deformed—so terrifyingly that he cannot bear to look at them. Totally disoriented, his hands hidden behind his back, Shadrack is expelled from the hospital and pushed out into the world—a lone, cringing figure in an alien landscape.

For Morrison, the psychological, like the sensual and sexual, is also historical. In a novel whose opening describes the leveling of a neighborhood and its transformation into the Medallion City Golf Course, Shadrack's experience of bodily fragmentation is the psychological equivalent of annihilating social upheaval, which he, as an army draftee, has been subjected to (the army being the first of capitalism's modern industrial machines to incorporate black men). Shadrack's imagined physical deformity is a figure for the equally monstrous psychological and social transformations which capitalism in all its modes (slavery, the military, and wage labor) has inflicted on the minds and bodies of black people.

Shadrack's affirmation of self, arising out of the moment he sees his image reflected in a toilet bowl and beholds the solid and profound reality of his blackness, ranks as one of the most powerful literary statements of racial affirmation. Race is the wellspring of Shadrack's inalienable identity. While all around him and within him may be subject to transformation, his blackness is forever. This sense of continuity in the face of chaos lies at the heart of Shadrack's cryptic, one-word message to the child Sula: "'Always,'" It is the basis for both Shadrack's and Sula's reinsertion into society as representations of freedom. As both messiah and pariah, Shadrack is marginal, accepted by, but never assimilated to, the black community. He, like Sula and Morrison's other social pariah, Soaphead Church, provides a point of perspective on the community which is both interior and exterior; and he allows the community to define itself against a form of freedom, which it, being a social unit, cannot attain. When Morrison remarks that the black community tolerates difference while the white bourgeois world shuts difference out, she underscores the fact that for the white world, under capitalism, difference, because it articulates a form of freedom, is a threat and therefore must be institutionalized or jailed.

In *Tar Baby*, bodily deformity takes a very different form. Because this novel describes an already sundered black community whose exiles have neither the wish nor the capacity to rediscover the source of black culture, freedom cannot be articulated (as it was in the previous novels) by an individual's moment of self-affirmation and reinsertion into society. Having no possible embodiment in the real world— not even as a pariah—freedom takes mythic form and defines the text's alternate, subterranean world, in which, in sharp contrast with the bourgeois world of manor house and leisure, a centuries-old band of blind black horsemen rides the swamps.

Blindness is another way of giving metaphoric expression to social difference and freedom.[13] It overlaps with the function of lack in that the lack of sight, which in bourgeois society is the basis for an individual's alienation, is in the mythic world the basis for the group's cohesion and absolute alternality. This is because blindness is not portrayed as an individual's affliction, but rather a communally shared way of being in the world. Once again the figure of deformity evokes an historical reality. The myth of the blind horsemen has it roots in the many real maroon societies whose very existence depended upon seclusion and invisibility. This is the social reality for which blindness is a metaphoric reversal.

A final metaphor for social otherness is self-mutilation.[14] Unlike lack and deformity, self-mutilation represents the individual's direct confrontation with the oppressive social forces inherent in white domination. Because it functions as a literary figure, self-mutilation is portrayed in Morrison's writing as liberational and contrasts sharply with all the other forms of violence done to the self. For instance, when Polly Breedlove lashes out at her child Pecola, berating her and beating her for spilling a berry cobbler while at the same time comforting and cuddling the white child in her charge, she internalizes her hate for white society and deflects the spontaneous eruption of violence away from its real object and towards a piece of herself. Unlike Polly Breedlove's violence toward the self, which locks her in profound self-hatred, self-mutilation is portrayed as a confrontational tactic which catapults the individual out of an oppressive situation. Because it involves severing a part of the body, self-mutilation coincides with the figure of lack and intensifies (by reason of its direct articulation) the potential for expressing freedom. In Morrison's writing, self-mutilation brings about the spontaneous redefinition of the individual, not as an alienated cripple—as would be the case in bourgeois society—but as a new and whole person, occupying a radically different social space.

When, as an adolescent, Sula is confronted by a band of teenage Irish bullies, she draws a knife. Instead of threatening the boys with it or plunging it into one of them, she whacks off the tip of her own finger. Sula's self-mutilation symbolizes castration and directly contests the white male sexual domination of black women which the taunting and threatening boys evoke. Her act, coupled with words of warning, "If I can do that to myself, what you suppose I'll do to you?" (S, p. 54), represents the refusal—no matter how high the cost—to accept and cower in the face of domination.

For its defiance of oppressive social norms as well as its symbolic nature, Sula's act of self-mutilation has its precedent in her grandmother's solution to a similar confrontation with bourgeois-dominated society. Abandoned by her husband, with three small children and nothing but five eggs and three beets among them, Eva Peace takes a truly radical course of action which lifts her out of the expected role of an abandoned black mother circa 1921, who could do no more than live hand-to-mouth, and gives her a very different future. Leaving her children in the care of a neighbor, she sets out. "Eighteen months later she swept down from a wagon with two crutches, a new black pocketbook, and one leg" (S, p. 34). Eva never confirms neighborhood speculation that she allowed a train to sever her leg because the way in which she lost it is not important. The real issue is what her self-mutilation enables her to achieve. As the juxtaposition between Eva's "new black pocketbook" and "one leg" suggests, monthly insurance checks make it possible for her to build a new life. The construction of a rambling, many-roomed house for family and boarders gives physical evidence of Eva's confrontation with and manipulation of the written laws of white society, whose unwritten laws would have condemned her to a life of poverty.

The most radical aspect of Eva's act is not the contestatory moment of self-mutilation, but the subsequent lack which allows a wholly new social collective to come into being around her. If the loss of a limb means that Eva practically never leaves her room, it does not signify withdrawal. Instead, Eva is "sovereign" of an entire household, which includes three generations of Peace women as its nucleus (Eva, Hannah, and Sula); their boarders (the young married couples and an alcoholic hillbilly); and their adopted outcasts (the three Deweys). For its fluid composition, openness to outsiders, and organization upon a feminine principle Eva's household represents a radical alternative to the bourgeois family model.

At one level, Morrison writes to awaken her reader's sensitivity, to shake up and disrupt the sensual numbing that accompanies social and psychological alienation. This is the function of her "eruptions of funk," which include metaphors drawn from past moments of sensual fulfillment as well as the use of lack, deformity, and self-mutilation as figures for liberation. At a deeper level, and as a consequence of these features, Morrison's writing often allows an alternative social world to come into being. When this happens, "otherness" no longer functions as an extension of domination (as it does when blackness is beheld from the point of view of racist bourgeois society, or when the crippled, blind, and deformed are compared to the terrorizing totality of a whole and, therefore, "perfect" body). Rather, the space created by otherness permits a reversal of domination and transforms what was once perceived from without as "other" into the explosive image of a utopian mode. Morrison's most radical "eruption of funk" is the vision of an alternative social world. It comes into view when Macon Dead peers into Pilate's window; when the child Nel, the product of her mother's stifled bourgeois morality, scratches at Sula's screen door; and when the intimidated and fearful Pecola visits her upstairs neighbors, the three prostitutes.

It is not gratutitous that in all these cases the definition of social utopia is based on a three-woman household. This does not imply a lesbian orientation, because in all cases the women are decidedly heterosexual. Rather, these are societies which do not permit heterosexuality as it articulates male domination to be the determining principle for the living and working relationships of the group, as it is in capitalist society.

Morrison's three-woman utopian households contrast dramatically with an earlier literary version which occurs in, of all places, Faulkner's *Absalom! Absalom!*. During the grinding culmination of the Civil War, the men all gone— siphoned off by the army—, the economy reduced to bare subsistence, the novel brings together three women: Judith, Sutpen's daughter and heir; Clytie, Sutpen's black non-heir; and the young spinstress, Miss Rosa, Sutpen's non-betrothed. Refuged in the shell of a once-prosperous manor house, they eke out their survival on a day-to-day basis:

> *So we waited for him. We led the busy eventless lives of three nuns in a barren and poverty-stricken convent: the walls we had were safe, impervious enough, even if it did not matter to the walls whether we ate or not. And amicably, not as two white women and a negress, not as three negroes or three whites, not even as three women, but merely as three creatures who still possessed the need to eat but took no pleasure in it, the need to sleep but from it no joy in weariness or regeneration, and in whom sex was some forgotten atrophy like the rudimentary gills we call the tonsils or the still-opposable thumbs for old climbing.*[15]

In considering the cataclysm of the Civil War and its destruction of traditional

Southern society, Faulkner is led to imagine the basis for a potentially radical new form of social organization, based on subsistence rather than accumulation, and women rather than men. However, the incipient possibility of social utopia dies stillborn, because the male principle and the system of patrimony have not been transformed or refuted, but merely displaced. Sutpen, even in his absence, is still the center of the household. Race, too, is not confronted or transcended. Rather, it, like sex, is simply dismissed. And with it go all vestiges of humanity.

The tremendous differences between Faulkner and Morrison, which include historical period, race, and sex, lie at the heart of their dramatically opposed images: the one, dystopian; the other, utopian. Rather than dwell on the social and historical factors which shape their fiction, I think it is more interesting in the study of literature to see the ways in which historical differences are manifested in the texts. Faulkner's dehumanized monads and the routinized lives they lead contrast sharply with Morrison's portrayal of Pilate's household, in which individual differences between the three women function to test the social dynamic within the group and between it and society at large. Faulkner's retrenched espousal of the male-dominated social model and his tenacious refusal to imagine anything else condition his bleak vision of society. On the other hand, Morrison's projection of a social utopia arises from its confrontation with and reversal of the male-dominated bourgeois social model. Rather than systematically leveling social problems, Morrison foregrounds them. The utopian aspect of her vision is produced by the totality of its opposition to society at large—not by its individual members. This makes her portrayal very different from classical literary utopias, whose individuals are presented as perfect and harmonious models. None of Morrison's individual characters in any of her three utopias is perfect. Rather than supplying answers to social problems, they give rise to questions about social relationships and society as a whole. Thus, Pilate demonstrates the insufficiency of the agrarian social mode to provide for its members once they are transplanted to urban consumer society. Her strength and resourcefulness cannot be passed on to her daughter and granddaughter because each is more distant from the rural society in which Pilate worked and grew up. Their experience of insufficiency leads to hollow consumption (Reba's of sex and Hagar's of commodities) and demonstrates the way consumer society penetrates and impoverishes human relationships.

When "funk" erupts as myth, its potential for estranging fetishized relationships is minimized because of its distance from the urban and suburban settings which condition the lives of more and more Americans—both black and white. Son's quest for the mythic community of blind maroon horsemen which ends *Tar Baby* may represent a dramatic departure from his previous endeavors, but it does not bring disruption into the heart of social practice, as occurs when the image of Pilate's household bursts upon Macon Dead's alienated and numbed sensibilities. Although *Song of Solomon* also has a mythic dimension, myth is not the novel's only form of "funk." Then, too, myth is integral to Milkman's concrete past, as he discovers by following his family's route back to slavery, whereas for Son, it represents a very distant cultural source not directly linked to his present.

"Funk" is really nothing more than the intrusion of the past in the present. It is most oppositional when it juxtaposes a not-so-distant social mode to those evolved under bourgeois society. It remains to be seen what form "funk" will take in Morrison's future work. Will it be mythic or social? Will it represent a wish fulfillment or the challenging struggle for social change?

CHAPTER 11

Fear of Flying:
Developing The Feminist Novel

Joan Reardon

Initial critical reaction to Erica Jong's *Fear of Flying* sold the book but did little to establish its considerable literary value. Particularly cutting, and more often than not, hostile, were the women who linked Jong's work to the tradition of Austen, Eliot, and the Brontës in their reviews and found the novel wanting. Ironically, the feminist critics were both negative and positive. For some, the book was trivial and did not state the case; others responded like Carol Tavris who said: "Jong has captured perfectly the dilemmas of the modern woman, the ironies of liberation and independence."[1] And still other reviewers joined Jane Crain in an unforgiving dismissal: "Taken one by one, no feminist novel really rewards critical scrutiny—they are all too steeped in ideology to pay the elementary respect to human complexity that good fiction demands."[2] With considerably more generosity, men tended to review the book as a good popular novel, a cut above *Diary of a Mad Housewife*, with the welcome addition of considerably more humor. Though Paul Theroux[3] and the anonymous *TLS* reviewer[4] were denigrating as well as negative and Alfred Kazin disregarded the work, Henry Miller praised it as "a female *Tropic of Cancer*."[5] To be sure, there were references to poor characterization, lack of irony or distance in the narration, but, on balance, John Updike's "...feels like a winner. It has class, and sass, brightness and bite. Containing all the cracked eggs of the feminist litany, her souffle rises with a poet's afflatus,"[6] seemed to be the prevailing male judgement.

Neither the reviewers nor readers read *Fear of Flying* within the context of Erica Jong's earlier statements about poetry and fiction nor did they treat the novel as a logical development of the themes and style of her poetry. More significantly, no critic pursued Christopher Lehmann-Haupt's passing observation that the novel was "sensitive to the ambiguities of growing up intelligently female these days,"[7] or examined the novel within the literary tradition of the *bildungsroman*.[8] Quite literally, *Fear of Flying* is the tale of Erica Jong's thinly disguised autobiographical heroine, Isadora Wing, on her journey from immaturity to maturity. As such, the plot follows the standard formula of the educational novel outlined by Jerome Buckley in *Season of Youth* in which a sequence of incidents involves a sensitive youth who leaves a provincial and constrained life in a small town, journeys to a cosmopolitan city, and begins his or her real education. After a series of initiating experiences, at least two love affairs, and a number of moral encounters, the character rearranges her/his values and pursues a career in earnest, leaving adolescence behind.[9]

The pattern, at least in its essential aspects, parallels *Fear of Flying*. That Isadora Wing is a sensitive character is made abundantly clear in her relationships and in her engagement with literature. Her parents, especially Isadora's mother, are portrayed as understanding and curiously disapproving as they encourage and discourage their gifted daughter. Fascinated by her desire to write and simultaneously hostile because she, unlike her sisters, rejects the role of motherhood, her family becomes increasingly antagonistic. Consequently, she leaves the repressive atmosphere of home by many routes—marriage, trips to Europe, analysis by at least six different psychiatrists, and, ultimately, by an affair with Adrian. When she does at last come of age, she returns "home" to her husband Bennett on her own terms, convinced of the "wisdom of her choice" of housewife as artist.

Isadora Wing, a character who is lost both literally and psychologically throughout most of the novel, finds herself on its final page. The circuitous routes always lead back. Familiar landmarks of the past—hotels, cafes, and trains—orient her to the present. The loss of contact with actual time frees her to listen to an inner rhythm, a resolute private timing which encompasses the twenty-eight-day time sequence of the novel. She finally comes to know where she is and what time it is as she resolves her fears—of flying, of driving, of "the man under the bed," of submitting her work to a publisher—and she comes of age. "I was determined to take my fate in my own hands. I meant that I was going to stop being a schoolgirl,"[10] she says at the end of the novel. And one can assume that she speaks with the authority of the author's voice.

The imagery of *Fear of Flying* supports the various stages of the heroine's coming of age and reveals the author's growing confidence in her own fictional voice. Illustrating the progress of Isadora Wing's "growing up female," Erica Jong uses the journey of Alice and Dante through fantasy and dream into a "wonderland" and an "inferno" from which her heroine eventually emerges with a clearer perception of herself. She refuses to be the perpetual child or the symbol of pure love. The rejection of Alice and Beatrice coincides, therefore, with Isadora's rejection of male definitions. Having exhausted the image of physical journey from place to place, Erica Jong finally employs the image of menstruation to convey the inward journey into her own womanhood.

Using Lewis Carroll and Dante to define the male image of woman as little girl and idealized lover is accomplished by Erica Jong with considerable panache. That Isadora ricochets between the two images is apparent throughout the novel. Furthermore, using the seemingly disparate authors unifies the journey motif employed extensively throughout the work—actual movement from America to Europe as well as movement in time from youth to maturity and, finally, the psychological movement toward self-understanding. Physical transport from place to place underpins the plot and supports the chapters which delineate earlier travels. Within the framework of the longer journey from New York to

Vienna, and to London, another important journey is undertaken. Isadora and Adrian leave "the Congress of Dreams" together, circle through Europe, and ultimately part company in Paris. In the context of these two major journeys, Isadora relates all other past trips, excursions, and travels which have in some way or other contributed to the present, including travel from New York to California and four different journeys from New York to Europe.

The recalled journeys, which interrupt the overall movement of the plot, serve to disorientate the reader as the narrative shifts from continent to continent as well as from present to past. However, the imposing pattern is always circular. Conversation spins round and round. "We seem to be talking in circles" (p. 83), Isadora says to Adrian as she has said to Bennett and Brian years earlier. Words echo words as the car "goes around in circles, dodging traffic" (p. 171). Similarly, dreams, nightmarish or benign, repeat Isadora's endless experiences with all the analysts in her life. The same story told and retold until she finally rejects analysis in the person of Dr. Kolner:

> Why should I listen to *you* about what it means to be a woman? Are you a woman? Why shouldn't I listen to *myself* for once? And to other women? I talk to them. They tell me about themselves—and a damned lot of them feel exactly the way I do—even if it doesn't get the Good Housekeeping Seal of the American Psychoanalytic. (p. 18)

With this first note of freedom, struck early in the novel, Isadora moves away from the analyst's couch into the labyrinth of Europe. From the phantasmal "dream of a zipless fuck" to the "dreams of Nazis and plane crashes" entire scenes assume the "swift compression of a dream." Dreams serve to confuse reality with unreality, actual occurrences with visionary happenings.

To a heightened degree, Alice, the prototypical child, exhibits this same sense of confusion in wonderland. Within the framework of her adventures, reality and fantasy, sense and nonsense, sanity and insanity are juxtaposed to create a dream-like world. Erica Jong's repeated references to Carroll's work clearly link Alice to Isadora. Because of their repetitiousness, Isadora describes her conversations with Adrian "like quotes from *Through the Looking-Glass*" (p. 83). In *Wonderland*, the Red Queen explains to Alice: "Now *here*, you see, it takes all the running *you* can do, to keep in the same place. If you want to get somewhere else, you must run at least twice as fast as that!"[11] Similarly, in the mirrored discotheque, Isadora and Adrian find themselves "lost in a series of mirrored boxes and partitions which opened into each other. . .I felt I had been transported to some looking-glass world where, like the Red Queen, I would run and run and only wind up going backward" (p. 82). In addition to the patterns of vertiginous motion, and to distorted patterns of size and shape, familiar characters also transfer from *Wonderland* to *Fear of Flying*. Adrian's grin is a continual reminder of the Cheshire cat. When Alice asks the cat, "Would you tell me, please, which way I ought to walk from here?" the cat replies, "That depends a good deal on where you want to get to."[12] Adrian, "smirking his beautiful smirk with his pipe tucked between his curling pink lips," tells Isadora, "you have to go down into yourself and salvage your own life" (p. 249).

Both Isadora and Alice live in a fantasy world which is more congenial to them than is reality. However, for Isadora, residence in wonderland is impossible to maintain. When the fantasy "of the zipless fuck," which Isadora pursues throughout the novel, becomes a reality, she realizes the disparity between eight-year-old naivety and twenty-nine-year-old delusion. She calls herself "Isadora in Wonderland, the eternal naif." The fantasy "instead of turning me on,. . .revolted me! Perhaps there was no longer anything romantic about men at all?" (p. 302). Isadora rejects one fantasy after another as Alice, weary of the Queen's tricks, seizes the table cloth and upsets her illusory dinner party. But most importantly, Isadora outgrows the role of "Isadora Wing, clown, crybaby, fool," and opts for a life that will satisfy her rather than repeatedly seeking some fantasy lover who will disappoint her.

However, all the aspects of her journey are not as felicitious as Alice's adventures in wonderland. Isadora, because she is "bloody Jewish. . .mediocre at other things, but at suffering you're always superb" (p. 251), must descend to the depths of Dante's hell in order to cleanse herself of yet another illusion—another masculine image of woman. Early in the novel, she assumes the Beatrice role by idealizing her various love-relationships, "Dante and Beatrice. . .Me and Adrian?" (p. 166). She also links Brian and herself to the well-known lovers, "What if he were Dante and I Beatrice?" (p. 198). She would be able to guide him through the hell of his madness. However, ultimately Isadora must identify with both the pilgrim Dante and some of the sinners he encounters on his way. She is the incontinent Francesca, "The book of my body was open and the second circle of hell wasn't far off" (p. 75); and Adrian, of course, is Paolo. As the Dantean lovers are whirled and buffeted through the murky air by a great whirlwind, so Isadora and Adrian are seen in various degrees of intoxication, moving through the purple mists of the "Congress of Dreams" and motoring in endless circles through Europe. However, Isadora's journey like Dante's is ever downward. When Adrian and Isadora venture into the bizzare, mirrored, and stroboscopic world of the discotheque, Isadora renames it "The Seventh Circle." Once inside they become lost in the maze of mirrors and with mounting panic they look for familiar faces in the crowd of strangers, "all the other damned souls." Isadora's relationship with her first husband establishes still more persistent links with the damned souls in the lowest depths of hell. Brian tells her, ". . .you're in hell and I'm in hell and we're all in hell," and calls her Judas when she consents to his hospitalization. He reminds her: "Didn't I know that I would go to the Seventh Circle—the circle of the traitors? Didn't I know mine was the lowest crime in Dante's book? Didn't I know I was already in hell?" (p. 205). The analogy is strengthened when Isadora experiences guilt, not for betraying him, but for surviving his madness "as if I were Dante and he were Ugolino and I would return from Hell and relate his story" (p. 285).

To complete his arduous journey through the triple world of the *Divine Comedy* Dante required the assistance of three guides—Virgil, Statius, and finally Beatrice—symbolic representations of reason, repentance, and love. Isadora's three lovers assume comparable roles on her journey to self-understanding. Brian, whose powerful mind is condemned to madness, is the antithesis of reason, but his "verbal pyrotechnics" and his way of looking at the world "through a poet's eyes" influence Isadora's desire to write. Her second husband Bennett withdraws into his guilt and silence until "he made his life resemble death. And his death was my death too" (p. 114). From Bennett, Isadora learns solitude and silence and proceeds to listen to the inner voice urging her to write. The heroine's third serious lover, Adrian, becomes an "idealized lover." Like Beatrice, he is passionately loved but never possessed, "that was part of what made him so beautiful. I would write about him, talk about him, remember him, but never have him. The unattainable man" (p. 261). He is the guide who ultimately shows Isadora the way to self-understanding, the way to salvage her life, hit rock bottom, and climb back up again.

After Adrian leaves her in Paris, she describes the terrifying experience of being alone "like teetering on the edge of the canyon and hoping you'd learn to fly before you hit bottom" (p. 271). Yet it is into this abyss that psychologically and emotionally she descends. After experiencing a period of numbness and fear, she looks into the mirror to affirm her physical identity. The reflection of her body assures her that she is still very much herself. She searches for her notebooks and begins to read the entries that record her past four years of married life with Bennett: "I am going to figure out how I got here. . .And where the hell was I going next?" (p. 287). Considering that question further, she realizes that running away from Bennett was the first step in reclaiming what she had surrendered long ago—to her parents, to Brian, to Bennett and only recently to Adrian—namely, her soul.

As Dante is instructed to wash the film of hell off his face in the morning's dew before he enters purgatory, Isadora washes herself before leaving the hotel room. She describes her trip from Paris to London as "purgatorial." The fog and cloud-cover veiling the island of England, leaving only the white cliffs of Dover visible, create the mixture of light and darkness which surrounds Dante's purgatorial mountain. Isadora enters through the customs gate like Dante passing through the gates of purgatory. The purifying bath of the last scene completes the rites of passage. Isadora has fulfilled her promise to return made earlier to Adrian. "Back where?" he questions. And she replies: "To Paradise" (p. 141), which, in the context of the novel, is a return to Bennett; however, now it is on her own terms.

The journeys form repetitious circular images, lending a vertiginousness and confusion appropriate to the immaturity of the heroine. Counterpointing the actual journey of Isadora—not in the traditional mode of the youthful hero from country to city but from New York to the twin capitals of the world, Paris and London—is the fantasy adventure of Alice and the pilgrimage of Dante, "midway this life" from sin to grace. The unusual blending of imagery from Carroll's *Alice's Adventures in Wonderland* and Dante's *Divine Comedy* reinforces the "novel of youth" and suggests as well a reappraisal of values, a purgation resulting from a process of painful soul-searching.

But these literary conventions as well as Isadora's previous twenty-eight years must be examined, evaluated, and ultimately rejected as part of what she considers the male definition. The novel of journey, the image of woman as child and icon must give way to the author's own feminine perceptions. Isadora angrily states: "I learned about women from men, I saw them through the eyes of male writers. Of course I didn't think of them as male writers. I thought of them as writers, as authorities, as gods who knew and were to be trusted completely" (p. 154). Within the tradition and yet apart from it, Erica Jong uses the image of the woman as child—the eternal Alice—and the woman as idealized lover—the eternal Beatrice—only to reject both roles and "survive."

Indeed the novel accomplishes more than that. It portrays not only the end of the journey but the journey itself on Erica Jong's own terms; namely, the awareness "of the fact of being female and going beyond it." In a paraphrase of her fictional heroine's words, Erica Jong has stated the case in "The Artist as Housewife/The Housewife as Artist":

> The reason a woman has greater problems becoming an artist is because she has greater problems becoming a self. She can't believe in her existence past thirty. She can't believe her own voice. She can't see herself as a grown-up human being. She can't leave the room without a big wooden pass.[13]

In a literary tradition where the standard of excellence is synonymous with male, the writer who is also a woman distrusts her own voice, undervalues her own experience and never really achieves a sense of self. According to Erica Jong, coming to terms with her own body, therefore, is the first corrective step for a creative woman to take, and *Fear of Flying* demonstrates precisely how this is accomplished. The result boldly stated by Isadora Wing is a literary work which is the antithesis of all those books throughout all of history which "were written with sperm, not menstrual blood" (p. 24).

However, the precedent for a "feminist style" had been established by a number of talented women poets before Erica Jong published *Fruits and Vegetables*. Discovery of the poetry of Anne Sexton and Sylvia Plath "came as a revelation," she said, because for the first time in her reading of literature, poetry ceased to be exclusively a "masculine noun." These contemporary women poets had come to terms with themselves as women and "wrote about their bodies and never attempted to conceal the fact that they were women."[14] They were attuned to the special rhythm which dominated their lives from menarche to menopause, and they were fearless in tapping "a kind of hidden power." In short, they expressed themselves in their own diction. Their images and symbols were chiefly drawn from the reality of daily experience rather than from the existing literary tradition.

Sylvia Plath charted new ground as she became more and more "attuned to her body harp." The casual and continued references to the interaction of psychological and physical states and the relationship of both to her ability to write at certain times found in both *Letters Home*[15] and some of her early poetry clearly indicate the extent to which Plath was preoccupied with the menstrual cycle.[16] The specific symbols which became the texture of her poetry, the ocean, the moon, pregnancy and sterility, revealed her deepest feelings about life and death. More often than not these feelings were expressed in the language of blood. In later poems like "The Munich Mannequins" menstruation becomes an image of repeated bankruptcy:

> Perfection is terrible, it cannot have children.
> Cold as snow breath, it tamps the womb
> Where the yew trees blow like hydras,
> The tree of life and the tree of life
> Unloosing their moons, month after month, to no purpose.

And she concludes, "The blood flood is the flood of love/The absolute sacri-fice."[17] Furthermore, birth, "There is no miracle more cruel than this,"[18] and the flow of blood in the afterbirth symbolized the ultimate creative act of poetry. Menstruation, signalling the failure to conceive, symbolized sterility. Because Plath was writing in her own terms about her own experiences, she opened the way for Erica Jong to explore with a surer sense the uncharted areas of female experience.

But Sylvia Plath was not alone in her efforts to create a more personal idiom in her poetry. In quite another style Anne Sexton adopts a valuable coarseness, a rude incapacity to be delicate in many of her confessional poems. Consider for a moment the titles, "In Celebration of my Uterus," and "Menstruation at Forty," poems belying their apparent flippancy and expressing, instead, a sub-jective and interior experience of time in relationship to the menstrual cycle, "That red disease. . ./year after year."[19] Rather than reject the experience of bodily pain, of hospitalization, of surgery and blood flow, Sexton utilizes all aspects of her physical and psychological states. In a poem on her childhood called "Those Times. . ." she contrasts the isolation of the child of six with the image of her future womanhood:

> I did not know the woman I would be
> nor that blood would bloom in me
> each month like an exotic flower.[20]

And in the poem, "The Break," the life of the roses in her hospital room is sym-bolically vitalized by blood:

> . . .My one dozen roses are dead.
> They have ceased to menstruate. They hang
> there like little dried up blood clots.[21]

In "Song for a Red Nightgown" she reinforces the connection between the lunar cycle and the menses:

> surely this nightgown girl,
> this awesome flyer, has not seen
> how the moon floats through her
> and in between.[22]

Anne Sexton is eminently qualifed to draw upon personal knowledge of her physical and mental states and to translate that knowledge into viable poetry. Notwithstanding the masculine opprobrium directed toward some of her poems, she remains true to her own words, "I cannot promise very much./I give you the images I know."[23]

These are some of the women writers, therefore, who have explored "the fact of being female and go beyond it, but never deny it."[24] Following their example, Erica Jong boldly incorporates certain private and female symbols, thought unmentionable in the past, into the artistic texture of her work. There is a noticeable evolution from the oral and sensual imagery of her first book of poems, *Fruits and Vegetables*, to the search for a genuine understanding of woman's role in the second volume, *Half-Lives*. However, the third book, *Love-root*, states the case most explicitly. For in virtually all these poems she is both iconoclastic about the traditional subject matter of poetry and sure about the necessity of woman's survival as both person and writer within the perimeters of feminine experience. More to the point, Erica Jong demonstrates in these poems that even the subject matter of a poem written by a woman can be, and indeed, must be different:

> I think women poets have to insist on their right to write like women. Where their experience of the world is different, women writers ought to reflect that difference. They ought to feel a complete freedom about subject matter. But most important, our definition of femininity has to change. As long as femininity is associated with ruffles and flourishes and a lack of directness and honesty, women artists will feel a deep sense of ambivalence about their own femaleness.[25]

In the volume *Half-Lives*, Erica Jong states the dilemma of the woman poet with uncompromising severity. "The Send-Off," a poem written to friends after she has sent her first book to the printer, poetically expresses the fear which was later to haunt Isadora Wing—the loneliness and half-life of the woman artist who is reminded month after month of the barrenness of her womb by the menstrual flow, the symbol of the non-event:

> *(Singing the Monthly Blues)*
> The book gone to the printer to die
> and the flat-bellied author
> disguised as me
> is sick of the anger of being a woman
> and sick of the hungers
> and sick of the confessional poem of the padded bra
> and the confessional poem of the tampax
> and the bad-girl poets
> who menstruate black ink.
>
> I am one!
> Born from my father's head
> disguised as a daughter
> angry at spoons and pots
> with a half-life of men behind me

and a half-life of me ahead
with holes in my shoes
and holes in my husbands
and only the monthly flow of ink to keep me sane
and only sex to keep me pure.

I want to write about something other than women!
I want to write about something other than men!
I want stars in my open hand
and a house round as a pumpkin
and children's faces forming in the roots of trees.
Instead
I read my fortune in the bloodstains on the sheet.[26]

The meaning is fairly obvious. The creation of the poem or novel is symbolized by the menses while the failure to conceive a child is visibly demonstrated by the discharge of the unfertilized egg, a pattern which imposes itself with idiotic, irrational punctuality on a woman's consciousness every twenty-eight days from menarche to menopause. In still another poem from the same volume, the polarity of the role of mother vs. artist is expressed in the imagery of exotic flowers:

I imagine the inside
of my womb to be
the color of poppies
and bougainvillea
(though I've never seen it).

But I fear the barnacle
which might latch on
and not let go
and I fear the monster
who might grow
and bite the flowers
and make them swell and bleed.

So I keep my womb empty
and full of possibility.

Each month
the blood sheets down
like good red rain.

I am the gardener.
Nothing grows without me.[27]

"Hook images," used earlier by Sylvia Plath to describe the demands of her two children on time and creative energy, appear in the poem. However, Erica Jong rejects "the barnacles which might latch on" and interprets the menstrual flow as a validation of her art and a symbol of its potency. As the last line suggests, she insists upon the right to make the final determination.

Despite the deliberateness and forcefulness of Erica Jong's poetry, it is to the novel *Fear of Flying* we must turn for a more subjective exploration of the multiple problems of "growing up female" and for more daring stylistic techniques of expressing the feminine experience. In addition to creating the sexually fanciful Isadora Wing, Erica Jong devised a subtle sequence of time to enclose the action of the novel. The Pan Am flight to Vienna, the ten-day Congress at the Academy of Psychiatry, the two-and-a-half week motor trip through Italy, Germany, and France, the climax in Paris and the short one-day trip to London is a little less than a month although the alternating chapters span the childhood, early education, university career, first marriage and almost five years of the second marriage of Isadora Wing. The elements of time present and time past merge into the climactic now by linking the climax—the end of the affair with Adrian—with the menstrual cycle.

The twenty-eight days of the novel chart the various biochemical changes, the physical experiences of ovulation and flow as well as the psychological movements of relaxation and tension which explain, at least in part, Isadora Wing's actions. In addition to the journey to a "wonderland" of sensuality and sexuality, to an "inferno" of guilt and eventual repentance, she must journey inward to define herself as a woman and to understand to what extent every woman is "tied to that body beat" month by month. Isadora's attraction to Adrian at the beginning of the Congress is directly associated with ovulation. She says:

> I seem to be involved with all the changes of my body. They never pass unnoticed. I seem to know exactly when I ovulate. In the second week of the cycle, I feel a tiny ping and then a sort of tingling ache in my lower belly. A few days later I'll often find a tiny spot of blood in the rubber yarmulke of the diaphragm. A bright red smear, the only visible trace of the egg that might have become a baby. I feel a wave of sadness then which is almost indescribable. Sadness and relief. (p. 47)

Isadora's observation describes the emotional tension which pervades the ten-day period of the Congress. Being physically and sexually attracted to Adrian, she is also melancholy at the thought of betraying her husband Bennett. She reels emotionally from lover to husband until the last session of the Congress is over. At that point she impulsively decides to tour Europe with Adrian.

After two and one half weeks of careening through Europe in Adrian's Triumph, the beer-drinking twosome reach Paris and part because Adrian has arranged to join his wife and children in Cherbourg that very evening. Having lost a sense of time as well as her heart, Isadora describes the situation:

> The enormity of his betrayal leaves me speechless. Here I am—drunk, unwashed, not even knowing what day it is—and he's keeping track of an appointment he made over a month ago. (p. 269)

Alone and still dazed by his desertion, Isadora is able "to gather my terror in my two hands and possess it" (p. 271). Overcoming her fear of strange rooms, her fear of "the man under the bed," she finally falls asleep and awakens the next morning to discover her menstrual period has begun. In the release of tension, signalled by the physical flow, she prepares to leave the hotel. The narrative is momentarily halted by Isadora's recollection of her first period and the subsequent case of anorexia she experienced at fourteen when she almost starved herself to death and stopped menstruating for a year and a half because someone told her that "if I had babies, I'd never be an artist" (p. 279).

Now twenty-nine years old and secure in the adult knowledge that menstruation cancels out the fear of pregnancy, she shampoos her hair, packs, and goes out into the sunny streets of Paris in search of a drug store and a cup of cappuccino. In her own words she is being given another chance. Anxiety over a possible pregnancy is dispelled. While her affair with Adrian has thrown her back on her own limited resources, there have been few consequences. Isadora concludes: "In a sense it was sad—but it was also a new beginning" (p. 299). After the overnight journey from Paris to London, Isadora gains admission to her husband's hotel room, and the bathtub scene concludes the novel. The purification by water is certainly appropriate to the Dantean journey; however, a more subtle meaning can be attached to the bath; namely the Jewish rite of *mikvah*, the ceremonial cleansing required of all orthodox women after the menstrual period before sexual relations can be resumed. The twenty-eight days of the novel are over; a new cycle begins.

It is impossible to read *Fear of Flying* and not recognize that more than any woman writer before her, Erica Jong is fully attuned to her own body. As a result, her prose as well as her poetry is vigorous and sensual and at one with the inner rhythms which she understands so well. In the complete physicality of language and image, she insists again and again that "one's body is intimately related to one's writing" (p. 285).

Perceiving the coming of age of the artist in the totality of female experience, she has structured a novel on one of the most personal experiences of female physiology, the menstrual cycle, and has achieved a correlation of subject matter and form which is both artistic and universal. Indeed, Erica Jong has done more than that, she has reached the sensibilities of her reading audience with a brave and brash voice and attempted in the words of Virginia Woolf, "to measure the heat and violence of the poet's heart when caught and tangled in a woman's body."[28] She is a writer who understands that a woman's perception of coming of age is:

> Every month,
> the reminder of emptiness
> so that you are tuned
> to your body harp,
> strung out on the harpsichord
> of all your nerves
> and hammered bloody blue
> as the crushed fingers

of the woman pianist
beaten by her jealous lover.

Who was she?
Someone I invented
for this poem,
someone I imagined. . .

Never mind,
she is me, you—

Tied to that bodybeat,
fainting on that rack of blood,
moving to that metronome—
empty, empty, empty.

No use.
The blood is thicker
than the roots of trees,
more persistent that my poetry,
more baroque than her bruised music.
It guilds the sky above the Virgin's head.
It turns the lilies white.

Try to run:
the blood still follows you.
Swear off children,
seek a quiet room
to practice your preludes and fugues.
Under the piano,
the blood accumulates:
eventually it floats you both away.

Give in.
Babies cry and music is your life.
Darling, you were born to bleed
or rock.
And the heart breaks
either way.[29]

To date, *Fear of Flying* is the most compelling statement of "growing up female in America: What a liability!" (p. 9). In the 311 pages of Isadora's journey from youth to maturity all the old idols fall and a woman novelist has had the courage to assert her freedom and liberation from the masculine ideal on her own terms. Isadora is neither Alice nor Beatrice, inspiration nor guide. She even rejects the most irresistible myth of all—motherhood—and dares the vagaries of print. The arduous journey from childhood, replete with the fantasies and dreams of youth and the search for the "wrong things in love," the borrowed wings which "never stayed on when I needed them," leads ultimately to the conclusion, "I really needed to grow my own" (p. 300). Isadora Icarus:

> Isadora White Stollerman Wing. . .B.A., M.A., Phi Beta Kappa. Isadora Wing, promising younger poet, Isadora Wing, promising younger sufferer. Isadora Wing, feminist and would-be liberated woman. Isadora Wing, clown, crybaby, fool. Isadora Wing, wit, scholar, ex-wife of Jesus Christ. Isadora Wing, with her fear of flying, Isadora Wing, slightly overweight sexpot with a bad case of astigmatism of the mind's eye. Isadora Wing, with her unfillable cunt and holes in her head and her heart. Isadora Wing of the hunger-thump. Isadora Wing whose mother wanted her to fly. Isadora Wing whose mother grounded her. Isadora Wing, professional patient, seeker of saviors, sensuality, certainty. Isadora Wing, fighter of windmills, professional mourner, failed adventuress. . .(p. 252).

Isadora Wing comes of age.

At this point it is difficult to assess the importance of the work of Erica Jong. Having been praised by John Updike and Henry Miller and dismissed by Alfred Kazin as a "Sexual Show-Off," she is as she has so cogently stated, "Exhibit A."[30] However, a strong case can be made for her ability to crystallize the dilemma of the woman writer and communicate that anguish in a brutally forceful way. And an even stronger case can be made for her artistic forging of a new and bold image of the "Housewife as Artist." If "woman writer" ceases to be a polite but negative label, it will be due in great measure to the efforts of Erica Jong.

NOTES

CHAPTER 2

1.   Nathaniel Hawthorne to William D. Ticknor, January 1855, quoted in Caroline Ticknor, *Hawthorne and His Publisher* (Boston: Houghton Mifflin Co., 1913), pp. 141-142; Leslie Fiedler, *Love and Death in the American Novel* (New York: Criterion Books, 1960), p. 257.

2.   Alexander Cowie, "The Vogue of the Domestic Novel: 1850-1870," *South Atlantic Quarterly* 41 (October 1942): 420. Cowie's interpretation is echoed by other critics. Henry Nash Smith observed that "popular fiction was designed to soothe the sensibilities of its readers by fulfilling expectation and expressing only received ideas. . . .The best-selling novels of the 1850s thus express an ethos of conformity." John T. Frederick's evaluation of the best sellers of the 1850s ascribed the same type of didacticism to novels and short stories. In her analysis of literature by and about women published in the four decades before the Civil War, Barbara Welter claimed that the stereotype of the ideal woman included four attributes—piety, purity, submissiveness, and a dedication to domesticity. Welter argued that such literature supported a traditional view of women as inferior, passive supporters of men. See Herbert Ross Brown, *The Sentimental Novel in America, 1789-1860* (Durham, N.C.: Duke University Press, 1940); Henry Nash Smith, "The Scribbling Woman and the Cosmic Success Story," *Critical Inquiry* 1 (September 1974): 47-70; John T. Frederick, "Hawthorne's Scribbling Women," *New England Quarterly* 48 (June 1975): 231-40; Barbara Welter, "The Cult of True Womanhood: 1820-1860," *American Quarterly* 18 (Summer 1966): 151-74.

3.   Cowie, pp. 420-21.

4.   Helen Waite Papashvily, *All the Happy Endings: A Study of the Domestic Novel in America, the Women Who Wrote It, the Women Who Read It, in the Nineteenth Century* (New York: Harper & Bros., 1956), p. xvii. Dee Garrison's and Ann Douglas's views parallel Papashvily's. All agreed that the writers were bitterly hostile toward males and Garrison claimed that "common to all these

bestsellers is a rejection of traditional authority, particularly in domestic life, in religious faith, and among class-ordered mankind." Douglas's article on Sara Parton argued that the writers urged women to remove themselves from the sphere of family and home. Papashvily, Garrison, and Douglas failed to note that the writers were not antagonistic to males per se, but to the individualistic and materialistic values of their time which men were thought to embody more than women. In her later book, Douglas more or less adopted the Cowie and Welter perspective. The heroine no longer wants liberation from the home and instead, as the ornamental middle-class housewife, has climbed atop her protected pedestal of leisure where she exhibits a "proto-consumer mentality." The latest study, Nina Baym's, presents a different perspective. Baym claimed that the fiction is generally and straightforwardly about the triumph of the feminine will: "Happily, our authors said, the world's hardships provide just the right situation for the development of individual character." For a woman, these authors maintained, children and husband "are not necessary for her identity" and "marriage cannot and should not be the goal toward which women direct themselves." See Dee Garrison, "Immoral Fiction in the Late Victorian Library," *American Quarterly* 28 (Spring 1976): 71-89; Ann Douglas Wood, "The 'Scribbling Women' and Fanny Fern: Why Women Wrote," *American Quarterly* 23 (Spring 1971): 3-24; Ann Douglas, "The Literature of Impoverishment: The Women Local Colorists in America, 1865-1914," *Women's Studies: An Interdisciplinary Journal* 1 (1972): 3-45; Ann Douglas, *The Feminization of American Culture* (New York: Alfred A. Knopf, 1977); Nina Baym, *Woman's Fiction: A Guide to Novels by and about Women in America, 1820-1870* (Ithaca, N.Y.: Cornell University Press, 1978).

5.   Papashvily, p. 95.

6.   I am considering the novels, short stories, letters, diaries, and journals of the following sentimentalists—Maria Cummins, Caroline Howard Gilman, Caroline Lee Hentz, Mary J. Holmes, Maria McIntosh, Sara Parton, Catharine Maria Sedgwick, E.D.E.N. Southworth, Harriet Beecher Stowe, Mary Virginia Terhune, Susan Warner, and Augusta Evans Wilson.

7.   As the sentimentalists clearly enunciated, the principle of a wife deferring to her husband was dictated by the tenets of Christianity. E.D.E.N. Southworth told her readers that the novelettes, "The Wife's Victory," and its sequel, "The Married Shrew," had been written "to illustrate that distinct principle of Christian ethics and social philosophy, indicated by the text of Scripture selected as [their] motto": "The husband is head of the wife, even as Christ is head of the Church; therefore, as the Church is subject to Christ, so let the wives be to their own husbands in everything" (Epn. 5:23-24). E.D.E.N. Southworth, *The Wife's Victory and Other Nouvellettes* (Philadelphia: T.B. Peterson, 1854), p. 27.

8.   Augusta Evans Wilson to Walter Clopton Harriss, 1856, quoted in William Perry Fidler, *Augusta Evans Wilson, 1835-1909* (University, Ala.: University of Alabama Press, 1951), p. 54.

9.   Griswold, William M., comp., *Descriptive Lists of American International Romantic and British Novelists*, Burt Franklin, Bibliography and Reference Series no. 135 (New York, 1968), pp. 63-64.

10.   Augusta Evans Wilson, *St. Elmo* (New York: G.W. Carleton, 1866), p. 238.

11. Ibid., p. 457.
12. Catharine Maria Sedgwick to William Ellery Channing, August 24, 1837. Catharine Maria Sedgwick Papers, Massachusetts Historical Society, Boston, Mass.
13. Mary Virginia Terhune [Marion Harland], *Phemie's Temptation* (New York: Carleton, 1869), p. 178.
14. Susan Warner to Dorothea Dix, August 27, 1852. Miscellany, Houghton Library, Harvard University, Cambridge, Mass.
15. Maria Cummins to Annie Adams Fields, September 16, 1862. Miscellany, Houghton Library, Harvard University, Cambridge, Mass.
16. Maria McIntosh, *Two Pictures; Or What We Think of Ourselves, and What the World Thinks of Us* (New York: D. Appleton & Co., 1863), pp. 358-59.
17. Maria Cummins, *Mabel Vaughan* (Boston: John P. Jewett & Co., 1857), pp. 9-10.
18. E.D.E.N. Southworth, *The Curse of Clifton* (Philadelphia: T.B. Peterson & Bros., 1867/1853), p. 309. Throughout the remainder of this paper the original publication date of the novel or collection of short stories is noted following the virgule.
19. Harriet Beecher Stowe to Henry Ward Beecher, undated, Beecher Family Papers, Manuscript Division, Yale University Library, New Haven, Conn.
20. Harriet Beecher Stowe, *My Wife and I, or Harry Henderson's History* (Cambridge, Mass.: Houghton Mifflin & Co., 1896/1871), pp. 33-34.
21. Sara Parton [Fanny Fern], "A Mother's Soliloquy," *Fern Leaves From Fanny's Portfolio* (Auburn, N.Y.: Derby & Miller, 1853), p. 157.
22. Caroline Lee Hentz, "The Sex of the Soul," *The Banished Son; and Other Stories of the Heart* (Philadelphia: T.B. Peterson, 1856), p. 269.
23. Mary Virginia Terhune [Marion Harland], "A Christmas Talk With Mothers," *The Christmas Holly* (New York: Sheldon & Co., 1867), p. 54.
24. Caroline Howard Gilman, *Recollections of a Southern Matron* (New York: Harper & Bros., 1838), p. 24.
25. Harriet Beecher Stowe, *The Minister's Wooing* (Cambridge, Mass.: Houghton Mifflin & Co., 1896/1859), pp. 567-68.
26. Catharine Maria Sedgwick, *Means and Ends, or Self-Training* (Boston: Marsh, Capen, Lyon, & Webb, 1839), p. 210.
27. Augusta Evans Wilson, *St. Elmo* (New York: G.W. Carleton, 1866), p. 526.
28. Maria McIntosh, *Woman in America: Her Work and Her Reward* (New York: D. Appleton & Co., 1850), p. 131.
29. Mary Virginia Terhune [Marion Harland], "Nobody to Blame," *Husbands and Homes* (New York: Sheldon & Co., 1865), p. 47.
30. D.H. Lawrence, *Studies in Classic American Literature* (Garden City, N.Y.: Doubleday Anchor Books, 1923), p. 13.
31. Caroline Lee Hentz, *Rena: or, the Snowbird* (Philadelphia: A. Hart, Late Carey & Hart, 1852) p. 265.
32. Caroline Howard Gilman [Mrs. Clarissa Packard], *Recollections of a Housekeeper* (New York: Harper & Bros., 1834), pp. 154-55.
33. Maria McIntosh, *Woman in America: Her Work and Her Reward* (New York: D. Appleton & Co., 1850), pp. 136-37.

34. Mary Virginia Terhune [Marion Harland], "Two Ways of Keeping a Wife," *Husbands and Homes* (New York: Sheldon & Co., 1865), p. 267.

35. Caroline Lee Hentz, *Helen and Arthur; or, Miss Thusa's Spinning Wheel* (Philadelphia: T.B. Peterson & Bros., 1856/1853), p. 213.

36. Caroline Lee Hentz, "Love after Marriage," *Love After Marriage; and Other Stories of the Heart* (Philadelphia: T.B. Peterson, 1857), p. 23.

37. Maria Cummins, *The Lamplighter* (Chicago: Rand, McNally & Co., n.d./ 1854), pp. 5-6.

38. Sara Parton [Fanny Fern], *Rose Clark* (New York: Mason Bros., 1856), p. 30.

39. Mary Virginia Terhune [Marion Harland], *Ruby's Husband* (New York: Sheldon & Co., 1869), p. 355.

CHAPTER 3

1. *Patriotic Gore* (New York: Oxford Univ. Press, 1966), p. 590.

2. *The Awakening*, with introduction by Kenneth Eble (New York: Capricorn, 1964), pp. vii-viii.

3. "Our Decentralized Literature: A Consideration of Regional, Ethnic, Racial, and Sexual Factors," from a paper delivered before the German American Studies Association in Heidelberg, June 5, 1971.

4. Ibid.

5. This quotation and all other quotations from *The Awakening* have been taken from the Capricorn edition (cited above) and will be identified in the text by page number. The hardcover edition Kate Chopin, *The Awakening*, Vol. 2 in *The Complete Works of Kate Chopin*, edited and with an introduction by Per Seyersted, foreword by Edmund Wilson (Baton Rouge: Louisiana State Univ. Press, [1969)], may be found in libraries but is not readily available to the general public.

6. Ronald D. Laing, *The Divided Self* (London: Penguin Books, 1965), p. 137.

7. See Laing, pp. 138-39.

8. Ibid., p. 113.

9. Laing cites a maneuver which is remarkably similar. "A patient, for instance, who conducted his life along relatively 'normal' lines outwardly but operated this inner split, presented as his original complaint the fact that he could never have intercourse with his wife but only with his own image of her. That is, his body had physical relations with her body, but his mental self, while this was going on, could only look on at what his body was doing and/or *imagine* himself having intercourse with his wife as an object of his imagination. . . .This is an example of what I mean by saying that phantasy and reality are kept apart. The self avoids being related directly to real persons but relates itself to itself and to the objects which it itself posits. *The self can relate itself with immediacy to an object which is an object of its own imagination or memory but not to a real person*" (p. 86).

10. Ibid., p. 77.

11.   Ibid.
12.   Ibid., p. 161.
13.   Sigmund Freud, "Civilization and its Discontents," in *The Standard Edition of the Complete Psychological Works*, ed. James Strachey (London: Hogarth Press, 1971), 21:71.
14.   Ibid., p. 68.
15.   Ibid., p. 79.
16.   Helene Deutsch, *The Psychology of Women* (New York: Grune and Stratton, 1971), 2:139.
17.   Ibid., p. 160.

CHAPTER 4

1.   Edith Wharton, *The House of Mirth* (New York: Holt, Rinehart and Winston, 1962), p. 82. All subsequent references are to this edition and will be included parenthetically within the text.
2.   Edith Wharton, *A Backward Glance* (New York: Charles Scribner's Sons, 1964), p. 207.
3.   *A Backward Glance*, p. 207.
4.   *Edith Wharton: A Study of Her Fiction* (Berkeley: Univ. of California Press, 1953), p. 55.
5.   *Edith Wharton: Convention and Morality in the Work of a Novelist* (Norman: Univ. of Oklahoma Press, 1959), p. 139.
6.   *The Novel of Manners in America* (Chapel Hill: Univ. of North Carolina Press, 1972), p. 127.
7.   "Introduction," *The House of Mirth* (New York: Holt, Rinehart and Winston, 1962), xxiv.
8.   The quote which provides the title for my essay is taken from an article by Dana Densmore called "On the Temptation To be A Beautiful Object." This article first appeared in *A Journal of Female Liberation* (November, 1968) and has been extensively anthologized in collections of contemporary feminist writing.
9.   "Edith Wharton's *The House of Mirth*," in *Twelve Original Essays on Great American Novels*, ed. Charles Shapiro (Detroit: Wayne State Univ. Press, 1958), p. 161.
10.   Nevius, p. 56.
11.   Nevius, p. 56.
12.   Howe, xix.
13.   Nevius, p. 56.
14.   Diana Trilling, "*The House of Mirth* Revisited," in *Edith Wharton: A Collection of Critical Essays*, ed. Irving Howe (Englewood Cliffs: Prentice-Hall, Inc., 1962), p. 108.

CHAPTER 5

1.   Terence Martin, "The Drama of Memory in *My Antonia*," *PMLA*, LXXXIV (March, 1969), 304-311.
2.   John H. Randall, III. *The Landscape and the Looking Glass: Willa Cather's Search for Value* (Boston: Houghton Mifflin Co., 1960), p. 149.
      See Cather's remark, "The best thing I've ever done is *My Antonia*. I feel I've made a contribution to American letters with that book," in Mildred Bennett, *The World of Willa Cather* (1951; reprinted, Lincoln: University of Nebraska Press, 1961), p. 203.
3.   Bennett, p. 212. Cather is quoted as saying, "If you gave me a thousand dollars for every structural fault in *My Antonia* you'd make me very rich."
4.   David Daiches, *Willa Cather: A Critical Interpretation* (Ithaca, N.Y.: Cornell University Press, 1951), pp. 43-61.
5.   1913; reprinted Boston: Houghton Mifflin, 1941, p. 259.
      When Emil finally approaches Marie to make love, she seems asleep, then whispers, "I was dreaming this. . .don't take my dream away!" The mergence of the real lover into the dream reminds me here of Keats's *The Eve of St. Agnes*— "Into her dream he melted." Here, too, the realization of love means facing the cold wintery world from which Madeline had been protected by her castle and her fantasy.
6.   1918; reprinted Boston: Houghton Mifflin Co., 1946, p. 2.
      All italics in quotations from *My Antonia* are in the original, and all subsequent references are to this text. I use this edition not only because it is readily available but also because the introduction by Walter Havighurst and the suggestions for reading and discussion by Bertha Handlan represent clearly the way the novel has been widely used as validating the American past.
7.   James E. Miller, "*My Antonia*: A Frontier Drama of Time," *American Quarterly*, X (Winter, 1958), 481.
8.   See Bennett, p. 148. Cather is quoted as saying, "The world broke in two about 1920, and I belonged to the former half." The year 1922 is given in her preface (later deleted) to *Not under Forty* (renamed *Literary Encounters*, 1937).
9.   E.K. Brown and Leon Edel, *Willa Cather: A Critical Biography* (New York: Alfred A. Knopf, 1953), p. 203. Italics mine.
10.   Miller, p. 482.
11.   Elizabeth Shepley Sergeant, *Willa Cather: A Memoir* (1953; reprinted Lincoln: University of Nebraska Press, 1963), p. 151.
12.   Brown and Edel, p. 202.
13.   Bennett, p. 47.
14.   Daiches says, "It is a remarkable little inset story, but its relation to the novel as a whole is somewhat uncertain" (p. 46). However, Daiches finds so many episodes and details "uncertain," "dubious," "not wholly dominated," or "not fully integrated," it might be his reading is flawed rather than the novel.
15.   Sergeant, p. 117.
16.   Martin, p. 311.
17.   See the "pictures from the Wm. Cather, M.D., period of Willa's life" in Bennett, especially the photograph of Cather as a child with "her first short

haircut." Note Cather's vacillating taste in clothes from the clearly masculine to feminine.

It is significant that in various plays at school and at the university, Cather assumed male roles—so convincingly that spectators sometimes refused to believe the actor was not a boy. See Bennett, pp. 175-176, 179.

18.　1925; reprinted Boston: Houghton Mifflin Co., 1938.

19.　Sergeant, p. 46.

20.　Ibid., p. 121.

CHAPTER 6

1.　Gertrude Stein, "Afterword," in *What Are Masterpieces?* by Gertrude Stein, ed. Robert Bartlett Haas (1940; rpt. New York: Pitman, 1970), p. 104.

2.　Together the following critical studies give a good sense of the lack of agreement about *Ida*, and the relative lack of attention accorded the novel: Richard Bridgman, *Gertrude Stein in Pieces* (New York: Oxford Univ. Press, 1970); John Malcolm Brinnin, *The Third Rose* (Boston: Little, Brown 1959); Carolyn Fauce Copeland, *Language and Time and Gertrude Stein* (Iowa City: Univ. of Iowa Press, 1975); Michael J. Hoffman, *Gertrude Stein* (Boston: Twayne Publishers, 1976); Rosalind S. Miller, *Gertrude Stein: Form and Intelligibility* (New York: Exposition Press, 1949); Allegra Stewart, *Gertrude Stein and the Present* (Cambridge, Mass.: Harvard Univ. Press, 1967); and Donald Sutherland, *Gertrude Stein: A Biography of Her Work* (New Haven: Yale Univ. Press, 1951).

3.　"Afterword," p. 104.

4.　Sutherland, p. 200.

5.　*A Room of One's Own* (New York: Harcourt, Brace and World, 1929), p. 91.

6.　Joanna Russ, "What Can a Heroine Do? Or Why Women Can't Write," in *Images of Women in Fiction*, ed. Susan Koppelman Cornillon (Bowling Green, Ohio: Bowling Green Univ. Popular Press, 1972), pp. 3-20.

7.　Gertrude Stein, "Ida," in *Gertrude Stein: Writings and Lectures 1909-1945*, ed. Patricia Meyerowitz (Baltimore: Penguin, 1971), p. 355. All further references to this work appear in the text.

8.　Sydney Janet Kaplan, *Feminine Consciousness in the Modern British Novel* (Urbana: Univ. of Illinois Press, 1975).

9.　*The Geographical History of America* (1936; rpt. New York: Vintage, 1973), p. 214.

10.　*Everybody's Autobiography* (1937; rpt. New York: Vintage, 1973), p. 102.

11.　Ibid., p. 69.

12.　*The Superstitions of Fred Anneday, Annday, Anday: A Novel of Real Life*," in *How Writing Is Written*, ed. Robert Bartlett Haas (Los Angeles: Black Sparrow Press, 1974), p. 29.

13.　Ibid., p. 27.

14.　Ibid., p. 28.

15.　"Afterword," p. 103.

16.　*Superstitions of Fred Anneday*, p. 25.

17. *Geographical History of America*, p. 58.
18. Ibid.
19. Ibid., p. 60.
20. Ibid., p. 223.

CHAPTER 7

1. *The Collected Stories of Katherine Anne Porter* (New York: Harcourt, 1965), p. 199. All subsequent page references, given in the text, will be from this volume.
2. William Nance, *Katherine Anne Porter and the Art of Rejection* (Chapel Hill: Univ. of North Carolina Press, 1963), p. 118.
3. "Reflections on Willa Cather," *The Collected Essays and Occasional Writings of Katherine Anne Porter* (New York: Delacorte, 1966), pp. 31-32.
4. George Hendrick, *Katherine Anne Porter* (New York: Twayne, 1965), pp. 61-62.
5. "Afterword," *Pale Horse, Pale Rider* (New York: New American Library, 1965), pp. 61-62.
6. Quoted in *Katherine Anne Porter: A Critical Symposium*, ed. Lodwick Hartley and George Core (Athens: Univ. of Georgia Press, 1969), p. 162.

CHAPTER 8

1. Pierre Teilhard de Chardin, *The Phenomenon of Man* (New York, 1959), p. 262.
2. Flannery O'Connor, *Mystery and Manners* (New York, 1969), p. 68.
3. Ibid., p. 44.
4. Teilhard, p. 291.
5. Ibid., p. 290.
6. Ibid., p. 289.
7. Gustav Janouch, *Conversations with Kafka* (New York, 1971), p. 90.
8. Teilhard, p. 309.
9. In the essay "The Fiction Writer and His Country," she declares "for me the meaning of life is centered in our Redemption by Christ." *Mystery and Manners*, p. 32.
10. See John Hawkes' essay, "Flannery O'Connor's Devil," *Sewanee Review*, LXX (Summer 1962), p. 400.
11. Quoted by Robert Fitzgerald in his introduction to *Everything That Rises Must Converge* (New York, 1965), p. xiii.
12. Teilhard, p. 256.
13. Flannery O'Connor is a remarkable synthesis of what Jung would call the personality characterized by *participation mystique* and that personality that "suffers in the lower stories, so to speak, but in the upper stories is singularly detached from painful as well as joyful events." ("Commentary on *The Secret of the Golden Flower*," in Jung's *Psyche and Symbol* (New York, 1958), p. 340.

CHAPTER 9

1.   "Sylvia Plath: A Partial Disagreement," *Harper's*, January 1972, p. 91. For an even stronger attack on Plath's art and on the Plath cult, see Paul West, rev. of *Crossing the Water*, *Book World* (*The Washington Post*), 9 January 1972, p. 8.

2.   See A. Alvarez, *The Savage God: A Study in Suicide* (New York: Random House, 1972), p. 21. Lois Ames refers to the same conversation in "Sylvia Plath: A Biographical Note," *The Bell Jar* (New York: Harper & Row, 1971), p. 293. All subsequent references to the text of *The Bell Jar* are to this edition.

3.   See Woolf, *A Writer's Diary* (London: Hogarth Press, 1953), p. 156.

4.   *The Divided Self*, Pelican ed. (1960; rpt. Baltimore: Penguin, 1970), p. 94.

5.   Ibid., p. 95.

6.   It is fascinating to compare this reference to Esther's infancy with the account given by the mother of "Julie," the chronic schizophrenic studied in the final chapter of *Divided Self*: "Julie was never a demanding baby. She was weaned without difficulty. Her mother had no bother with her from the day she took off nappies completely when she was fifteen months old. She was never 'a trouble' " (pp. 182-83). Similar case histories are found in R.D. Laing and A. Esterson, *Sanity, Madness and the Family*, Pelican ed. (1964; rpt. Baltimore: Penguin, 1970), *passim*.

7.   *Divided Self*, p. 109.

8.   When asked in an interview what she held the function of poetry at the present time to be (1962), Sylvia Plath responded: "Surely the great use of poetry is its pleasure—not its influence as religious or political propaganda. Certain poems and lines of poetry seem as solid and miraculous to me as church altars or the coronations of queens must seem to people who revere quite different images." For this representative statement of Plath's noninvolvement, see *London Magazine*, new series 1 (Feb. 1962), 45-46.

9.   Lois Ames cites a letter that Aurelia Plath wrote to Harper and Row in 1970: "Practically every character in *The Bell Jar* represents someone—often in caricature—whom Sylvia loved; each person had given freely of time, thought, affection, and in one case, financial help during those agonizing six months of breakdown in 1953. . . .As this book stands by itself, it represents the basest ingratitude. That was not the basis of Sylvia's personality. . ." (p. 295). Here Mrs. Plath unintentionally reveals that, precisely like the mother in the novel, she could only regard her daughter's mental illness as an insult to herself. In view of Sylvia Plath's subsequent suicide, it seems strangely irrelevant to talk of her "basest ingratitude."

10.   *New York Times Book Review*, 11 April 1971, p. 7.

11.   "Art as Technique," in *Russian Formalist Criticism, Four Essays*, trans. and ed. Lee T. Lemon and Marion J. Reis (Lincoln, Neb.: University of Nebraska Press, 1965), pp. 12-13.

12.   *The Politics of Experience* (New York: Pantheon Books, 1967), p. 79.

13.   *Ariel* (New York: Harper, 1966), p. 27.

CHAPTER 10

1.   Toni Morrison, *The Bluest Eye* (1970; rpt. New York: Pocket Books, 1972), pp. 103-104. Subsequent page references are to this edition and are prefaced by the abbreviation *TBE*.

2.   Much of the criticism of Toni Morrison's work is done from a sociological point of view. See, for example, Joan Bischoff, "The Novels of Toni Morrison: Studies in Thwarted Sensitivity," *Studies in Black Literature*, 6, No. 3 (1975), 21-23; Phyllis Klotman, "Dick-and-Jane and the Shirley Temple Sensibility in *The Bluest Eye*," *Black American Literature Forum*, 13 (1979), 123-25; Barbara Lounsberry and Grace Anne Hovet, "Principles of Perception in Toni Morrison's *Sula*," *Black American Literature Forum*, 13 (1979), 126-29. These studies focus on the erosion of the individual's sensitivity by white cultural domination on the one hand, and ordering mechanisms within the black neighborhood on the other. The critics tend to agree that, while Morrison regrets the loss of sensitivity, she favors a practical and pragmatic point of view.

   Without denying the objective social facts or the importance of literary studies which document the social in literature, I am more interested in how texts subvert the limitations within which they are written. The focus of this study is, thus, on those instances in Morrison's writing in which the literature does something more than simply monitor and confirm social fact.

3.   The surrealist metaphors of the Negritude poets resist being read in the way we can read through Morrison's metaphors, progressively constructing their referents and meaning. An example from *Césaire's Cahier d'un Retour au Pays Natal* exemplifies the difference between the poetics of Negritude and Morrison's use of metaphor.

   Conjuring up the Congo, Césaire depicts a rich natural setting:
   où l'eau fait
   likouala—likouala
'Where the water goes likouala—likouala.' This is followed by one of the most complex and condensed examples of surrealist metaphor:
   où l'éclair de la colere lance sa hache vedâtre
   et force les sangliers de la putréfaction dans
   la belle orée violente des narines
Reading the metaphor produces something like this: 'Where the lightning bolt of anger hurls its green axe and forces the wild boars of putrefaction over the beautiful and violent edge of the nostrils.'

   Overall, the image evokes the powerful and driving force of nature and the hunt. Individual words are themselves metaphors, linked together to form a total metaphoric image whose meaning does not reside in a particular referent, but in the myriad cross-references pulled into the whole.

   The "lightning bolt of anger" captures the essence of the poem as a whole, for it voices the enraged outcry of black people and reverses the image of the meek, long-suffering "poor old Negro" produced by colonialism. The image of "wild boars pouring over the nostrils" (like snot) extends the notion of putrefaction, which is itself a code word for the effects of colonialism. This is developed at length in the poem's opening pages where the Antilles are portrayed—

not as a tropical island paradise—but a degraded, diseased, and decayed speck of land:

> Here the parade of contemptible and scrofulous bubos, the gluttony of very strange microbes, the poisons for which there are no known alexins, the pus of very ancient wounds, the unforeseeable fermentations of species destined to decay.

Bodily orifices, too, are in more than one instance related to the visage of colonialism. But these observations do not translate what the metaphor says. Rather, they are embraced by it. There is no single, comprehensive way to decipher Césaire's metaphor as there is for Morrison's. This is because, while history infuses the image, the metaphor resists being tied to any specific referent, or set of referents. The effect is finally an explosion of meanings, created out of the convergence of many possible interpretations, as opposed to, in Morrison, the revelation of meaning, made possible by linking images to referents.

4.   Harriette Arnow's *The Dollmaker*, an account of an Appalachian family's migration to Detroit during World War II is very similar to Morrison's portrayal of black Southern migration. Notably, it documents the initial experience and assimilation to wage labor, the erosion of folk culture, and the fragmentation of the family unit. In Arnow, as in Morrison, the individual's experience of alienation is portrayed in relation to fetishization under the commodity form. For a brief discussion of this novel, see my article, "A Literary Lesson in Historical Thinking," *Social Text*, No. 3 (1980), pp. 136ff.

5.   See Georg Lukacs, "Reification and the Consciousness of the Proletariat," in *History and Class Consciousness* (London: Merlin Press, 1971), p. 83. According to Luckas, reification occurs when the "commodity structure penetrates society in all its aspects and remoulds it in its own image." This differentiates bourgeois society from previous social modes, in which the commodity form may have pertained to certain endeavors or may have been only partially developed. Reification means the transformation of all human functions and qualities into commodities "and reveals in all its starkness the dehumanized and dehumanizing function of the commodity relation."

6.   Toni Morrison, *Song of Solomon* (1977; rpt. New York: New American Library, 1978), pp. 314-15. Subsequent page references are to this edition and are prefaced by the abbreviation *SOS*.

7.   Referred to as "The Principal Beauty of Maine," Margaret Lenore from *Tar Baby* comes closest to embodying bourgeois reification. Her characterization may well be a literary allusion to another great beauty and bourgeois stereotype in contemporary fiction: "The Most Beautiful Woman in the World," in Gabriel García Marquez's *One Hundred Years of Solitude*. Both Margaret Lenore and Marquez's "Most Beautiful Woman" are first beheld by their future husbands as beauty contest winners, draped in ermine and in a parade. However, neither Margaret Lenore nor Marquez's Remedios define total reification. First of all, neither is originally of the bourgeois class: Remedios being the sole survivor of a transplanted and bankrupt Spanish aristocracy, and Margaret Lenore the daughter of struggling Italian immigrants. Both develop forms of hysteria

as a result of the discontinuity between their pasts and presents and imperfect assimilation to bourgeois culture. Margaret Lenore abuses her infant son and Remedios develops a relationship with "imaginary doctors," who she hopes will cure her bodily ailments through telepathic surgery (a situation not unlike Margaret Lenore's long-distance telephone conversations with her son, which, because no one witnesses or overhears them, appear to be imaginary).

8.   In Morrison's writing, candy is often associated with capitalism. In *Song of Solomon*, it is the symbolic payoff given by the boss's wife when Guitar's father is crushed in a mill accident. In *The Bluest Eye*, it is a penny's worth of sweetness in the life of a little girl who will never find satisfaction in human terms. And in *Tar Baby*, it is a metaphor for all of capitalist production. The association is not gratuitous, for the connection between candy and capitalism extends far beyond the current glut of sugary breakfast cereals and junk foods. As Wallerstein explains in *The Modern World System*, sugar production in the New World was essential to the rise of capitalism. Rather than simply satisfying luxury consumption, a lot of the sugar produced under slavery in the Caribbean found its way into the daily diet of the growing European proletariat. With many peasants leaving the countryside to seek jobs in the cities, there was an increased need for food production and a shrinking rural labor force. The need for more food was neither met by increased cereal production (which would have required substantial transformation in production techniques) nor was it met by increasing meat production (which was basically intended for the bourgeoisie). Rather, sugar became—and remains today—a substitute for real food. Capable of providing increased energy output at the expense of long-term health, sugar is the opiate of the working class under capitalism.

9.   Toni Morrison, *Tar Baby* (New York: Knopf, 1981), p. 61. Subsequent page references are to this edition and are prefaced by the abbreviation *TB*.

10.   Toni Morrison, *Sula* (New York: Knopf, 1974), p. 3. Subsequent page references are to this edition and are prefaced by the abbreviation *S*.

11.   Abandoned at birth by his mother, rejected by his father for the sake of a poker game, and having experienced the ultimate moment of objectification when two white hunters catch him in his first sex act, Cholly Breedlove finds absolute freedom in the realization that he has nothing to lose. In many ways he is Pilate's antithesis—his freedom being a barrier, rather than a bridge, to others. As opposed to Pilate, who similarly did not know her mother's name, who lost her father and also experienced the freezing "look" of others for her lack of a navel, Cholly can neither communicate nor share his freedom.

12.   Many modernist novels from the Third World include "mythic heroes" very similar to Faulkner's Thomas Sutpen. In Vargas Llosa's *La Casa Verde*, Don Anselmo bursts upon a stodgy, backwater town, shrouded in mystery, apparently without a past or a name. Like Sutpen, he embarks upon an enterprise which the townspeople marvel at and, at first, do not comprehend. What Don Anselmo builds symbolizes exploitation in the Third World: a brothel.

The "mythic hero" creates a distance from society, which enables its estrangement once it is revealed that what was first perceived as very different and foreign is nothing more than that society's ultimate representation.

13.   The otherness of blindness and the fear it instills in a repressive bourgeois society are developed in *Sobre Heroes y Tumbas*, the great historical novel by the Argentinian Ernesto Sabatú. Similar to Morrison's portrayal, Sabatú conjures up an underground society of the blind whose otherness, perceived as grotesque from the point of view of the Peronist social model, is the basis for the group's solidarity and resistance to assimilation by the forces of domination.

14.   The relationship between forms of mutilation and freedom is not unique to Morrison, but recurs in the history of slavery and its literature. In his mythic account of the Haitian Revolution, Alejo Carpentier portrays the mutilation of Mackandal, an early slave leader, in terms that coincide with Morrison's treatment. His arm crushed in a cane mill, and amputated, Mackandal is unfit for most forms of plantation labor. Freed from the most grueling forms of toil, he wanders the countryside, watching over his master's livestock. There he discovers and studies plant and animal life, learning the secrets of science and voodoo. Mutilation is, thus, the means for Mackandal's liberation from labor and access to learning. Furthermore, because Mackandal, as voodoo priest, is capable of undergoing various metamorphoses, his human body and its mutilation are not perceived of as permanently disabled, but as one more manifestation of transitory and transitional matter. Mackandal's spiritual liberation—made possible by his mutilation—finally transcends his earthly form.

15.   William Faulkner, *Absalom! Absalom!* (1936; rpt. New York: Random House, 1972), p. 155.

CHAPTER 11

1.   Carol Tavris, rev. of *Fear of Flying*, by Erica Jong, *Psychology Today*, 8 (1975), 114.

2.   Jane L. Crain, "Feminist Fiction," *Commentary*, Dec. 1974, p. 59.

3.   Paul Theroux, "Hapless Organ," *New Statesman*, 19 April 1974, p. 87.

4.   "Altitude Sickness," rev. of *Fear of Flying* by Erica Jong, *Times Literary Supplement*, 26 July 1974, p. 813.

5.   Henry Miller, "Erica Jong's Tropic," *New York Times*, 20 August 1974, p. 38, cols. 2-3.

6.   John Updike, "Jong Love," *New Yorker*, 17 Dec. 1973, p. 149.

7.   Christopher Lehmann-Haupt, "Nuances of Woman's Lib," *New York Times*, 6 Nov. 1973, p. 35.

8.   "The *Bildungsroman* in its pure form has been defined as the 'novel of all-around development or self-culture' with a more or less conscious attempt on the part of the hero to integrate his powers, to cultivate himself by his experience," Susanne Howe, *Wilhelm Meister and His English Kinsman* (New York: Columbia University Press, 1930), p. 6; Jerome Hamilton Buckley, "Autobiography in the English Bildungsroman," Morton W. Bloomfield, ed., *The Interpretation of Narrative: Theory and Practice* (Cambridge, Mass.: Harvard University Press, 1970), p. 95; and *Season of Youth: The Bildungsroman from Dickens to Golding* (Cambridge, Mass.: Harvard University Press, 1974), p. 13.

9.   Ibid., pp. 17-18.

10.   Erica Jong, *Fear of Flying* (New York: New American Library, Inc., 1973), p. 304. All subsequent quotes from the novel will be annotated in the text.

11.   Lewis Carroll, *Alice's Adventures in Wonderland and Through the Looking-Glass* (London: Oxford University Press, 1971), p. 145.

12.   Ibid., p. 57.

13.   Erica Jong, "The Artist as Housewife/The Housewife as Artist," *Here Comes and Other Poems* (New York: New American Library, 1975), p. 253. This article first appeared in *Ms.*, December 1972.

14.   Ibid., p. 264.

15.   *Letters Home by Sylvia Plath: Correspondence 1950-1963*. ed. Aurelia Schober Plath (New York: Harper and Row, 1975), p. 217.

16.   Ibid., p. 111.

17.   Sylvia Plath, *Ariel* (New York: Harper and Row, 1961), p. 73.

18.   Sylvia Plath, *Winter Trees* (New York: Harper and Row, 1972), p. 44.

19.   Anne Sexton, *Live or Die* (Boston: Houghton Mifflin Co., 1966), p. 52.

20.   Ibid., p. 32.

21.   Anne Sexton, *Love Poems* (Boston: Houghton Mifflin Co., 1967), p. 24.

22.   Ibid., p. 17.

23.   Anne Sexton, *All My Pretty Ones* (Boston: Houghton Mifflin Co., 1961), p. 32.

24.   "Artist as Housewife," p. 264.

25.   Ibid., p. 261.

26.   Erica Jong, *Half-Lives* (New York: Holt, Rinehart and Winston, 1971), pp. 56-57.

27.   Ibid., pp. 83-84.

28.   Quoted in Erica Jong, *Loveroot* (New York: Holt, Rinehart and Winston, 1975), p. 47.

29.   Ibid., pp. 47-48.

30.   Erica Jong, "Introductory Remarks" to a paper delivered in Seminar 117: Modern Poetry by Women: A New Tradition," Eighty-Ninth Annual Convention of the Modern Language Association of America, December 28, 1974, New York, N.Y.